Professional
SAS®
Programmer's
Pocket
Reference

5th edition

Rick Aster

BREAKFAST

Also by Rick Aster:
PROFESSIONAL SAS PROGRAMMING SHORTCUTS
PROFESSIONAL SAS PROGRAMMING LOGIC

PROFESSIONAL SAS PROGRAMMER'S POCKET REFERENCE

5th edition   ISBN 1-891957-12-0   9-781891-957123

©2004 Rick Aster

Published by Breakfast Communications Corporation, P.O. Box 176, Paoli, PA 19301-0176 U.S.A., http://www.breakfast.us. Breakfast is a registered trademark of Breakfast Communications Corporation.

Any updates to this book will be posted at the author's web site at http://www.globalstatements.com.

Printed in Canada   1

Contents

Preface

In today's difficult computer problems, it is often SAS programming that holds the complex mix of technologies together. It puts the data in the data warehouse or keeps track of the customers in one-to-one marketing. Whether these SAS programs are written by SAS specialists or not, it is important for the programming process to be quick and accurate. The new design of this edition is meant to make this easier by providing quick answers to routine questions about SAS features. You can use this book as the one place you look for most of the answers you need as you are writing SAS programs, whether you work with SAS every now and then or every day.

   Other changes in this tenth anniversary edition come in response to the rapid change in operating system environments. More than 90% of new SAS projects developed this year will be moved to a new platform or at least a new operating system version within five years. There is more reason now to program with SAS's portable features; this edition focuses mainly on these cross-platform features and marks more clearly any platform dependencies. Add in the many new SAS features to support important computing standards such as XML and Unicode, and what you have is a formula that figures to keep SAS in the mix for a long time to come.

Notation

Syntax entries in this book use these notational conventions:

CODE FONT   Use these characters as shown.

italic code font   Substitute appropriate values, names, or terms.

or   Alternatives; use one.

. . .   Pattern can continue; additional terms are allowed.

options   / *options*   *optional*   (*options*)   Omit these terms if they do not apply.

'*text*'   "*text*"   Character constants.

n   Whole-number constant.

item list   One or more items, separated by spaces.

=(*list*)   The parentheses are not required if there is only one item.

1

The SAS Environment

SAS programming is not like programming in an ordinary programming language because the environment that the SAS System supplies goes far beyond the ordinary idea of a run-time environment. The SAS environment provides a data model, high-level access to data files, a library of routines, options, a macro language, and much more.

The SAS Data Model

To make data fully available in the SAS environment, you have to organize it as a SAS dataset, which may be thought of as an ordinary data table. Create as many SAS datasets as you need to hold the data you will be using. Write a data step to create a SAS dataset from data that is already in a file.

The data elements of a SAS dataset are called variables. Besides providing values for each variable, the SAS dataset also provides attributes which tell you about the variable and determine the way it is used. The most important attributes are the variable's name, its data type, its length, and the format used to write it. The part of the SAS dataset that contains the attribute information is called the header.

The records in a SAS dataset are called observations, and each observation contains a value for each variable. The observations are considered to be in a specific sequence, and a SAS dataset is usually read sequentially, reading all the observations one at a time, in order. There is no set limit on the number of observations a SAS dataset may contain.

The various kinds of SAS datasets all use this same logical structure. The one kind of SAS dataset you are sure to use is the SAS data file of the BASE engine.

SAS treats SAS datasets as members of libraries. A few other types of files, especially catalogs, may also be stored in libraries. The name of a SAS file is a combination of the library name and the member name. For example, WORK.LIST is a SAS file LIST in the WORK library. The one-word name of a library is a libref; when you create libraries, write LIBNAME statements to define librefs for them.

Text Files

SAS also uses one-word names to identify text data files for either input or output. These one-word names are filerefs and are sometimes called file shortcuts. Use FILENAME statements to define filerefs. Use a data step with INFILE and INPUT statements to read data from an input text data file; use a data step with FILE and PUT statements to write data to an output text data file.

In SAS, binary files are treated as text files, and you can read and write them using the same statements that are used for text files.

Print Files

Print files are text files with control characters to break them into pages. Two print files are automatically available to receive output from a SAS program.

The log is a sequential record of the actions of the SAS program. It contains program lines of the programs you run, messages about the programs, some other kinds of output, and any messages you want to add. To write to the log, use the LOG fileref or the PUTLOG statement in a data step. In an interactive session, you can see the log in the Log window.

The standard print file contains text reports that are generated in SAS programs. To write to the standard print file in a data step, use the PRINT fileref. In an interactive session, you can see the standard print file in the Output window, and a list of its contents in the Results or Output Manager window. If you want something more than plain text as output, you can send output to another destination using the options of the ODS statement.

Routines

SAS provides six essential kinds of routines that are used in SAS programs.

Procedures, or procs, are specialized applications programs that do a wide range of things. You write a proc step to use a procedure.

Functions and CALL routines do familiar kinds of calculations and provide access to some of the features of the SAS environment.

Informats interpret text data to create data values. Formats convert data values to text data for display or output. It is possible to create your own informats and formats in the FORMAT procedure.

Engines provide access to SAS files. If you want to create a library that contains a specific kind of SAS file, you can do that by selecting an engine for the library.

Data Types

SAS supports only two data types. The numeric data type may contain any kind of measurement or mathematical value. Special informats, formats, and functions allow the numeric data type to work with time data. A numeric value is an 8-byte floating-point value, often described as a double-precision value.

The character data type can hold text data or any kind of data. It has a maximum length of 32,767 bytes. In ordinary text data, each character occupies one byte. If you are storing a character variable in a SAS dataset, it is important to give the variable a length that is not especially long, because the entire length of the variable is stored in every observation, and this can use up a lot of space quckly.

Informats and formats also have data types. Use character informats and formats with character variables, and numeric informats and formats with numeric variables.

Products, Releases, and Environments

SAS is published by SAS Institute Inc. as a set of products. This book mainly addresses the main product, base SAS, which is the only product that most SAS programs rely on. Other products add routines that provide specialized capabilities. This book includes some of the statements, options, and other features of SAS/ACCESS, SAS/CONNECT, and SAS/SHARE, products that provide additional data access capabilities for databases, servers, and shared libraries, respectively. Features that require a specific product are marked with the symbol ○.

This edition covers SAS versions 8 and 9 and is updated with features of SAS 9.1. For newer features, a note such as ○ 9.1+ tells you when the feature was first supported.

A few features belonging to specific operating systems are mentioned, and these use similar notes to identify the operating systems in which the feature is supported. These notes show W for Microsoft Windows, z for z/OS (including OS/390), and X for Linux and most other environments. Primary features that are not broadly supported have gray headings.

SAS Learning Edition 1.0 is a subset of features from SAS 8.2. It has a data-size limitation of 1,000 observations or records and runs only in selected Microsoft operating systems. These limitations aside, it generally runs programs the same way as the production version of SAS. To access the programming environment in SAS Learning Edition, launch the file sas.exe, which you can find installed in the application's main directory.

Session

Many of the properties of the SAS environment persist only for the duration of the SAS session. A session is a single period of activity for SAS; you start a new session every time you launch SAS.

It is possible to run each SAS program as a separate session. To do this, run the SAS programs in batch mode, using the SYSIN system option. The way this looks depends entirely on the operating system you are using and the way you configured SAS when you installed it. In a typical Linux installation of SAS, the operating system line command to run the SAS program myprogram.sas might be

```
sas myprogram.sas
```

Batch mode is the simplest approach when you know exactly what you want SAS to do. When you are trying things out, the SAS windowing environment provides countless helpful interactive features. To start an interactive windowing session, start without the SYSIN system option. You can then create, edit, open, and save SAS programs. You can submit an entire SAS program to execute, or you can run it one step at a time. If you find an error when you run a program, or if you just change your mind about it, you can recall the program, revise it, and run it again. You can run any number of programs, one after another, in a single interactive session.

System options are the fundamental settings of a SAS session. You can set some of them only when you start up; others can be changed at any point along the way. Use system options such as CONFIG and AUTOEXEC to customize your SAS session.

The WORK library is provided automatically as a place to store SAS files during a session. It is automatically deleted at the end of the session, so if you are creating SAS files that you want to save for another SAS session, create another library to store them in. To save files that are in the WORK library, use the COPY procedure to copy them to another library. You can omit the WORK libref when you refer to SAS files in the WORK library.

Macro language allows you to create text objects, called macros and macro variables, that you can use to construct a SAS program. Macros and macro variables are automatically deleted at the end of the SAS session.

Many other objects and settings you might use, such as title lines, page numbers, informats and formats you create with the FORMAT procedure, librefs, and filerefs, are also lost at the end of the session. You can save any of these items by saving a SAS program that contains the statements to create or define them. To save the log and standard print files from an interactive session, save the contents of the Log and Output windows.

The data step debugger provides an interactive way to troubleshoot logical errors in a data step. You might use it if the problems in a data step are too subtle to find by examining data files or writing diagnostic log notes. With the debugger, you can suspend execution of a data step at any selected point to display values of variables. This can help you find exactly where the program's actions differ from the actions you expected. To run a data step with the debugger, use the DEBUG option in the DATA statement.

2

Programming

While there are many ways to work with SAS, the easiest is by programming. The idea of writing a computer program might seem like a strange new world to some people, but it is fundamentally no different from anything else that involves a computer. Think of the SAS program you write as simply a single document that spells out the complete set of actions you want SAS to take.

The SAS Language

The SAS programming language is a high-level language that provides both general programming features and product-oriented features that connect you to the specific capabilities of the SAS System. In some ways, the SAS language resembles the traditional general programming languages C, Fortran, Basic, Pascal, and PL/I. But other aspects of SAS are tuned to the SAS data model and the kinds of work people do in SAS.

If you have done programming before, the biggest surprise you will find in SAS is the way it divides a program into sequential program units called steps. This approach lets SAS use memory efficiently and makes it possible to work with data files of any size. It makes it easy to plug in SAS's procedures to do most of the work of a program. It also makes a program easier to read because you can trace though it sequentially, step by step. However, if you are used to structured programming and dividing a program's logic into modules, you will have to change your way of thinking in order to create programs that divide into steps.

There are two kinds of steps in SAS. A data step creates SAS datasets and does general programming. A proc step runs a procedure. There are also a few statements that do not belong to steps. These global statements execute between steps.

Data Step Programming

The data step is what makes the SAS language a general programming language. In a data step, you can create variables, compute values, and work with files. A data step can include control flow statements to allow programming of any degree of complexity. As the name of the DATA statement implies, the most common use of the data step is to create SAS datasets.

A data step starts with a DATA statement, which names the SAS datasets that the step creates. After this, there are two main things: actions and declarations. Executable statements spell out events that actually occur when the data step runs. The order of the statements determines the order of the actions. Declaration statements set things up, but they don't correspond to any specific action. The order of declarations is less critical. Often, programmers put all the declaration statements at the beginning of the step, right after the DATA statement.

Data steps can draw data from various sources, including text data files, SAS datasets, or a window in which the user can enter data. The data step's statements execute repeatedly as long as there is more input data in an automatic loop sometimes called the observation loop. Each time through the loop, an observation is written to the output SAS dataset. The SAS dataset includes all the variables of the data step.

One common task is to create a SAS dataset from a CSV file, such as you might export from a spreadsheet or database program. This requires only a few statements, as shown in this example:

```
DATA WORK.MEASURE;
   LENGTH NAME $ 22 HEIGHT WEIGHT 8;
   INFILE MYIMPORT DELIMITER=',' DSD;
   INPUT NAME HEIGHT WEIGHT;
RUN;
```

This example reads a CSV file that contains three variables. The LENGTH statement defines the variables for the data step, the INFILE statement identifies the input file, and the INPUT statement tells how to obtain the variables from the input record. The DATA statement indicates that the step creates the output SAS dataset WORK.MEASURE.

The RUN statement marks the end of a step. Using a RUN statement is not required as a matter of syntax, but it is frequently helpful.

Data steps often use these additional statements and terms:

- A subsetting IF statement to select parts of the input data that have a particular characteristic.
- Informats and pointer controls in the INPUT statement for formatted input.
- Programming statements to create additional variables or to recode variables.
- Dataset options in the DATA statement to alter the way that the output SAS dataset is written, such as the KEEP= dataset option to select variables to be stored in the SAS dataset or the COMPRESS= option to control whether the SAS dataset is

stored in compressed format.
- PUT or PUTLOG statements to write messages in the log.
- PUT statements together with a FILE statement to produce an output text file or print file.
- FORMAT, LABEL, and other statements to set the attributes of the variables in the step. The variable attributes from the data step are also stored in the output SAS dataset.

These are other common variations of the data step:

- A data step with no output SAS dataset, using the DATA _NULL_; statement.
- Data read from an input SAS dataset using a SET statement.
- Data read from a combination of two or more SAS datasets in a MERGE or SET statement.
- Dataset options for the input SAS datasets, such as the OBS= option to limit the number of observations read.
- Creating two or more SAS datasets, with OUTPUT statements and control flow statements to determine which observations are written to which output SAS datasets. When a data step contains OUTPUT statements, observations are written only when an OUTPUT statement is executed.
- Creating two or more SAS datasets with the same observations, but with different sets of variables, according to the KEEP= dataset option in the DATA statement.
- Programming statements with no source of input data. There is no automatic loop, and the data step stops when the last statement or a RETURN statement is reached.

Control flow statements, such as DO, IF-THEN, and GOTO, can be used to control the order in which executable statements are executed. Control flow statements do not affect declaration statements. A few control flow statements use statement labels to refer to other statements. A statement label is a name that comes before an executable statement and is followed by a colon, as in this example:

HERE: VOLUME = NUMBER*AMOUNT;

Each step in a program is independent, so the control flow statements of one data step have no effect on any other data step.

Example
This data step creates a SAS dataset, WORK.FREEZE, that contains selected observations from another SAS dataset, WORK.WEATHER:

```
DATA WORK.FREEZE;
  SET WORK.WEATHER;
  IF TEMPERATURE < 0;
RUN;
```

Proc Step Programming

Almost every procedure has a range of capabilities. When you run the procedure, options and statements in the proc step control the details of its actions.

The PROC statement that starts a proc step identifies the procedure to run. For many procedures, this is enough. For example, this step runs the OPTIONS procedure:

```
PROC OPTIONS;
RUN;
```

The OPTIONS procedure writes the values of system options in the log. By adding an option to the PROC statement, the OPTIONS procedure can write the value of one specific system option, the PAGENO option:

```
PROC OPTIONS OPTION=PAGENO;
RUN;
```

Most procedures work with the data of a SAS dataset, which you identify in the DATA= option of the PROC statement. For example, to print the SAS dataset WORK.OUTCOME, you can use the PRINT procedure, as shown here:

```
PROC PRINT DATA=WORK.OUTCOME;
RUN;
```

Other statements in a proc step control other details. One of the most common is the VAR statement, which tells which variables to use. For example, by adding a VAR statement to the example above, you can print just two variables from the SAS dataset:

```
PROC PRINT DATA=WORK.OUTCOME;
  VAR TIME MEASURE;
RUN;
```

Each procedure has its own set of statements and syntax rules, but there are a few statements that work essentially the same way in every procedure. The BY statement, for example, identifies groups of observations, and the INFORMAT, FORMAT, and LABEL statements, as in the data step, provide attributes for variables.

For most procedures, the RUN statement marks the end of the step. However, some procedures can run a few statements at a time, and for these run-group procedures, the RUN statement merely tells the procedure to run the statements that have come so far. If necessary, you can use the QUIT statement to mark the end of the proc step.

Example

This step sorts the SAS dataset HOME.EXTENT by the variable DATE:

```
PROC SORT DATA=HOME.EXTENT;
  BY DATE;
RUN;
```

3

General Rules

A few general rules of syntax create the characteristic look of the SAS language. These rules apply to all statements throughout any SAS program. They also apply, with minor modifications, to all other languages implemented by the SAS System.

Tokens and Spacing

A program is made of meaningful units called tokens. Most tokens are words, consisting of letters and often digits. Other common tokens are symbols, made up of one or more special characters, and constants, which represent data values.

A space is often required between two consecutive tokens, but is not required before or after a symbol. Any amount of whitespace — spaces, line breaks, and similar characters — can appear between any two tokens. Spaces usually cannot be added between the characters that make up a token; there are exceptions for symbols and compound words.

SAS words are keywords, which have a specific syntactical meaning, and names, which identify the objects that the program uses. The first character of a word must be a letter or underscore. Subsequent characters can be letters, underscores, and digits. Uppercase letters and lowercase letters are equivalent to each other and can be used interchangeably. In many cases, the SAS language lets you use one word in place of another. For example, instead of the word GRAY you can write GREY or A. GREY and A are said to be aliases of GRAY.

A quoted string is a character string that represents an exact sequence of characters in a program. Quote it with either double or single quotation marks. A quoted string can be a character literal, or it can be followed by a letter to identify it as a special kind of constant or a name.

Quoted String Modifiers   X   Character hexadecimal constant.
D   Date constant.   T   Time constant.   DT   Datetime constant.
N   Name.   B   Bit mask.   **Example** "This Name"N is a name.

When a quoted string contains the same quote character you use to quote the sting, write the quote character twice wherever it appears in the string. This notational rule prevents the quote character from appearing to mark the end of the quoted string.

Example   Write *it's* as a constant as either 'it''s' or "it's".

Character Equivalents

The EBCDIC character set of z/OS does not include the caret character ^, so SAS uses the EBCDIC logical not character ¬ as the equivalent of the caret. In addition, these symbol characters can be used as substitutes for characters used in SAS symbol tokens:

> ~ for ^ (ASCII) or ¬ (EBCDIC)
> ! for |

Comments

A comment can be delimited by the symbols /* and */ and can appear between any two tokens. Alternatively, you can use a comment statement, which begins with an asterisk (*). A comment statement can appear between any two statements.

Statements

A program is made up of statements. A semicolon (;) marks the end of each statement. The first token in a statement is usually a keyword that is the name of the statement. A few statements, especially the assignment statement, do not begin with a keyword.

A name and a colon (:) before a statement represent a statement label and are not part of the statement's syntax. Statement labels are used only occasionally, and only on executable statements in the data step.

Names

A SAS program uses a name to identify almost anything it may have to refer to: variables, arrays, statement labels, SAS datasets, librefs, filerefs, and other objects. These names must follow the rules for SAS words. Additional restrictions apply to the names of some objects. Notably, the names of informats and formats cannot end in a digit, and the names of character informats and formats must begin with a dollar sign ($).

The length allowed for a name is limited, usually to 8 or 32 characters. Some objects have multilevel names, which consist of two to four words (called levels) connected by periods (called dots). Each level of a multilevel name must meet the rules for a SAS name. There is no separate limit on the length of the multilevel name as a whole.

Examples

LIBRARY.FORMATS is a two-level name.

SASUSER.PROFILE.DMKEYS.KEYS is a four-level name.

Maximum Length of Names

8   Libref, fileref, catref, engine, password

16   Procedure, function, CALL routine

28   Generation dataset

31   Informat

32   Variable, array, statement label, window, macro, member, entry, format

In SAS version 8 and previous versions, format names have a maximum length of 8 and informat names have a maximum length of 7. When you count the length of the names of character informats and formats, the dollar sign is the first character of the name.

Mixed Case in Variable Names

SAS stores and displays the case of variable names you create according to the way the name first appears. This means that you can use any combination of upper- and lowercase letters for names of variables. SAS routines display the same capitalization in reports and descriptions of the variables. Capitalization works the same way for names of indexes and integrity constraints. However, like other words in a SAS program, names are not case-sensitive, so that a SAS name is the same name even if the capitalization changes. If you prefer, you can have SAS ignore the case of names in the program and treat them as uppercase; set the system option VALIDVARNAME to UPCASE.

When you must use an arbitrary string of characters as a variable (or table) name, write the name as a quoted string followed by the letter N. Also, for variable names, set the system option VALIDVARNAME to ANY. In versions 8 and 9, there is limited support for names that are not SAS names; if these names cause problems, use the RENAME= dataset option to change the names to SAS names.

Abbreviated Variable Lists

A list of names is formed using spaces as separators. These forms of abbreviated lists can also be used in some statements:

NAME1-NAME5   Represents: NAME1 NAME2 NAME3 NAME4 NAME5

NAME5-NAME1   Represents: NAME5 NAME4 NAME3 NAME2 NAME1

NAME08-NAME10   Represents: NAME08 NAME09 NAME10

ALL   All

CHARACTER *or* _CHAR_   All character variables

NUMERIC   All numeric variables

FROM--TO   A sequential range of consecutive variables

FROM-NUMERIC-TO   Numeric variables in a sequential range

FROM-CHARACTER-TO   FROM-CHAR-TO   Character variables in a sequential range *prefix*: All variable names that begin with the prefix (especially in proc steps)

Character Encoding

SAS version 9 has specific support for standard character encodings through the ENCODING= system option and various other options. The character encoding of a SAS dataset is stored with the SAS dataset so that character values can be interpreted correctly when the SAS dataset is read. These are examples of character encoding names:

latin1   Western Latin
latin2   Central European Latin
latin5   Turkish Latin
latin6   Baltic Latin
latin9   European Latin
utf-8   Unicode
arabic   Arabic
hebrew   Hebrew
greek   Greek
cyrillic   Cyrillic
thai   Thai
ebcdic037   North American EBCDIC
ebcdic500   International EBCDIC
aiceland   Macintosh Icelandic
pcoem865   IBM PC Nordic
wlatin1   Windows Western Latin
wvietnamese   Windows Vietnamese
ibm-935   IBM Simplified Chinese
ibm-939   IBM Japanese
macos-1   Macintosh Japanese
macos-3   Macintosh Korean

Colors

SAS commands and statements use a standard set of named colors and video attributes, each with a one-letter abbreviation.

Colors

A	GRAY GREY	N	BROWN
B	BLUE	O	ORANGE
C	CYAN	P	PINK
G	GREEN	R	RED
K	BLACK	W	WHITE
M	MAGENTA	Y	YELLOW

Video attributes

B Blinking.
H Highlight.
R Reverse.
U Underline.

4

Global Statements

Global statements are executed between steps in a SAS program. Any global statements that appear before the end of a step are executed before the step is executed.

The %PUT and %INCLUDE statements can be categorized as global statements, but they are implemented as macro statements, and other macro statements can have functionality that is similar to that of a global statement; see chapter 8.

❧

`* text ;`   Comment statement. It contains text that describes the program, but it is not executed as part of the program.

CATNAME ⊘ 7+

CATNAME *catref* or *libref.catref* (*catalog option . . .*);   Associates the catref with the catalog(s).   **Option** ACCESS=READONLY

CATNAME *catref* or *libref.catref* or _ALL_ CLEAR;   Clears the catref.

CATNAME *catref* or *libref.catref* or _ALL_ LIST;   Lists information about the catref in the log.

DM

DM '*commands*' *options*;   DM *window* '*commands*' *options*;
Executes the commands. If a window is named, commands are executed for that window.

Options

window   Activates this window after executing the commands.

CONTINUE   If the statement activates a window, this option activates that window again after all submitted statements are executed.

Example
DM 'CLEAR LOG; CLEAR OUTPUT';

ENDRSUBMIT

See **RSUBMIT**.

ENDSAS

ENDSAS;   Ends the current SAS process. If there is only one SAS process, ending it ends the SAS session.

ENDSAS *process ID . . . or* ALL *or* _ALL_;   Ends the SAS process(es). ↻ 8+

FILENAME

FILENAME *fileref optional device* '*physical file or directory name*' *options*;   Associates the fileref with the physical file name.

FILENAME *fileref device options*;   Associates the fileref with the device.

FILENAME *fileref optional device* ('*physical file name*' . . .) *options*;   Associates the fileref with the concatenated physical files. ↻ 7+

FILENAME *fileref or* _ALL_ CLEAR;   Clears the fileref.

FILENAME *fileref or* _ALL_ LIST;   Lists information about the fileref in the log.

Options

LINESIZE *or* LS=*n* Line size: the maximum number of characters used in a record.

For output files: PAGESIZE *or* PS=*n* Page size: the number of lines on a page.   MOD Starts writing records at the end of the file.

File system options: RECFM= LRECL= BLKSIZE=   See chapter 10.

Example
FILENAME RES 'SYS.RES';

FOOTNOTE

FOOTNOTE*n* '*text*' . . . ; $1 \le n \le 10$ Sets the specified footnote line to the text string specified. Resets all higher-numbered footnote lines.

FOOTNOTE*n*; $1 \le n \le 10$ Resets the footnote line and all higher-numbered footnote lines.

KILLTASK ↻ SAS/CONNECT ↻ 8.2+

KILLTASK *task name*;   Ends the remote session or task.

LIBNAME

LIBNAME *libref optional engine* '*physical file name*' *options*;
Associates the libref with the physical file name.

LIBNAME *libref optional engine* ('*physical file name*' *or libref* . . .) *options*;   Associates the libref with the concatenated libraries. ↻ 7+

LIBNAME *libref or* _ALL_ CLEAR;   Clears the libref.

LIBNAME *libref or* _ALL_ LIST;   Lists information about the libref in the log.

Options

ACCESS=READONLY Read-only. ACCESS=TEMP Scratch.

File system options: see chapter 10.

REPEMPTY=YES *or* NO   Equivalent to the dataset option. ○ 8+

OUTREP=   File format for new members: WINDOWS   OS2   MAC
RS_6000_AIX   SOLARIS   HP_UX   MVS ○ 8+

INENCODING=   OUTENCODING=   Character set. ○ 9+

TRANTAB=*name*   Translation table for character conversion. ○ 8+

SHORTFILEEXT   LONGFILEEXT ○ W 8+

MEMLIB ○ W 8+

SERVER=*session ID*   ACCESS=READONLY   RMTVIEW=YES NO
SLIBREF=*libref*   RENGINE=*engine*   ROPTIONS="*engine options*"
○ SAS/CONNECT, SAS/SHARE

USER=   PASSWORD=   SAPW= ○ SAS/SHARE

USER=   PASSWORD=   DATASRC=   DATABASE=   SERVER=   PATH=
ACCOUNT= *etc.* ○ SAS/ACCESS

Examples
LIBNAME MAX 'NEWSMAX.SDL';
LIBNAME MAX CLEAR;

LISTTASK ○ 8.2+

LISTTASK   ALL_ *or task name*;   Writes information about asynchronous tasks of the SAS session in the log.

LOCK

LOCK *libref or SAS file or entry*;   Locks the file.

LOCK *libref or SAS file or entry* CLEAR;   Unlocks the file.

LOCK *libref or SAS file or entry* LIST;   States in the log whether the
file is locked.

MISSING

MISSING *characters*;   *characters*: A, a, B, b, . . . , _   Allows the specified characters to be read as special missing values by most numeric
informats. **Example** MISSING L X l x;

Null

;   No effect.

ODS ○ 7+

ODS *destination driver options*;   Opens a destination with the
ODS driver and/or sets options for it.

ODS *destination* CLOSE;   Closes the ODS destination.

ODS _ALL_ CLOSE;   Closes all open ODS destinations. ○ 8.2+

ODS *optional destination* SELECT *or* EXCLUDE *objects*;   Adds
the objects to the selection list or exclusion list. **Objects** ALL All
objects. Resets the list.   NONE No objects. Resets the list.   *path or
label* A specific object.   *object#n* The *n*th occurrence of the object.
object PERSIST Keeps the object in the list in subsequent steps.

ODS *optional destination* SHOW;   Writes a log note showing the
selection or exclusion list.

ODS PATH *item store (optional access mode)* . . . ;   Locations to search for style and table definitions. **Access modes** READ   WRITE   UPDATE   **Default** SASUSER.TEMPLAT (UPDATE)   SASHELP.TMPLMST (READ)

ODS VERIFY *value*;   Action when a style or table definition is not supplied as part of the SAS System: OFF   Writes the output parts. ON   Writes the output parts and writes a warning message.   ERROR   Writes an error message and does not write the output parts.

ODS TRACE ON / *options*;   Writes log notes identifying output parts. **Options** LABEL   Also writes label paths.   LISTING   Writes the notes in the Listing destination.

ODS TRACE OFF;   Stops writing log notes identifying output parts.

ODS RESULTS ON;   Sends output to the Results window.   ↻ 9+

ODS RESULTS OFF;   Stops sending output to the Results window. ↻ 9+

ODS *options*;   Sets driver-independent options. **Options** PROCTITLE   Writes a title line with the name of the procedure. NOPROCTITLE   Does not write the name of the procedure.   ↻ 8.2+ Default alignment of numeric columns: DECIMAL_ALIGN   At decimal point.   NO_DECIMAL_ALIGN   Right-aligned.   ↻ 9+   USEGOPT   Use graphics options for text output.   NOUSEGOPT   Uses ODS settings only to format text output.   ↻ 9.1+

ODS GRAPHICS ON / *options*;   Turns on ODS statistical graph generation. **Options** ANTIALIAS=ON   ANTIALIAS   Provides antialiasing (smoothing) for graph symbols and curves under some conditions.   ANTIALIAS=OFF   NOANTIALIAS   Does not provide antialiasing for graphs.   IMAGENAME=*file name*   Provides a name for the image file.   PERSIST   Clears the graph data cache at run boundaries.   PERSIST=RUN   Maintains the graph data cache across run boundaries.   PERSIST=PROC   Maintains the graph data cache across step boundaries.   ↻ 9.1+

ODS GRAPHICS OFF;   Turns off ODS statistical graph generation. ↻ 9.1+

Destination

driver   A single open destination for the driver.

tagset   A destination for the Markup driver using the indicated tagset to create a destination format.   ↻ 9+

driver ID=*n or name*   A destination identified by a name or number that you provide when you open it. Use this form to open more than one destination at the same time for a driver. Each destination uses its own files and options.   ↻ 9+

Drivers ↻ 9+

Each file type associated with Markup or Printer can be used as an alias for the driver. See chapter 11 for descriptions and options.

DOCUMENT   ODS document.

MARKUP   Markup languages and other unpaginated visual or textual output. **File types** XML   RTF   HTML   HTMLCSS   HTML3   CHTML   PHTML   DOCBOOK   WML   IMODE

PRINTER   Printer page description languages and other output divided into pages. **File types** PS   PDF   PCL

LISTING   Print file (paginated monospaced text). ◌ 7+

OUTPUT   SAS data file. ◌ 7+

(Versions 7–8 provide a limited set of drivers and file types.)

OPTIONS

OPTIONS *system options*;   Sets the values of system options.

Alias OPTION

Example
OPTIONS COMPRESS=NO NODATE PAGENO=1;

PAGE

PAGE;   Starts a new page in the log.

RSUBMIT ◌ SAS/CONNECT

RSUBMIT *options*; *statements* ENDRSUBMIT;   Submits statements to the remote session for execution.

Options
REMOTE=*session ID*   WAIT=Y N   LOG=   OUTPUT=
MACVAR=*name*   STATUS=Y N   CSYSRPUTSYNC=YES NO   SCRIPT=
USERID=   PASSWORD=

SASFILE ◌ 8.1+

SASFILE *SAS file   action*;   Loads a SAS data file into memory.

Actions
OPEN   Opens the file and prepares to load it into memory. The file is loaded into memory when a subsequent step accesses it.

LOAD   Opens the file and loads it into memory.

CLOSE   Closes the file and releases the memory it occupied.

SIGNON ◌ SAS/CONNECT

SIGNON *options*;   Starts a remote session.

Options
REMOTE=*session ID*   WAIT=Y N   LOG=   OUTPUT=
MACVAR=*name*   STATUS=Y N   SCRIPT=   USERID=   PASSWORD=
NOTIFY=YES NO

SIGNOFF ◌ SAS/CONNECT

SIGNOFF *options*;   Ends a remote session.

Options
REMOTE=*session ID*   MACVAR=*name*   SCRIPT=

SKIP

SKIP;   Skips a line in the log.

SKIP *n*;   Skips *n* lines in the log.

STARTSAS ☉ 8+

STARTSAS *system options*;   Starts a new SAS process.

Example
STARTSAS SYSIN="info.sas" LOG="info.log";

SYSTASK ☉ 8+

SYSTASK COMMAND '*command*' options;   Executes the operating
system command. **Options** WAIT   NOWAIT   TASKNAME=*name*
MNAME=*macro variable name*   STATUS=*macro variable name*

SYSTASK LIST _ALL_ *or task name*;   Writes information about
asynchronous tasks in the SAS session in the log.

SYSTASK KILL *task name* . . . ;   Terminates the task.

TITLE

TITLE*n* '*text*' . . . ;   1 ≤ *n* ≤ 10   Sets the specified title line to the text
string specified. Resets all higher-numbered title lines.

TITLE*n*;   1 ≤ *n* ≤ 10   Resets the title line and all higher-numbered
title lines.

Example
TITLE1 'Star Trek';
TITLE2 'Enterprise';

WAITFOR ☉ 8+

WAITFOR *selection option task name . . . timeout option*;   Waits
for an asynchronous system task to complete.

Selection options
ANY Wait for any one of the listed tasks to complete.
ALL Wait until all the listed tasks complete.

Timeout option
TIMEOUT=*n* Waits no longer than *n* seconds.

WAITSAS ☉ 8+

WAITSAS *process ID* . . . ;   Waits for the other SAS process(es) to
end. There is no wait if the process ID is not valid, the process is the
current process, or the process has already ended.

Example
WAITSAS &SYSSTARTID;

X

X '*command*';   Executes the operating system command.

X;   Temporarily exits to an operating system shell.

5

Data Step Statements

The DATA statement marks the beginning of a data step; a RUN or DATALINES statement marks its end. If nothing else intervenes, the end of the step is found at the beginning of the next step or the end of the SAS session.

A RETURN statement is implied at the end of every data step. A RETURN statement, either written or implied, includes the effect of an OUTPUT statement, but there are exceptions.

- If there is a MODIFY statement, the RETURN statement implies UPDATE rather than OUTPUT.
- If the step contains an OUTPUT, UPDATE, or REMOVE statement, the RETURN statement does not imply any output action, and it is the same as a DELETE statement.
- The LINK statement and the HEADER= option of the FILE statement can change the meaning of a RETURN statement.

It is important to distinguish between the executable statements that set forth the actions of a data step and the declarations that define objects and set options. Write executable statements in the order that properly indicates the sequence of actions you intend. Usually, you can place all declarations at the beginning of the step. If you use declarations to set the data type of variables and the length of character variables, it is especially important for these statements to appear before the action statements that refer to the same variables. These symbols identify the main kinds of statements:

Δ executable (action)
   66 declaration
   2 secondary

ABORT △

ABORT *options*;   Stops execution of the data step (and, in batch mode, stops processing of observations for the rest of the SAS program).

Options RETURN ABEND Ends the SAS session immediately.
n An error code returned to the operating system.

ARRAY ❝

ARRAY *array* {*subscript range, . . .* } *optional length or* $ *length optional variable list or* _TEMPORARY_ / *optional* (*initial value, . . .*);   Declares an array, using the variables listed as elements of the array. If no variables are listed, variable names are constructed by appending 1, 2, 3, etc., to the array name. Use the keyword _TEMPORARY_ for an array of temporary variables. All the elements must be of the same type. If a length term is used, it sets the length for any variables created by the ARRAY statement. Initial values can optionally be provided for all the elements in the array.

Subscript range

The dimension(s) produced by the subscript range(s) must match the number of variables listed as elements.

n Subscripts from 1 through *n*.

n:n Subscripts that cover the indicated range.

* Subscripts from 1 through the number of variables listed (for a one-dimensional array only).

Example
ARRAY MSB{3, 5} $ 6 MSB1-MSB15;

Assignment △

variable = expression;   Assigns the value of the expression to the variable. If the type of the expression is different from the type of the variable, an automatic type conversion is done.

SUBSTR(*character variable, position, optional length*) = *expression*;
Assigns the value of the expression to the segment of the character variable.

Examples
DF = DC*1.8 + 32;
WORD = 'now';
SUBSTR(WORD, 2, 1) = 'e'; * Changes WORD to "new";

ATTRIB ❝

ATTRIB *variable list attributes . . .* ;   Declares one or more attributes for a variable or variables.

Attributes

LENGTH=*n or* LENGTH=$ *n* The length of the variable, in bytes. Use $ for a character variable.

INFORMAT=*informat* The informat used when the user enters a value for the variable.

FORMAT=*format* The format used when the variable is displayed.

LABEL='*label*' A descriptive phrase, up to 256 characters long.

TRANSCODE=YES Permits transcoding of the character variable; treats values as text. TRANSCODE=NO Prevents transcoding of the character variable; treats values as binary data. ↻ 9.1+

BY 2

BY *sort order option*; Indicates that the input SAS dataset(s) is (are) sorted or grouped by the indicated variables. Creates the automatic FIRST. and LAST. variables for each BY variable.

Use this statement only after a SET, MERGE, MODIFY, or UPDATE statement.

Sort order

The sort order clause lists one or more variables that define the sort key:

options variable Sorted by this variable. **Options** DESCENDING In descending order. GROUPFORMAT Grouped according to the formatted values of the variable.

Option

NOTSORTED The input data is grouped but not necessarily sorted.

CALL Δ

CALL *routine*(*arguments*); Executes the CALL routine.

CARDS

See **DATALINES**.

CARDS4

See **DATALINES4**.

CONTINUE Δ

CONTINUE; Branches to the bottom of the (innermost) DO loop. Use only in a DO loop.

DATA

DATA *SAS datasets or* _NULL_ / *option*; Names the output SAS dataset(s) of the data step.

DATA; The same as DATA _DATA_; .

DATA PGM=*compiled data step* (*password option*); Accesses or executes a compiled data step.

DATA VIEW=*data step view* (*password option*); DESCRIBE; Accesses a data step view to write its source code in the log.

Options

VIEW=*SAS dataset* (*options*) Creates a view from the data step and stores it in the SAS dataset named. The SAS dataset must be one of the output SAS datasets named in the statement. **Options** *password options source option*

PGM=*SAS file* (*options*) Compiles the data step and stores it in the file named. **Options** *password options source option*

DEBUG   Uses the data step debugger when running the step.

Source option

SOURCE=   Storage of the source code for a data step view or compiled data step: SAVE   Stores it in the file.   ENCRYPT   Stores it in encrypted form. This requires an ALTER password.   NOSAVE   Does not store it.

DATALINES

DATALINES;
data lines
;

Marks the end of the step and the beginning of data lines. Data lines continue until a line that contains a semicolon is reached.

Alias CARDS, LINES

DATALINES4

DATALINES4;
data lines
;;;;

The same as the DATALINES statement, except that a semicolon does not mark the end of the data lines. Data lines continue up to a line of four semicolons.

Alias CARDS4, LINES4

DECLARE Δ ⟲ 9+

DECLARE *class object*;   Declares a component object.

DECLARE *class object* ( );   Declares and instantiates a component object.

DECLARE *class object* (*constructor argument, . . .*);   Declares and creates a component object.

Classes

HASH   Hash. A lookup table with key variables and data variables.

HITER   Hash iterator. Retrieves items from a hash object in sequence.

Constructor arguments

For HASH (all arguments are optional):

HASHEXP: *n*   Creates a hash of size 2^n. (This does not limit the number of data items in the hash object.) **Default** 8

DATASET: '*SAS dataset*'   A SAS dataset that supplies data values for the object.

ORDERED: The order in which data values are returned: 'YES'   'Y' 'ASCENDING'   'A'   In ascending order.   'DESCENDING'   'D'   In descending order.   'NO'   'N'   In an arbitrary order.   **Default** 'NO'

For HITER: '*hash*'   The hash object that the object refers to.

Alias DCL

DELETE Δ

DELETE;   Stops execution of the current repetition of the observation loop; branches to the top of the observation loop.

DESCRIBE ⊙ 8+

DESCRIBE;   Writes source code from the data step view or compiled data step to the log.

DISPLAY Δ

DISPLAY *window or window.group options*;   Displays a window as defined in the WINDOW statement. If a group is specified, the fields in that group are displayed. By default, the window remains displayed until the data step ends. The user can enter the END command in the window to stop execution of the data step.

If the automatic variable _MSG_ has a value, that value is displayed in the message line of the window. If the user enters a command that is not recognized as a display manager command, the command line is assigned to the automatic variable _CMD_.

Options

BLANK   Previously displayed fields in the window are erased.

NOINPUT   Does not allow user input.

BELL   Beeps.

DELETE   Closes the window immediately after the DISPLAY statement executes.

Example

```
DATA _NULL_;
   WINDOW GREETING
      #7 @9 'This is a data step window'
      #9 @9 'Press enter to continue';
   DISPLAY GREETING BLANK;
   STOP;
RUN;
```

DO Δ

DO; *statements* END;   Forms a simple block. A block is treated as a unit for control flow purposes.

DO *iteration control*; *statements* END;   Forms a loop. The statements in the loop execute repeatedly until a stopping condition is reached.

Iteration control

variable = value iteration options, . . .   The variable is set to the value. **Iteration options** TO *stop* The increment value, or the default 1, is added whenever the bottom of the loop is reached. The loop stops when the value of the variable passes the stop value. Use this form only with a numeric variable.   BY *increment* The increment value. The default is 1.   WHILE(*condition*) Iteration stops if the condition is false.   UNTIL(*condition*) Iteration stops after the first time through if the condition is true.

WHILE(*condition*)   The loop stops if the condition is false.

UNTIL(*condition*)   The loop stops after the first time through if the condition is true.

Example

```
DO I = 1 TO 8;
   SQUARE = I*I;
   PUT I= SQUARE=;
   END;
```

DROP ᴬ

DROP *variable list*;   Equivalent to the DROP= dataset option for all output SAS datasets in the step. If the KEEP= or DROP= dataset option is also used on an output SAS dataset, the DROP statement is applied first.

ELSE 2

ELSE *action*   Immediately following an IF-THEN statement, it executes the action if the condition in the IF-THEN statement is false.

END 2

END;   Marks the end of a block. See **DO**, **SELECT**.

ERROR Δ

ERROR . . . ;   Sets the value of the automatic variable _ERROR_ to 1. Additional terms can be used in the statement, as in the PUT statement, to write a message to the log.

EXECUTE ○ 8+

EXECUTE;   Executes the compiled data step. This statement is necessary only if the DESCRIBE statement is also present.

FILE Δ

FILE *fileref or 'physical file name' options*;   Sets the current output text file to the file indicated.

Options

PRINT   A print file.   NOPRINT   A nonprint file.

PAD   Pads short records (shorter than the logical record length) with trailing spaces. This is the default for fixed-length records.   NOPAD Does not pad with trailing spaces. This is the default for variable-length records.

LINESIZE *or* LS=*n*   Line size: the maximum number of characters that can be written to a record.

Action when the PUT statement attempts to write beyond the end of a record: DROPOVER   It takes no action and does not write the fields that do not fit in the record.   FLOWOVER   It continues writing at column 1 of the next record.   STOPOVER   It creates an error condition, and the step stops running.

OLD   Starts writing records at the beginning of the file.   MOD   Starts writing records at the end of the file.

TITLES   TITLE   Writes title lines on each page of output. This is the default.   NOTITLES   NOTITLE   Does not write title lines.

FOOTNOTES FOOTNOTE Writes footnote lines on each page of output. NOFOOTNOTES NOFOOTNOTE Does not write footnote lines. This is the default. ⚙ 7+

N=*n or* PAGESIZE *or* PS The number of lines that are available to the output pointer. For a print file, the only values allowed are 1 and PAGESIZE or PS.

PAGESIZE *or* PS=*n* Page size: the number of lines on a page. Overrides the system option of the same name.

HEADER=*statement label* When a PUT statement writes the end of a page in the file, it branches to the statement label to execute a group of statements there until a RETURN statement is reached. Control then returns to the PUT statement.

COLUMN *or* COL=*variable* A numeric variable that the PUT statement sets to the column pointer location.

LINE=*variable* A numeric variable that the PUT statement sets to the line pointer location.

LINESLEFT *or* LL=*variable* A numeric variable that shows the number of lines left on the page, including the current line pointer location.

NBYTE=*variable* A numeric variable that determines the number of bytes to write to a stream record format.

DELIMITER *or* DLM='*char*' *or character variable* The delimiter character for list output. The default action is to skip a column without writing a delimiter. With the DSD option, the default delimiter character is a comma. ⚙ 7+

DSD Writes an output value as a quoted string if it contains the delimiter character, when writing list output ⚙ 7+

FILE=*character variable* Creates a character variable that contains the output buffer for the file. ⚙ 7+

FILENAME=*variable* A character variable that shows the physical name of the file. **Note** Declare the length of the character variable in an earlier LENGTH statement.

FILEVAR=*variable* A character variable that can be used to change the physical output file. Changing the value of the variable causes the FILE statement to close the input file and open the file whose physical name is the value of the variable.

DCB=*fileref* DEVTYPE=*variable* VOLUME=*variable*
DSCB=*variable* JFCB=*variable* UCBNAME=*variable* ⚙ z

File system options: RECFM= LRECL= DEVICE= BLKSIZE= See chapter 10.

ODS ODS=(*ODS suboptions*) Writes an ODS output object instead of writing print output directly. This option is valid only for fileref PRINT. ⚙ 7+

ODS suboptions
COLUMNS=(*columns*) The output columns.
VARIABLES=(*variables*) The output variables.
Column *column optional* =*variable optional* (*attribute=value* . . .)
Variable *variable optional* =*column optional* (*attribute=value*

. . .) **Attributes** FORMAT=*format* LABEL='*label*' DYNAMIC=
GENERIC=

DYNAMIC=(*name or name=variable or constant* . . .) Makes a
variable or constant value available for use in dynamic attributes of
the template.

GENERIC=ON Uses a column definition for a class of variables.

GENERIC=OFF Uses a column definition only for a single, specified
variable.

LABEL='*label*' The column label for all columns that are not given a
label in the template or the COLUMNS= or VARIABLES= suboption.

TEMPLATE='*path*' The template that produces the output object.

OBJECT=*object* The name of the output object.

OBJECTLABEL='*label*' The label of the output object.

FORMAT **“**

FORMAT *variable list format . . . options*; Sets the format
attribute of one or more variables.

FORMAT *variable list*; Clears the format attribute of one or more
variables.

Options

DEFAULT=*format* . . . Default character or numeric format for
variables that have no format attribute.

GOTO Δ

GOTO *label*; Branches to the indicated statement label.

IF Δ

IF *condition*; Subsetting: continues executing the current repetition
of the observation loop only if the condition is true.

IF . . . THEN Δ

IF *condition* THEN *action* Executes the action if the condition is
true.

Example

IF X >= 0 THEN ROOT = SQRT(X);
ELSE ROOT = -SQRT(-X);

INFILE Δ

INFILE *fileref or 'physical file name' options*; Sets the current
input text file to the file indicated.

Options

Action when the INPUT statement reaches the end of a record before
finding values for all its variables: MISSOVER It assigns missing
values to the remaining variables. TRUNCOVER The same as
MISSOVER, except that a short field at the end of the record is used
where available. FLOWOVER It continues reading at column 1 of
the next record. STOPOVER It creates an error condition, and the
step stops running. SCANOVER The same as FLOWOVER, except

that scanning continues on subsequent records if it is the scanning operation that reaches the end of the record. ⊙ 7+

PAD Pads short records (shorter than the logical record length) with trailing spaces. This is the default for fixed-length records. NOPAD Does not pad with trailing spaces. This is the default for variable-length records.

LINESIZE *or* LS=*n* Line size: the maximum number of characters used in a record.

FIRSTOBS=*n* The first record to be read from the input file.

OBS=*n* The last record to be read from the input file.

N=*n* The number of lines available to the input pointer.

UNBUFFERED UNBUF Does not look ahead at the next record when reading a record.

EOF=*statement label* An INPUT statement branches to this statement label when it attempts to read past the end of the file.

END=*variable* A numeric variable that the INPUT statement sets to 1 when it reads the last record of the file. However, it does not do so for an unbuffered input file.

COLUMN *or* COL=*variable* A numeric variable that the INPUT statement sets to the column pointer location.

LINE=*variable* A numeric variable that the INPUT statement sets to the line pointer location.

INFILE=*variable* Creates a character variable that contains the input buffer. ⊙ 7+

LENGTH=*variable* A numeric variable that contains the length of the automatic variable _INFILE_. Changing the value of this variable changes the length written when the variable _INFILE_ is written in the PUT statement. START=*variable* A numeric variable whose value indicates the first character to be used when the variable _INFILE_ is written in the PUT statement.

DELIMITER *or* DLM='*chars*' *or variable* Delimiters used in list input. The default is DELIMITER=' '.

DSD In list input, the INPUT statement treats each delimiter character separately (when two or more delimiter characters are consecutive) and interprets quoted strings (unless the ~ scanning control is used).

EXPANDTABS Converts tab characters to blanks, using tab stops every 8 columns. NOEXPANDTABS Does not convert tabs. This is the default.

PRINT A print file (interpreting print control characters). NOPRINT A nonprint file (or reading print control characters as data). ⊙ 7+

NBYTE=*variable* A numeric variable that determines the number of bytes to read from a stream record format.

EOV=*variable* A numeric variable that is set to 1 when the first record of each concatenated physical file is read.

FILENAME=*variable* A character variable that shows the physical name of the file. **Note** Declare the length of the character variable in an earlier LENGTH statement.

FILEVAR=*variable*   A character variable that can be used to change the physical input file. Changing the value of the variable causes the INFILE statement to close the input file and open the file whose physical name is the value of the variable.

SHAREBUFFERS   SHAREBUFS   Uses the same buffer for input and output when the same fileref is used in an INFILE and a FILE statement in the same step. This makes it possible to modify a text file by rewriting selected fields or records.

DCB=*fileref*   CCHHR=*variable*   DEVTYPE=*variable*
VOLUME=*variable*   DSCB=*variable*   JFCB=*variable*
UCBNAME=*variable* ◌ z

File system options: RECFM=   LRECL=   DEVICE=   BLKSIZE=   See chapter 10.

Example
INFILE NEWDATA DLM="," DSD;

INFORMAT ❝

INFORMAT *variable list informat . . . options*;   Sets the informat attribute of one or more variables.

INFORMAT *variable list*;   Clears the informat attribute.

Options
DEFAULT=*informat . . .*   Default character or numeric informat for variables that have no informat attribute.

INPUT Δ

INPUT *terms*;   Reads from the current input text file.

Terms
@*n*   @(*numeric expression*)   @*numeric variable*   Moves the pointer to the indicated column.

@'*constant*'   @(*character expression*)   @*character variable*   Moves the pointer after the indicated character value. The action taken if the character value is not found in the current record depends on the SCANOVER, TRUNCOVER, or other option in the INFILE statement.

+*n*   +(*numeric expression*)   +*numeric variable*   Advances the pointer by the indicated number of columns.

/   Moves the pointer to the next record.

#*n*   #(*numeric expression*)   #*numeric variable*   Moves the pointer to the indicated line.

At the end of the INPUT statement: @   Holds the current input line(s). The input lines are released at the bottom of the observation loop.   @@   Holds the current input line(s). The input lines can be carried over to the next repetition of the observation loop.

(*variable list*) (*informat list*)   Applies informats and pointer control terms to a list of variables. **Variable list terms** *variable variable list   array element* **Informat list terms** *pointer control options   n*   options   informat*

variable or array element options   Reads a value for a variable.

Options for a variable

= Indicates named input: the variable name appears in the input record, followed by an equals sign and the variable value. Other variables can also appear in the input record.

$ Indicates a character variable.

: Scans. & Scans and allows single embedded blanks. Scanning extracts a word and removes leading and trailing spaces. ~ Scans and allows quoted strings that may contain delimiter characters if the DSD option is used in the INFILE statement. The quoted string is read intact, without being interpreted.

? Suppresses data error messages. ?? Ignores data errors.

informat Shows how to interpret the input data. *n   n-n* Reads from the indicated column or columns in the input line, using the standard informat. *n-n .n* Reads from the indicated column or columns with the indicated number of implied decimal places. Otherwise, the variable is read using list input, using the variable's informat attribute or the default informat.

Examples

List input:

```
LENGTH NAME $ 18 STATE $ 2;
INPUT NAME & AGE STATE;
```

Reading a fixed-field record:

```
INPUT @1 A 7. @8 B 7. @15 C $CHAR4. @20 D $CHAR1.;
or
INPUT A 7. B 7. C $CHAR4. +1 D $CHAR1.;
```

KEEP «

KEEP *variable list*;   Equivalent to the KEEP= dataset option for all output SAS datasets in the step. If the KEEP= or DROP= dataset option is also used on an output SAS dataset, the KEEP statement is applied first.

LABEL «

LABEL *variable*='*text*' . . . ;   Sets the label attribute of one or more variables. A label is descriptive text up to 256 characters long.

LEAVE ∆

LEAVE;   Branches to the first statement after the (innermost) DO loop or SELECT block. Use only in a DO loop or SELECT block.

LENGTH «

LENGTH *variable list n or $ n . . . option* ;   Declares the length in bytes and the data type of variables. Use $ for character variables.

Option

DEFAULT=*n* Sets the default length in bytes of numeric variables.
Default 8

LINK Δ

LINK *label*;   Branches to the indicated statement label, then returns when a RETURN statement is executed.

Example

```
DATA . . . ;
  . . .
  IF REPORTS < 1 THEN LINK MSG1;
  . . .
  RETURN;
MSG1:
  PUTLOG 'No reports indicated for '
    ID $CHAR. '. One report assumed.';
  REPORTS = 1;
  RETURN;
```

LIST Δ

LIST;   Causes the input lines to be written to the log when the bottom of the observation loop is reached.

LOSTCARD Δ

LOSTCARD;   Discards one record from the current input text file and restarts the current repetition of the observation loop.

MERGE Δ

MERGE *SAS dataset SAS dataset . . . option*;   Unmatched merge: observations from two or more input SAS datasets are combined one at a time. The step stops when the end of all input SAS datasets is reached.

MERGE *SAS dataset SAS dataset . . . option*; BY . . . ;   Match merge: observations with matching values of BY variables from two or more input SAS datasets are combined. The step stops when the end of all input SAS datasets is reached.

Option

END=*variable*   A numeric variable whose value is set to 1 when the last observation is read.

MODIFY Δ

MODIFY *SAS dataset options*;   Reads an observation from a SAS dataset open for editing. The SAS dataset must also be named in the DATA statement. Use the REPLACE statement later to save changes to the observation, the REMOVE statement to delete the observation, or the DELETE statement to discard changes to the observation.

MODIFY *SAS dataset SAS dataset options*; BY . . . ;   Modifies values from the first SAS dataset with values from the second SAS dataset. The first SAS dataset must also be named in the DATA statement.

Options

END=*variable* A numeric variable whose value is set to 1 when the last observation is read or when the indexed search fails to find a matching observation.

POINT=*variable* A numeric variable whose value determines the observation number of the next observation to read. To read an observation using direct access, assign a value to the POINT= variable, then execute the MODIFY statement with the POINT= option. The POINT= option cannot be used in combination with the BY statement.

NOBS=*variable* A numeric variable whose value is the number of observations in the input SAS dataset(s) when the step begins.

KEY=*index*/UNIQUE Indicates an indexed search for the first observation that matches the values of the key variables in the data step.

KEY=*index* Indicates an indexed search for observations that match the values of the key variables.

UPDATEMODE=MISSINGCHECK Does not read standard missing values from the second SAS dataset. Thus, only nonmissing and special missing values from the second SAS dataset replace values from the first dataset. This is the default. UPDATEMODE=NOMISSINGCHECK Reads all values, including missing values, from the second SAS dataset. Values from the second SAS dataset replace values from the first SAS dataset.

Null △

;   No action.

object.method △ 9+

object.method();   *object.method*(*argument name: value,* . . .);
Executes the object method. If the action is unsuccessful, a log message describes the error. See the discussion of component objects and methods in chapter 7, "Expressions."

OTHERWISE 2

OTHERWISE *action*   Executes the action if none of the WHEN statements of the SELECT block apply. Use only in a SELECT block.

OUTPUT △

OUTPUT;   Writes an observation to all output SAS datasets in the data step, using the current values of data step variables.

OUTPUT *SAS dataset* . . . ;   Writes an observation to the indicated SAS dataset(s). The SAS dataset(s) must have been named in the DATA statement. Dataset options cannot be used in the OUTPUT statement.

PUT △

PUT *terms*;   Writes to the current output text file.

Terms

@*n* @(*numeric expression*) @*numeric variable* Moves the pointer to the indicated column.

+*n* +(*numeric expression*) +*numeric variable* Advances the pointer by the indicated number of columns.

/ Moves the pointer to the next record.

#*n* #(*numeric expression*) #*numeric variable* Moves the pointer to the indicated line.

At the end of the PUT statement: @   @@   Holds the current output line(s).

In a print file: _PAGE_ Starts a new page. _BLANKPAGE_ Starts a new page even if the current page is blank.

character constant Writes the character constant.
n*character constant Writes the character constant *n* times.

(*variable list*) (*format list*)   Applies formatting and pointer-control terms to a list of variables. **Variable list terms** *variable variable list   array element* **Format list terms** *pointer control options n*options format alignment option   character constant*

ALL Similar to (_ALL_)(=), except that it also includes automatic variables in the output.

ODS Writes variable values to empty columns in the ODS buffer. ᗆ 7+

variable or array element options Writes a variable.

Options for a variable

= Named output: the variable name is written followed by an equals sign and the variable value with leading and trailing spaces removed and a blank appended.

$ Indicates a character variable.

: Removes leading and trailing spaces. Writes the delimiter character after the value, or advances one column if there is no delimiter character.

format alignment option Shows how to format the value.
n n-n Writes to the indicated column or columns in the output line, using the variable's format attribute or the standard format.
n-n .n Writes to the indicated columns in the output line, with the indicated number of decimal places. Otherwise, the variable is written using list output, equivalent to using the colon (:) modifier with the variable's format attribute or the default format.

Alignment options -L Left. -C Center. -R Right.

Examples

Writing a message:

```
PUT 'There were ' COUNT :COMMA11. 'observations in '
   PLACE +(-1) '.';
```

Writing a fixed-field record:

PUT @1 A 7. @8 B 7. @15 C $CHAR4. @20 D $CHAR1.;

Using a format list:

PUT (N1 X1 N2 X2 N3 X3 N4 X4 N5 X5) (8. +1 $CHAR2. +2);

PUTLOG ∆ ⊙ 9+
PUTLOG . . . ;   Writes a message to the log. Use the same terms as in the PUT statement.

REDIRECT
REDIRECT INPUT *or* OUTPUT *logical name–actual name* . . . ;
Changes the name of an input or output SAS dataset of a compiled data step. Use only after a DATA PGM= statement.

REMOVE ∆
REMOVE;   REMOVE *SAS dataset* . . . ;   Deletes an observation that was previously read with the MODIFY statement. If you use both the REMOVE and OUTPUT statements, execute the REMOVE statement before the OUTPUT statement.

Example
This step removes some observations from the SAS dataset NEW. The REMOVE statement removes an observation, while the DELETE statement leaves the observation unchanged.

```
DATA NEW;
  MODIFY NEW;
  IF NAME IN (' ', 'X') THEN REMOVE;
  ELSE DELETE;
RUN;
```

RENAME ••
RENAME *variable(s)=new name(s)* . . . ;   Equivalent to the RENAME= dataset option for output SAS datasets. If this statement is used with the KEEP=, DROP=, or RENAME= dataset option on an output SAS dataset, the statement is applied before the dataset option.

REPLACE ∆
REPLACE;   REPLACE *SAS dataset* . . . ;   Updates an observation that was previously read with the MODIFY statement. If you use both the REPLACE and OUTPUT statements, execute the REPLACE statement before the OUTPUT statement.

RETAIN

RETAIN *variables optional value or* (*value list*) . . . ; Keeps the variables from being automatically reset to missing and initializes them to the indicated value. **Variable terms** *variable array array element variable list* **Value list terms** *constant n*constant n**(*value list*)

RETAIN; Keeps all variables from being automatically reset to missing.

RETURN Δ

RETURN; After a LINK statement, it branches back to the statement following the LINK statement. After a HEADER= branch, it returns control to the PUT statement. Otherwise, it ends the current repetition of the observation loop; also it writes an observation to all output SAS datasets using the current values of the data step variables, unless an OUTPUT (or REPLACE or REMOVE) statement appears somewhere in the data step.

A RETURN statement is implied after the last statement in a data step.

RUN

RUN; Marks the end of the step.

RUN CANCEL; Cancels the step.

SELECT Δ

SELECT(*expression*); WHEN(*expression*, . . .) *action* . . . OTHERWISE *action* END; Executes the action for the first WHEN expression that matches the SELECT expression, or executes the OTHERWISE action if no WHEN expression matches.

SELECT; WHEN(*condition*, . . .) *action* . . . OTHERWISE *action* END; Executes the action for the first true WHEN condition, or executes the OTHERWISE action if no WHEN condition is true.

Example

```
SELECT(NUMBER);
   WHEN(0) WORD = 'None';
   WHEN(1) WORD = 'One';
   OTHERWISE WORD = 'Some';
   END;
```

SET Δ

SET *SAS dataset options*; Reads an observation from an input SAS dataset.

SET; The same as SET _LAST_; .

SET *SAS dataset SAS dataset* . . . *options*; Concatenate: reads an observation from one of the SAS datasets listed. The SAS datasets are combined end-to-end.

SET *SAS dataset SAS dataset* . . . *options*; BY . . . ; Interleave: reads the next observation from one of the SAS datasets listed. The SAS datasets are combined in sorted order.

Options

END=*variable* A numeric variable whose value is set to 1 when the last observation is read or when the indexed search fails to find a matching observation.

POINT=*variable* A numeric variable whose value determines the observation number of the next observation to be read. To read an observation using direct access, assign a value to the POINT= variable, then execute the SET statement with the POINT= option. The POINT= option cannot be used in combination with the BY statement.

NOBS=*variable* A numeric variable whose value is the number of observations in the input SAS dataset(s).

KEY=*index*/UNIQUE Indicates an indexed search for the first observation that matches the values of the key variables in the data step.

KEY=*index* Indicates an indexed search for observations that match the values of the key variables.

OPEN=DEFER Opens only the first SAS dataset during compilation. Use this option only when concatenating multiple SAS datasets that have the same variables.   OPEN=IMMEDIATE Opens all the SAS datasets during compilation. This is the default. ⟳ 8+

Statement Label

label: Provides a label for the statement that follows. A statement label is a SAS name up to 32 characters long and must be different from all other statement labels in the same step.

Use statement labels only for executable (**Δ**) statements. The statement label and the reference to it must appear in the same data step.

STOP Δ

STOP;   Stops execution of the data step.

Sum Δ

numeric variable + *expression*;   Adds the expression (if not missing) to the numeric variable. The numeric variable is initialized to 0 and is not automatically reset to missing.

UPDATE Δ

UPDATE *master SAS dataset transaction SAS dataset options*;
BY . . . ;   Modifies observations from the master SAS dataset with values from observations in the transaction SAS dataset that have the same values of BY variables. There should be only one observation in the master SAS dataset for each combination of values of BY variables. The default behavior of the observation loop is modified so that an implied OUTPUT occurs only after the last transaction observation is processed for a master observation. To avoid conflicts, do not use the UPDATE statement in combination with any other source of input data in a step.

Options

END=*variable*   A numeric variable whose value is set to 1 when the last observation is read.

UPDATEMODE=MISSINGCHECK   Does not read standard missing values from the transaction SAS dataset. Thus, only nonmissing and special missing transaction values replace master values. This is the default.   UPDATEMODE=NOMISSINGCHECK   Reads all values, including missing values, from the transaction SAS dataset. Transaction values replace master values.

WHEN 2

WHEN(*condition or expression*) *action*   Executes the action if the condition is true or the expression equals the SELECT expression. Use only in a SELECT block.

WHERE 66

WHERE *condition*;   Equivalent to the WHERE= dataset option for all input SAS datasets.

WINDOW 66

WINDOW *name window options field . . . and/or group . . .* ;
Defines a window that can then be displayed by the DISPLAY statement.

Window options

COLOR=*color*   The background color for the window.

ROWS=*n* COLUMNS=*n* IROW=*n* ICOLUMN=*n*   Sets the window size and location.

MENU=*PMENU entry*   The window displays the menu bar that is defined by the PMENU entry.

KEYS=*KEYS entry*   The function key definitions of the KEYS entry are used in the window.

Fields

A field can be a constant field, a protected variable field, or an unprotected variable field. A window must have at least one field or group.

pointer controls 'constant' *field options*   A constant field: the constant value is displayed at the indicated location.

pointer controls variable optional format PROTECT=YES *field options*   A protected variable field: the value of the variable is displayed at the indicated location. If the format is omitted, the variable's format attribute or the standard format is used.

pointer controls variable optional informat/format field options
An unprotected variable field: the value of the variable is displayed at the indicated location and can be modified by the user. The format must also be a valid informat. If the format is omitted, the variable's informat and format attributes or the standard informat and format are used.

Pointer controls

#n *#numeric variable* *#(numeric expression)* Moves the pointer to the line indicated.

/ Moves the pointer to the next line.

If no line pointer control is used, a field is placed on the same line as the previous field, or on line 1.

@n *@numeric variable* *@(numeric expression)* Moves the pointer to the indicated column.

+n *+numeric variable* *+(numeric expression)* Advances the pointer by the indicated number of columns.

If no column pointer control is used, a field is placed immediately after the preceding field, or at the beginning of the line.

Field options

COLOR *or* C=*color* The color of text displayed in the field.

ATTR *or* A=(*video attribute, . . .*) Video attributes of text displayed in the field. HIGHLIGHT Highlighting. REV_VIDEO Reverse video. BLINK Blinking. UNDERLINE Underlining.

PROTECT *or* P=YES A protected variable field. PROTECT *or* P=NO An unprotected variable field (user entry field). This is the default.

PERSIST=YES The contents of a field remain displayed when the screen is redisplayed. PERSIST=NO The contents of the field disappear when the screen is redisplayed. This is the default.

REQUIRED=YES A user is not allowed to leave the field blank. Use this only for unprotected variable fields. REQUIRED=NO A user is allowed to leave the field blank. This is the default.

AUTOSKIP *or* AUTO=YES Moves the cursor to the next unprotected field in the window after the user types a character in the last position of the field. AUTOSKIP *or* AUTO=NO Does not automatically move the cursor. This is the default.

DISPLAY=YES Displays the field. This is the default. DISPLAY=NO Hides the field.

Groups

A window can have one or more groups that are displayed separately. A group is defined as:

GROUP=*name field . . .*

A group must contain at least one field.

NEW Δ ⏺ 9+

object = _NEW_ *class* (*constructor argument, . . .*);   Creates a component object. (First declare the object in the DECLARE statement.)

Constructor arguments

For HASH (all arguments are optional):

HASHEXP: *n* Creates a hash of size 2^n. (This does not limit the number of data items in the hash object.) **Default** 8

DATASET: '*SAS dataset*'   A SAS dataset that supplies data values for the object.

ORDERED: The order in which data values are returned: 'YES'   'Y'   'ASCENDING'   'A'   In ascending order. 'DESCENDING'   'D'   In descending order.   'NO'   'N'   In an arbitrary order.   **Default** 'NO'

For HITER: '*hash*'   The hash object that the object refers to.

6

Proc Step Statements

The statements you can use in a proc step depend on the procedure you run. However, a common set of proc step statements can be used in most procedures.

The PROC statement is the first statement in a proc step. Often, any additional statements can be written in any order.

For the WEIGHT and FREQ statements and PROC statement options having to do with the way observations are handled when statistics are calculated, see chapter 12, "Descriptive Statistics."

ATTRIB

ATTRIB *variable attributes* . . . ;   Declares one or more attributes for a variable.

Attributes

LENGTH=*n* or LENGTH=$ *n*   The length of the variable, in bytes. Use $ to indicate a character variable.

INFORMAT=*informat*   The informat used when the user enters a value for the variable.

FORMAT=*format*   The format used when the variable is displayed.

LABEL='*label*'   A descriptive phrase, up to 256 characters long.

TRANSCODE=YES   Permits transcoding of the character variable; treats values as text.   TRANSCODE=NO   Prevents transcoding of the character variable; treats values as binary data. ○ 9.1+

BY

BY *sort order option*;   Indicates that the input SAS dataset is sorted or grouped by the indicated variables. Most procedures process each BY group separately.

Sort order

The sort order clause lists one or more variables that define the sort key:

option variable Sorted by this variable. **Option** DESCENDING In descending order.

Option

NOTSORTED The input data is grouped but not necessarily sorted.

FORMAT

FORMAT *variable list format* . . . ; Sets the format attribute of one or more variables.

FORMAT *variable list*; Clears the format attribute of one or more variables.

INFORMAT

INFORMAT *variable list informat* . . . ; Sets the informat attribute of one or more variables.

INFORMAT *variable list*; Clears the informat attribute of one or more variables.

LABEL

LABEL *variable*='*text*' . . . ; Sets the label attribute of one or more variables. A label is descriptive text up to 256 characters long.

PROC

PROC *proc options*; The first statement in a proc step. Identifies the procedure being run and supplies options for the procedure.
Alias PROCEDURE

Option

DATA=*SAS dataset* The input SAS dataset for the step.

QUIT

QUIT; Marks the end of the step.

RUN

RUN; In most procedures, this statement marks the end of the step. In run-group procedures, it marks the end of a run group.

RUN CANCEL; Cancels the step or, in a run-group procedure, the run group.

VAR

VAR *variables*; The analysis variables or primary set of variables to process from the input SAS dataset.

WHERE

WHERE *condition*; Equivalent to the WHERE= dataset option for the input SAS dataset.

7

Expressions

An expression is a way to arrive at something. Most often, the
result is a single value to be used in a program. A SAS expression can
be a constant, variable, or array element, or it can combine constants
and variables with function calls and operators. Expressions are used
mainly in the data step and in WHERE conditions. Constants are also
used at various other places in SAS programs.

A SAS expression belongs to one of two data types. The numeric
data type holds numeric data in a double-precision format. The character data type can hold any kind of data and can have a length of up to
32,767 bytes (prior to version 7, it was limited to 200 bytes).

Variables

Variables can be referred to by their names or as array elements. The
name of a variable cannot be the same as the name of an array in the
same step. Variables are used in expressions, as arguments to some
routines, and in some statement options. Within a data step, a variable
can have only one data type. The data type is determined by the first
appearance of the variable in the step.

In addition to variables that are named in the data step and those
that are created as array elements, a data step can contain the automatic
variables listed here.

CMD
Text entered by the user in the command line of a data step window
that SAS does not recognize as a display manager command.

ERROR
Boolean: 1 if an error has been detected in the current repetition of
the observation loop, or 0 otherwise.

INFILE ↻ 7+

The current input record buffer of the current input text file. This is a pseudo-variable that refers to different physical variables if you use INFILE statements to select different input text files.

IORC

A system return code from an I/O action on an observation in a SAS dataset. This variable is set by the MODIFY statement and the SET statement with the KEY= option.

MSG

A message to be displayed in a data step window.

_N_

Counts the repetitions of the observation loop, starting with 1.

FIRST.*variable*

Boolean for each BY variable: 1 if the current observation is the first one in the group that is formed by the BY variable and all earlier BY variables, 0 otherwise.

LAST.*variable*

Boolean for each BY variable: 1 if the current observation is the last one in the group that is formed by the BY variable and all earlier BY variables, 0 otherwise.

Constants

Constants are data values that appear in a program.

Decimal

Decimal constants represent the ordinary way of writing numbers, except that commas are not used. A minus sign (the hyphen character) can be used to indicate a negative number.

Examples
23
-.03125
50000

Missing

A numeric missing value indicates the absence of a number in a place where a numeric value is expected. A standard missing value is represented by a period. A special missing value is represented by a period followed by a letter or underscore.

Scientific

Scientific notation follows a decimal constant with an E (or D) and an integer that indicates a power of 10.

Examples

6.02E23 is 602,000,000,000,000,000,000,000.

1E-12 is 0.000000000001.

Hexadecimal

Hexadecimal notation is a way of writing whole numbers in base 16, with the letters A–F used as the digits 10–15. The constant value is followed by an X and cannot begin with a letter. Write an initial 0 if necessary.

There is no way to write a negative or fractional value as a hexadecimal constant.

Example

0C053X

SAS Date

A SAS date is a number that represents the number of days elapsed since the beginning of 1960. A SAS date constant is an integer value represented in date form, with the day of month, 3-letter month abbreviation, and year, quoted and followed by the letter D.

Example

'31DEC1999'D

SAS Time

A SAS time is the number of seconds since midnight. A SAS time constant shows hours, minutes, and optionally seconds, separated by colons, quoted, and followed by the letter T.

SAS time constants can also be written using a 12-hour clock, with AM or PM at the end of the value to indicate the day half. ○ 8+

Examples

'15:38:00.00'T
'3:38 PM'T

SAS Datetime

A SAS datetime is the number of seconds since the beginning of 1960. A SAS datetime constant combines the notation of a SAS date constant and a SAS time constant. It is quoted and followed by the letters DT.

Example

'01JAN1960 00:00:00'DT

Character Literal

A character literal is an ordinary character constant. It is a quoted string. The characters in the quoted string are the actual constant value.

To represent the quote character in the character constant (or in any quoted string), write the quote character twice.

Examples

'constant'
'Isn''t'

Character Hexadecimal

Character hexadecimal notation uses two hexadecimal digits to represent each byte of data. A character hexadecimal constant must contain an even number of digits. It is quoted and followed by the letter X.

Example
'7E5C'X

Operators

An operator acts on one or two expressions to form a new expression. Most operators form values of a particular data type, indicated by **N** or **$** in the entries below. Each SAS operator uses either one operand or two, as indicated in the code model for the operator.

The comparison operators produce numeric values, either a 1 (indicating true) or a 0 (indicating false). The logical operators treat nonzero numbers as true, and 0 and missing values as false.

When missing values are used with the comparison and MAX and MIN operators, they compare less than numbers.

*

$a*b$ **N**   Multiplication: a times b.

**

$a**b$ **N**   Exponentiation: a raised to the power of b.

+

$+a$ **N**   Identity; a.
$a + b$ **N**   Addition: a plus b.

—

$-a$ **N**   Negation: the negative of a.
$a - b$ **N**   Subtraction: a minus b.

/

a/b **N**   Division: a divided by b.

AND

a AND b **N**   And: 1 if a and b are both true, 0 otherwise. **Alias** &

Comparison

$a < b$ Is less than. **Alias** LT
$a <= b$ Is less than or equal to. **Alias** LE
$a = b$ Equals. **Alias** EQ
$a >= b$ Is greater than or equal to. **Alias** GE
$a > b$ Is greater than. **Alias** GT
a NE b Does not equal.
a IN (*constant, . . .*)   Is in. The expression is equal to one of the constant values. (The commas are not required.)

a NOTIN (*constant*, . . .)   Is not in. The expression is not equal to any of the constant values.

N   Comparison: 1 if the comparison is true, 0 otherwise. With character operands of unequal lengths, the shorter operand is treated as padded with blanks to the length of the longer operand.

a <: *b*   *a* <=: *b*   *a* =: *b*   *a* >=: *b*   *a* >: *b*   *a* NE: *b*
a IN: (*constant*, . . .)   *a* NOTIN: (*constant*, . . .)
Aliases LT: LE: EQ: GE: GT:

N   Character comparison with truncation: 1 if the comparison, with the longer operand treated as being truncated to the length of the shorter operand, is true, 0 otherwise.

a = '*bit mask*'B   **Alias** EQ

N   Bit testing. The bit mask is a string of 0s, 1s, and periods. Spaces can also be included for clarity. Each character in the bit mask represents a bit. The bit mask is compared to the value *a* bit by bit. If the value is numeric, it is converted to a 32-bit integer and right-aligned against the bit mask. If the value is character, it is left-aligned. The comparison is true if all the 0s and 1s in the bit mask match the corresponding bits in the expression.

Also see **NOT**

MAX

a MAX *b*   **$N**   Maximum; the greater of the values *a* and *b*.
Alias <>

MIN

a MIN *b*   **$N**   Minimum; the lesser of the values *a* and *b*.
Alias ><

NOT

NOT *a*   **N**   Logical not: 1 if *a* is false, 0 otherwise.

a NOT *comparison operator b*   **N**   Negative comparison; logical not applied to the comparison; equivalent to
NOT (*a comparison operator b*).

Alias ∧, ¬, ~

OR

a OR *b*   **N**   Or: 1 if either *a* or *b* is true, 0 if both *a* and *b* are false.
Alias |

||

a || *b*   **$**   Concatenation: *a* with *b* added to the end.

Compound Expressions

In an expression with more than one operator, parentheses can be used to control the order in which the operators are applied.

If parentheses are not used to isolate each operator, the sequence of operations is determined by the priority of each operator. When two or more operators have the same priority, they are executed in order, either left to right or right to left. Operator priorities are shown in this table:

Operators	Priority	Order
Prefix (NOT, +, -), MIN, MAX, **	1 (first)	right to left
*, /	2	left to right
+, - (addition, subtraction)	3	left to right
||	4	left to right
Comparison	5	left to right
AND	6	left to right
OR	7 (last)	left to right

Examples

In A/(B + C), the addition operation is done first because it is enclosed in parentheses.

A OR B AND C is evaluated as A OR (B AND C) because AND has a higher priority than OR.

A - B - C is evaluated as (A - B) - C because the subtraction operator is evaluated from left to right.

Multiple Comparison Operators

When an expression contains multiple comparison operators (not including the IN operator), each operator is evaluated separately and the results combined with an AND operation.

Example

0 < X <= 1 is evaluated as 0 < X AND X <= 1.

WHERE Operators

WHERE expressions are conditions used in the WHERE statement, WHERE= dataset option, and elsewhere to subset SAS datasets. They can use constants, variables in the SAS dataset, SAS function calls, and operators.

The NE operator can be written <>.

The MAX operator can be used, but must be written MAX, not <>.

These additional comparison operators can be used in WHERE clauses:

a BETWEEN *b* AND *c*   **N**   Boolean: 1 if *a* is in the range between *b* and *c*, inclusive, 0 otherwise.

a CONTAINS *b*   *a* ? *b*   **N**   Boolean: 1 if *b* is a substring of *a*, 0 otherwise.

a IS NULL   *a* IS MISSING   **N**   Boolean: 1 if *a* is a missing (or blank) value, 0 otherwise.

a LIKE *b*   **N**   Character comparison with wild-card characters; similar to the = operator, but in *b*, _ matches any character in *a*, and % matches any sequence of characters.

a =* *b*   *a* EQ* *b*   **N**   Sounds-like: tests whether two character operands sound the same, according to the Soundex algorithm.

These are the negative forms of the comparisons:

a NOT BETWEEN *b* AND *c*
a NOT CONTAINS *b*
a NOT ? *b*
a IS NOT NULL
a IS NOT MISSING
a NOT IS NULL
a NOT IS MISSING
a NOT LIKE *b*
a NOT =* *b*
a NOT EQ* *b*

A logical operator, the SAME AND operator, may be useful when a WHERE expression already exists, especially for run group processing. A WHERE expression that starts with the SAME AND operator adds more conditions to the existing WHERE expression. The SAME AND operator has a lower priority than any other operator.

SAME AND *a*   **N**   Boolean. 1 if the existing WHERE condition and *a* are both true, 0 otherwise.

Examples
WHERE AGE BETWEEN 14 AND 59.5;
WHERE LAST =* 'ASTR' AND LAST NOT CONTAINS 'O';

Character Sets

A computer's character set, or collating sequence, determines what characters the computer can display and the comparison order of character data.

ASCII

Most computers use the ASCII character set with additional characters. The characters beyond hexadecimal 7F may vary depending on the font, operating system options, or the selection of character set. The ASCII character codes are also used in the Unicode character set.

	0	1	2	3	4	5	6	7	8	9	A	B	C	D	E	F
0	null										tab					
1																
2	space	!	"	#	$	%	&	'	(	)	*	+	,	-	.	/
3	0	1	2	3	4	5	6	7	8	9	:	;	<	=	>	?
4	@	A	B	C	D	E	F	G	H	I	J	K	L	M	N	O
5	P	Q	R	S	T	U	V	W	X	Y	Z	[	\	]	^	_
6	`	a	b	c	d	e	f	g	h	i	j	k	l	m	n	o
7	p	q	r	s	t	u	v	w	x	y	z	{	|	}	~	

EBCDIC

This character set is found on IBM mainframe computers.

	0	1	2	3	4	5	6	7	8	9	A	B	C	D	E	F
0	null					tab										
1																
2																
3																
4	blank										¢	.	<	(	+	|
5	&										!	$	*	)	;	¬
6	-	/									¦	,	%	_	>	?
7										`	:	#	@	'	=	"
8		a	b	c	d	e	f	g	h	i						
9		j	k	l	m	n	o	p	q	r						
A		~	s	t	u	v	w	x	y	z						
B																
C	{	A	B	C	D	E	F	G	H	I						
D	}	J	K	L	M	N	O	P	Q	R						
E	\	~	S	T	U	V	W	X	Y	Z						
F	0	1	2	3	4	5	6	7	8	9						

Arrays

An array is a named list of variables in a data step. It is defined in the ARRAY statement. The name of an array should not be the same as the name of a variable in the same data step or the name of a SAS function.

After an array is defined, a variable in the array can be used by referring to the array. An array reference is formed by following the array name with the subscript value in braces:

array{subscript}

The subscript can be any numeric expression, but you should make sure it resolves to an integer value within the array's subscript range. You can use parentheses in place of braces.

For a multidimensional array, two or more subscripts are separated by commas:

array{subscript, subscript}

Array names can be used as abbreviated variable lists in some statements. A previously defined array name can be listed in a RETAIN statement to provide initial values for the array elements.

In a PUT or INPUT statement, you can list all the elements of an array by using * in place of an array subscript:

PUT *array*{*};

Lengths of Character Expressions

The length of a character expression results from the variable and constant values and the operators and functions that make up the expression. If a character expression is assigned to a character variable with a different length, the expression is altered to fit the length of the variable. If the expression is shorter than the variable, trailing spaces are added, a process called blank padding. If the expression is longer than the variable, characters are omitted from the end of the expression. That process is called truncation.

Example
LENGTH A $ 4;
A = 'INFORMATION';
PUT A=;

A=INFO

Automatic Type Conversion

In a data step, if a numeric expression is assigned to a character variable or used in another place where a character expression is expected, a character value is created by applying the BEST format to the numeric value. The resulting character value often contains leading spaces.

Similarly, character expressions in data steps are automatically converted to numeric values as needed using the standard numeric informat. If the character expression does not contain a valid numeral, this results in an error.

In other places where expressions are used, such as WHERE clauses and SQL, data types are not automatically converted and using an incorrect data type results in an error.

Missing Values

Numeric missing values are numeric values that represent the absence of a number. Blank character values are also missing values. Missing values can appear in input text data or as constant values in the program. They are also generated in many situations when a program is run. By default, ordinary variables in a data step are initialized to missing, and many of them are reset to missing at the beginning of each repetition of the observation loop. Missing values are also created by the SET statement when SAS datasets contain different variables and by the MERGE statement when not all observations match.

Numeric missing values result when invalid values are read from input files or are used as arguments to functions, when missing values are used as operands for arithmetic operators, and when an automatic type conversion of a character value to a numeric value is unsuccessful. In comparisons, numbers are considered to be greater than missing values.

Special missing values are 27 distinct missing values that you can read and assign, using the 26 letters and the underscore. Uppercase and lowercase letters are equivalent. Use the MISSING statement before you read special missing values from input data. Special missing value constants are written as a period followed by an underscore or letter. In comparisons, different special missing values are considered to be unequal.

Sort order of numeric values

._ .   .A – .Z   *negative numbers*   0   *positive numbers*

Component Objects ○ 9+

Data step component objects are used in data step programming to accomplish tasks that would be difficult to do with data step variables. A component object belongs to an object class that defines a particular arrangement of data and a set of actions, called methods.

Object-Dot Syntax

The object-dot syntax emphasizes the connection between an object and its attribute or method by writing their names in combination. Write the object name, a dot (period), and the attribute or method.

object.attribute   An object attribute. Use an attribute in the same manner as a variable in expressions and assignment statements.

object.method(*argument*, . . .)   An object method. This takes an action that involves the object. Use an object method in the same manner as a function. If there are named arguments, write the argument name and a colon before the argument value. For some methods, an argument name may be used more than once. If there are no arguments, the parentheses are still required. The method returns an error code; a nonzero value indicates that the action was unsuccessful. You can also use an object method as a complete statement, without assigning the error code to a variable. If the action is unsuccessful, a log note describes the error.

DECLARE *class object*(*argument*, . . .);   *object* = _NEW_ *class*(*argument*, . . .);   An object constructor. This is a special object method that creates a new object.

Examples

This statement assigns the number of items in the hash object TABLE to the variable SIZE:

SIZE = TABLE.NUM_ITEMS;

These statements define and set up the hash object TABLE with two key variables and three data variables:

DECLARE HASH TABLE(ORDERED: 'A');
TABLE.DEFINEKEY('PART', 'SEQUENCE');
TABLE.DEFINEDATA('PART', 'SEQUENCE', 'RATING');
TABLE.DEFINEDONE();

In this statement, the variable RC tells whether the hash object TABLE contains an item with values of A and 100 for the key variables.

RC = TABLE.CHECK(KEY: 'A', KEY: 100);

Object Classes

HASH

A hash object; a lookup table containing key values and data values. The key values must be unique; a hash object cannot add an item that duplicates an existing key value. The hash object looks up an item based on the values of the key variables and retrieves values for the data variables from the item.

Constructor arguments

All arguments are optional.

HASHEXP: *n*   Creates a hash of size 2^n. (This does not limit the number of data items in the hash object.) **Default** 8

DATASET: '*SAS dataset*'   A SAS dataset that supplies data values for the object.

ORDERED: The order in which data values are returned: 'YES' 'Y' 'ASCENDING' 'A' In ascending order. 'DESCENDING' 'D' In descending order. 'NO' 'N' In an arbitrary order. **Default** 'NO'

Attribute

object.NUM_ITEMS   The number of items in the object.

Methods

object.DEFINEKEY('*variable*', . . .)   Declares key variables.

object.DEFINEKEY(ALL: 'YES')   Uses all variables from the SAS dataset as key variables.

object.DEFINEDATA('*variable*', . . .)   Declares data variables.

object.DEFINEDATA(ALL: 'YES')   Uses all variables from the SAS dataset as data variables.

object.DEFINEDONE()   Call this method after DEFINEKEY and DEFINEDATA to indicate that the initialization process is complete.

object.ADD() Adds data using the current values of the key and data variables.

object.ADD(KEY: *value*, . . . , DATA: *value*, . . .) Adds data using the indicated values of the key and data variables.

object.REPLACE() Adds or replaces data using the current values of the key and data variables.

object.REPLACE(KEY: *value*, . . . , DATA: *value*, . . .) Adds or replaces data using the indicated values of the key and data variables.

object.REMOVE() Removes data using the current values of the key variables.

object.REMOVE(KEY: *value*, . . .) Removes data using the indicated values of the key variables.

object.CHECK() Checks for the existence of an item using the current values of the key variables. Returns 0 if the item exists, an error code if it does not.

object.CHECK(KEY: *value*, . . .) Checks for the existence of an item using the indicated values of the key variables. Returns 0 if the item exists, an error code if it does not.

object.FIND() Retrieves data variables using the current values of the key variables.

object.FIND(KEY: *value*, . . .) Retrieves data variables using the indicated values of the key variables.

object.OUTPUT(DATASET: *SAS dataset*, . . .) Stores data variables from the object in a SAS dataset.

object.DELETE() Deletes the object.

HITER

A hash iterator; retrieves data in sequence from a hash object. It obtains the values of the data variables of the hash object.

Constructor argument

'*hash object*' The hash object that the hash iterator object refers to.

Methods

object.FIRST() Retrieves the first item.

object.LAST() Retrieves the last item.

object.NEXT() Retrieves the next item.

object.PREV() Retrieves the previous item.

8

Macro Language

Macro objects are text objects that can be used to construct SAS statements and commands. Macro language is a language that can be used to act on macro objects. You can use macro language anywhere in a SAS program or on the command line.

Macro Variables

A macro variable is a string of characters associated with a name. You can assign a value to a macro variable with the %LET statement or the SYMPUT routine. To refer to a macro variable, use an ampersand (&) followed by the macro variable name, optionally followed by a period:

&name or &name.

The period is required if the macro variable reference is immediately followed by a letter, digit, underscore, or period.

In addition to macro variables you define, you can refer to the automatic macro variables listed below. Those marked **(a)** can also be assigned new values in order to change the state of the session.

&SQLOBS   Number of rows processed by an SQL statement.

&SQLOOPS   Number of loop iterations of an SQL statement.

&SQLRC   Error code from an SQL statement.

&SQLXRC   SQL pass-through return code. ○ SAS/ACCESS

&SQLXMSG   SQL pass-through error message. ○ SAS/ACCESS

&SYSCC   Error code of the current SAS process. **(a)** ○ 7+

&SYSCHARWIDTH   Character width, 1 (narrow) or 2 (wide). ○ 7+

&SYSCMD   An unrecognized command from a macro window.

&SYSDATE   The date when the SAS session started, as written by the DATE7. format.

&SYSDATE9 The date when the SAS session started, as written by the DATE9. format. ⟲ 7+

&SYSDAY The name of the day of the week when the SAS session started.

&SYSDEVIC Equivalent to the system option DEVICE=. **(a)**

&SYSDMG Error code that indicates a reaction to damaged SAS datasets. **(a)** ⟲ 7+

&SYSDSN Libref (characters 1–8) and member name (characters 9–40) of the _LAST_ SAS dataset. **(a)**

&SYSENV FORE in foreground modes if TERMINAL system option is in effect, BACK otherwise.

&SYSERR The error code from a step. **(a)**

&SYSFILRC The error code from the FILENAME statement. **(a)**

&SYSINDEX How many macros have started executing in the SAS session.

&SYSINFO Diagnostic information from some procedures. **(a)**

&SYSJOBID The user ID or job number of the SAS session.

&SYSLAST The _LAST_ SAS dataset. **(a)**

&SYSLCKRC The error code from the LOCK statement. **(a)**

&SYSLIBRC The error code from the LIBNAME statement. **(a)**

&SYSMACRONAME The name of the current macro (blank if there is no current macro). ⟲ 7+

&SYSMAXLONG The maximum value of a long integer. ⟲ 7+

&SYSMENV S if a macro was invoked in a program, D if a macro was invoked in a command.

&SYSMSG A message to be displayed in the message line of a macro window. **(a)**

&SYSNCPU The number of available central processors as indicated in the CPUCOUNT system option. ⟲ 9+

&SYSPARM The parameter string from the SYSPARM= system option. **(a)**

&SYSPBUFF Text of macro parameters (in a macro compiled with the PARMBUFF option). **(a)**

&SYSPROCESSID The process ID of the current SAS process. ⟲ 7+

&SYSPROCESSNAME The process name of the current SAS process. ⟲ 7+

&SYSPROCNAME For the current step, the procedure name or DATASTEP (blank if there is no current step). ⟲ 8.2+

&SYSRC The return code from an operating system command.

&SYSSCP The operating system, abbreviated.

&SYSSCPL The specific operating system, abbreviated.

&SYSSITE The SAS site number.

&SYSSTARTID The most recent SAS process ID. ⟲ 7+

&SYSSTARTNAME The most recent SAS process name. ⟲ 7+

&SYSTIME The time of day when the SAS session started.

&SYSUID The user ID associated with the job. ☾ z

&SYSUSERID The user ID. ☾ 7+

&SYSVER The SAS release number.

&SYSVLONG The extended SAS release number, including the maintenance (technical support) level.

Macro Statements

Macro statements are executed when the macro processor reaches them. Macro statements in macros are executed as the macro is resolved. Macro statements can appear just about anywhere in statements and commands in a SAS session. Some (marked **M...**) can be used only within the definition of a macro.

To execute macro statements during the execution of a data step, use the CALL EXECUTE routine.

%*

%* *text* ; Macro comment statement. no effect on session. Unlike the regular comment statement, a macro comment statement can appear anywhere a macro statement is allowed. Macro comment statements are not treated as part of a macro definition. Any quote characters in the comment text must match (that is, they must be present in an even number).

Macro language references in macro comment statements are not resolved. (By contrast, SAS comment statements in a macro definition are treated as constant text, and macro language references in them are resolved as the macro is resolved.)

%ABORT M... ☾ 9+

%ABORT *options*; Ends execution of a macro with an error condition. Also ends execution of the current data step, if any, with an error condition. **Options** ABEND RETURN *n*

%COPY ☾ 9.1+

%COPY *macro / options*; Copies a macro to a text file.

Options

LIBRARY=*libref* LIB=*libref* The location of the macro (a libref other than WORK).

OUT=*text file* OUTFILE=*text file* The destination. **Default** LOG

SOURCE SRC Uses the stored source code of the macro (from the SOURCE option in the %MACRO statement).

%DISPLAY

%DISPLAY *window or window.group options*; Displays a macro window. In a macro, the window closes automatically when the macro ends. Elsewhere, the window closes automatically as soon as the user responds. **Options** BLANK BELL NOINPUT DELETE (See the data step DISPLAY statement for descriptions.)

%DO . . . %END M...

%DO; *macro expression* %END;   Forms a macro block.

%DO %WHILE(*condition*) or %UNTIL(*condition*) or
macro variable name = *start* %TO *stop optional* %BY *increment*;
macro expression %END;   Forms a macro loop. The macro
expression is resolved repeatedly. (See the data step DO statement for
descriptions of keywords.)

%ELSE M...

%ELSE *macro expression*;   Generates the macro expression if
the %IF condition is false. Use only immediately after a %IF-%THEN
statement.

%GLOBAL

%GLOBAL *macro variable name . . .* ;   Declares global macro
variables.

%GOTO M...

%GOTO *macro label*;   Branches to the macro label. The label must
be in the same macro. A macro label has the form %*label*:

%IF . . . %THEN M...

%IF *condition* %THEN *macro expression*;   Generates the macro
expression only if the condition is true.

%INCLUDE

%INCLUDE *fileref or fileref(member)* or '*physical file*' . . . / *options*;
Includes the text file as part of the SAS program.

Options

SOURCE2   Statements in the included file appear in the log.
NOSOURCE2   Statements in the included file do not appear in the log.
JCLEXCL   Excludes JCL lines. ○ z

S2=*n*   Uses only the first *n* characters from each line in the file.

Alias %INC

Example
%INC 'HERE.SAS';

%LET

%LET *macro variable name* = *macro expression*;   Assigns a value
to the macro variable.

Examples
%LET I = 0;
%LET DAILY = %QUOTE(AMT = M(DAY)*RATE(DAY););

%LOCAL M...

%LOCAL *macro variable name . . .* ;   Declares local macro variables.

%MACRO . . . %MEND

%MACRO *macro optional* (*parameters*) / *options*; *macro expression* %MEND . . . ;   Defines a macro. The macro expression is

resolved when the macro is invoked. The parameters, if used, define local macro variables that can be set when the macro is invoked.

Options
STMT   Allows statement-style invocation.

CMD   Allows command-style invocation.

DES='*label*'   Stores a description with the catalog entry.

STORE   Stores the compiled macro in the current macro catalog.

SOURCE   SRC   Also stores the source code.   ☉ 9.1+

PARMBUFF   Assigns the parameter list, including parentheses, to the automatic macro variable SYSPBUFF when the macro is called.

Example
```
%MACRO RESETP;
PROC PRINTTO PRINT=PRINT;
RUN;
TITLE1 ' ';
FOOTNOTE;
OPTIONS PAGENO=1 NODATE NUMBER;
%MEND;
```

%PUT
%PUT *terms*;   Writes information in the log.

Terms
text   Writes text (after resolving).

Writes the scope, name, and value of macro variables, each on a separate line: _ALL_   All macro variables. _AUTOMATIC_   Automatic macro variables. _GLOBAL_   Global macro variables. _USER_ Global macro variables and local macro variables of all executing macros. _LOCAL_   Local macro variables of the current macro only.

Example
%PUT SYSMENV IS &SYSMENV;

%RETURN   M... ☉ 9+
%RETURN;   Ends execution of a macro.

%SYMDEL   ☉ 8.2+
%SYMDEL *name* . . . ;   Deletes the global macro variables.

%SYSCALL
%SYSCALL CALL *routine name*(*macro variable name*, . . .);
Executes a CALL routine using macro variables as arguments. Supply names of macro variables (without ampersands) for the arguments.

%SYSEXEC
%SYSEXEC;   %SYSEXEC *command*;   Equivalent to the X statement.

%SYSLPUT   ☉ SAS/ACCESS ☉ 8+
%SYSLPUT *remote macro variable name* = *macro expression* / *option*;   Assigns a value to the macro variable in the remote session. Execute this statement in the local session.

Option REMOTE=*session ID* ☉ 9+

%SYSRPUT ○ SAS/ACCESS

%SYSRPUT *macro variable name = remote macro expression*;
Assigns a value from the remote session to the local macro variable.
Execute this statement in the remote session.

%WINDOW

%WINDOW *window window options field definitions and/or group definitions*;   Defines a macro window. The syntax of options, fields, and groups is the same as in the data step WINDOW statement, with these differences: Informat/format terms are not used. Instead, a number indicates the length of the field. Macro variables, instead of data step variables, are displayed in variable fields.

Macro Operators

The arithmetic, comparison, and logical operators can be used with macro variables and other macro objects. Arithmetic operators work only with integer parts of values. Comparison operators do character comparisons, unless both operands are integers. Use the %EVAL function to evaluate a macro expression that uses macro operators, unless it appears as part of a macro statement.

The symbol # is an alias for the IN operator. The MINDELIMITER= system option selects the delimiter that separates values in the list of values that is the right operand of the IN operator. ○ 9.1+

Macro Functions

Macro functions take one or more macro expressions as arguments and return a macro expression. Usually the returned value is a modified form of one of the arguments.

Many of these macro functions are actually implemented as macros. As long as the macro library is correctly installed, there is little practical difference between using a macro function and using a function-style macro.

Quoting

The macro quoting functions modify the way the macro processor tokenizes and resolves a macro expression.

%STR(*macro expression*)   Quotes the unresolved macro expression and treats it as constant text.

%NRSTR(*macro expression*)   Quotes the unresolved macro expression, treats it as constant text, and prevents it from being rescanned.

%QUOTE(*macro expression*)   Quotes the resolved macro expression.

%NRQUOTE(*macro expression*)   Quotes the resolved macro expression and prevents it from being rescanned.

%BQUOTE(*macro expression*)   Quotes the resolved macro expression and treats it as constant text.

%NRBQUOTE(*macro expression*)   Quotes the resolved macro expression, treats it as constant text, and prevents it from being rescanned.

%SUPERQ(*macro variable name*)   A macro variable reference: substitutes the value of the macro variable and prevents it from being scanned.

%UNQUOTE(*macro expression*)   Unquotes: removes the effects of quoting functions.

String

The macro string functions treat a macro expression as a character string. Most correspond to SAS functions of the same names. These functions always return an unquoted result, even if the arguments are quoted.

%CMPRES(*string*)   Removes leading and trailing spaces and converts multiple blanks to single blanks.

%INDEX(*string, substring*)   Corresponds to the INDEX function.

%LEFT(*string*)   Removes leading spaces.

%LENGTH(*string*)   Returns the actual length of the (resolved) argument (including leading and trailing spaces, if quoted). Returns 0 for a null argument.

%LOWCASE(*string*)   Corresponds to the LOWCASE function.

%SCAN(*string, n*)   **%SCAN**(*string, n, delimiters*)   Corresponds to the SCAN function.

%SUBSTR(*string, start*)   **%SUBSTR**(*string, start, length*) Corresponds to the SUBSTR function

%TRIM(*string*)   Removes trailing spaces.

%UPCASE(*string*)   Corresponds to the UPCASE function.

%VERIFY(*string, characters*)   Corresponds to the VERIFY function.

String Quoting

The macro string quoting functions duplicate macro string functions, but return a quoted result.

%QCMPRES(*string*)

%QLEFT(*string*)

%QLOWCASE(*string*)

%QTRIM(*string*)

%QSCAN(*string, n*)   **%QSCAN**(*string, n, delimiters*)

%QSUBSTR(*string, start*)   **%QSUBSTR**(*string, start, length*)

%QUPCASE(*string*)

Expression

%DATATYP(*macro expression*)   Data type: returns NUMERIC for a numeric constant in regular or scientific notation, CHAR otherwise.

%EVAL(*macro expression*)   Evaluates a macro expression that contains macro operators.

%SYSEVALF(*numeric expression, optional effect code*)   Evaluates a numeric expression and applies a numeric effect to the result. This function is useful for floating-point arithmetic and for converting fractional values to whole values. **Effect codes** CEIL FLOOR INT INTEGER TRUNC BOOLEAN

%SYSFUNC(*function name (argument, . . .), optional format*) Executes a SAS function. Supply the function's arguments as macro expressions; do not quote character arguments. When a function requires a variable as an argument, supply a macro variable name (without an ampersand). The returned value is converted to a macro expression.

%QSYSFUNC(*function name (argument, . . .), optional format*) Executes a SAS function and quotes the returned value.

Environment

%SYMEXIST(*macro variable name*)   Returns 1 if the macro variable exists, 0 otherwise. ⊙ 9.1+

%SYMGLOBL(*macro variable name*)   Returns 1 if the global macro variable exists, 0 otherwise. ⊙ 9.1+

%SYMLOCAL(*macro variable name*)   Returns 1 if the local macro variable exists, 0 otherwise. ⊙ 9.1+

%SYSGET(*variable or symbol name*)   Returns the value of the environment variable or operating system variable or symbol.

%SYSPROD(*name*)   Equivalent to the SYSPROD function.

Macros

A macro is a macro expression that is given a name and stored as a catalog entry of type MACRO. Macros are typically used to generate SAS statements that make up an entire SAS program or a part of a SAS program.

A macro is defined by the %MACRO and %MEND statements. After the macro is defined, it can be invoked by using its name preceded by a percent sign:

```
%MACRO macro;                    %* macro definition;
macro expression
%MEND;
. . .
%macro                           %* macro invocation;
```

Usually a macro has parameters, which are local macro variables that can be given values when the macro is invoked. Parameters are listed in parentheses, separated by commas, after the macro name. In the %MACRO statement, the parameter names are given. In the macro invocation, values are given for the parameters.

There are two kinds of parameters. Positional parameters appear first in the list. Values for positional parameters must be supplied every time the macro is invoked and must appear in the correct order.

Keyword parameters can appear after the last positional parameter. In the %MACRO statement, the keyword parameter name is followed by an equals sign and a default value. In the macro invocation, a different value can optionally be supplied for the keyword parameter, using the same syntax. Keyword parameters can appear in any order at the end of the parameter list.

```
%MACRO macro(positional parameter name, . . . ,
        keyword parameter=default value, . . . );
macro expression
%MEND;
. . .
%macro(positional parameter value, . . . ,
        keyword parameter name=value, . . . )
```

In the macro, parameters are local macro variables that can be used in the same way as any macro variables.

Macros that are defined with the STMT option can also be invoked using a statement syntax:

```
macro  positional parameter value . . .
        keyword parameter name=value . . . ;
```

Command-style invocation works about the same way, but it allows a macro to be used as a command

When the MAUTOSOURCE system option is in effect, a set of macros can be used in a program without having to be defined in the same program. Each autocall macro is defined in a separate member of an autocall library, which is a library of SAS programs that is identified by the SASAUTOS= system option. The SAS System also provides a set of utility macros.

Example

These macro statements define the macro CLOSE with positional and keyword parameters:

```
%MACRO CLOSE(X1, X2, TOL=.00001);
(ABS((&X1) - (&X2)) <= ABS(&TOL))
%MEND;
```

Later, the macro can be called with values supplied for the positional parameters and, optionally, the keyword parameter:

```
%CLOSE(THICK, 2.0072, TOL=.0002)
```

The Macro Processor

The macro processor intercepts program lines and command lines in a SAS session and resolves macro language references. It scans the incoming text and does the following:

- executes macro statements
- substitutes values for macro variables, macros, and macro functions
- deletes macro comment statements
- converts double ampersands to single ampersands

It then rescans any text generated from macro objects, and repeats the process until no macro language references remain.

Macro language references are resolved in constants that are enclosed in double quotes, but are not resolved inside constants that are enclosed in single quotes.

Examples

The scanning examples below use these macro variables and macro:

```
%LET LA = 6;
%LET LETTER = L;
%MACRO A(X);
MISSING %UPCASE(&X) %LOWCASE(&X);
%MEND;
```

When the macro processor scans this text:

```
&&&LETTER.A..4
```

it converts && to & and &LETTER. to L:

```
&LA..4
```

On rescanning, the text resolves to:

```
6.4
```

Scanning works the same way when macros and macro functions are involved. This reference:

```
%&LETTER(A B C D E)
```

becomes, in succession:

```
%A(A B C D E)
```

```
MISSING %UPCASE(&X) %LOWCASE(&X);
```

```
MISSING %UPCASE(A B C D E) %LOWCASE(A B C D E);
```

```
MISSING A B C D E a b c d e;
```

9

System Options

System options allow you to control the way things work in a SAS session.

Most system options can be changed at any time during the SAS session. Some, marked **Init.** in the entries that follow, are initialization options that can be set only at the beginning of the SAS session, either in the command line or configuration file. Those marked **Start** can also be set at the beginning of a SAS process.

During a session, options are changed in the OPTIONS statement. When starting a SAS process, options can be set in the STARTSAS statement. In these statements, keyword options can appear simply as the option name to turn the option on, or the option name prefixed by NO to turn the option off. For keyword-value options, the option name is followed by an equals sign (=) and an appropriate value for the option. A few options can take either a value or the NO prefix; in that case, the NO prefix is equivalent to a blank value or no value assigned to the option.

Keyword options indicate Boolean values (1 and 0), and they might also be shown as check boxes. Check boxes in the following entries represent the on (☑) and off (☐) states of keyword options. Where it is not specifically described, the off state of an option represents the opposite or absence of the on state.

Option groups organize system options for display and reporting purposes. These are option group names:

COMMUNICATIONS   DATAQUALITY   EMAIL   ENVDISPLAY
ENVFILES   ERRORHANDLING   EXECMODES   EXTFILES
GRAPHICS   HELP   INPUTCONTROL   INSTALL
LANGUAGECONTROL   LISTCONTROL   LOG_LISTCONTROL
LOGCONTROL   MACRO   MEMORY   META   ODSPRINT
PERFORMANCE   SASFILES   SORT

ALTLOG=

Start *'physical file name' or device* A copy of the log is directed to this file. □

ALTPRINT=

Start *'physical file name' or device* A copy of the standard print file is directed to this file. □

APPLETLOC= ○ 8+

Start *'url or physical file name' or device* Location of Java applets.

APPEND= ○ W X

Start *system option 'physical file name'* Adds the physical file name to any already in the system option. **System option** CONFIG ECHO HELPLOC MAPS MSG SAMPLOC SASAUTOS SASHELP MSG SASSCRIPT

ASYNCHIO ○ 8+

Init. ☑ Executes other tasks at the same time as I/O. □ Waits for I/O to complete before starting any other tasks.

AUTOEXEC=

Init. *'physical file name'* SAS statements in this file are executed at the beginning of the session. □

AUTOSAVELOC= ○ 9.1+

file The Program Editor autosave file.

AUTOSIGNON= ○ SAS/CONNECT ○ 8.1+

YES Allows actions such as the RSUBMIT statement to start a remote session. NO Requires a SIGNON statement to start a remote session. This is the default.

AWSCONTROL= ○ W

Init. The SAS AWS has: TITLE A title bar. NOTITLE No title bar, window control menu, or minimize/maximize buttons. SYSTEMMENU A window control menu. NOSYSTEMMENU No window control menu. MINMAX Minimize/maximize buttons. NOMINMAX No minimize/maximize buttons. **Default** TITLE SYSTEMMENU MINMAX

AWSDEF= ○ W

Init. *row percent column percent height percent width percent* The size and location of the SAS AWS.

AWSMENU ○ W

☑ Displays AWS menu bar. □

AWSMENUMERGE ○ W

☑ Menus include menu items specific to the operating system. □

AWSTITLE= ↺W
Init. "*title*" The title of the SAS AWS.

BATCH
Start ☑ Uses the batch mode defaults for system options SOURCE, PAGESIZE=, LINESIZE=, and OVP. ☐ Uses the interactive default settings.

BINDING= ↺7+
The binding edge when printing on both sides: DEFAULTEDGE DEFAULT LONGEDGE LONG SHORTEDGE SHORT

BLKSIZE=
n *n*K Block size for a SAS data library. ↺Xz

BLKSIZE(*storage device* or OTHER)=*size* Block size for SAS data libraries on specific storage devices. **Storage device** DISK DASD *device number* **Size** *n* *n*K OPT MAX FULL HALF THIRD FOURTH FIFTH ↺z

BLOCKALLOC ↺z
Sets LRECL and BLKSIZE when a SAS data library is: ☑ Allocated. ☐ First accessed.

BOTTOMMARGIN= ↺7+
size "*size unit*" The size of the bottom margin. **Unit** IN CM

BUFNO=
n The number of buffers to use for a SAS dataset. 0 A SAS dataset uses the default number of buffers.

BUFSIZE=
n *n*K *n*M The buffer size for each SAS dataset created. 0 Each SAS dataset created uses the default buffer size.

BYERR
When an attempt is made to sort a SAS dataset with no variables: ☑ An error is generated. ☐ No action is taken.

BYLINE
☑ Procedures print BY lines that identify each BY group. ☐ Procedures do not print BY lines. Each BY group starts on a separate page.

BYSORTED ↺9+
When a step processes BY groups for a SAS dataset that is not in sorted order: ☑ An error is generated. ☐ The step processes whatever groups are present.

CAPS
Lowercase letters in data values in the SAS program file are treated as: ☑ Capital letters. ☐ Lowercase letters.

CAPSOUT ⟳z

☑ All print output is converted to uppercase. ☐

CARDIMAGE

☑ Source and data lines are processed as 80-character lines. Tokens can be split between lines. ☐ The last nonblank character is treated as the end of the line of input and is a token boundary.

CATCACHE=

Init. *n* The specified number of SAS catalogs are kept open (cached).

CBUFNO=

n The number of extra buffers to use for each catalog.

CENTER

☑ Title lines, footnote lines, and most print output from procedures are centered horizontally on the page. ☐ Print output is left-aligned on the page. **Alias CENTRE**

CHARCODE

☑ Special character combinations can be used to substitute for characters that are not on the keyboard:

?: for `   ?, for \   ?(for {   ?) for }   ?= for ∧ or ¬
?- for _   ?/ for | ?< for [?> for]

☐ Substitute character combinations are not recognized.

CLEANUP

Automatically frees memory: ☑ Continuously, by removing unnecessary resources. Prompts the interactive user only for a disk-full condition. ☐ As needed, by removing unnecessary invisible resources. Prompts the interactive user to decide how to respond to any out-of-resource condition.

CMDMAC

The macro processor: ☑ Checks every command to see if it is a command-style macro call. ☐ Does not recognize command-style macro calls.

CMPOPT= ⟳9.1+

Uses compiler optimizations: ALL All. NONE None.
(*list*) Specific selections: EXTRAMATH   NOEXTRAMATH
MISSCHECK   NOMISSCHECK   PRECISE   NOPRECISE   GUARDCHECK
NOGUARDCHECK

COLLATE ⟳7+

When printing multiple copies of multiple pages: ☑ Collate copies.
☐

COLORPRINTING ⟳7+

☑ Prints in color, if available. ☐

COMAMID= ○ SAS/CONNECT, SAS/SHARE

TCP/IP   APPC   XMS   The communications access method.

COMDEF= ○ W

Init.   TOP *or* CENTER *or* BOTTOM   LEFT *or* CENTER *or* RIGHT
The location for the Command dialog box. **Default** BOTTOM
CENTER

COMPRESS=

YES   CHAR   BINARY   NO   Equivalent to the dataset option.

CONFIG=

Init.   '*physical file name*'   The file that contains system options that
are set at the start of the session. Valid only on the command line or
in an environment variable that holds SAS system options.

CONNECTPERSIST ○ SAS/CONNECT ○ 9+

After a remote submit ends: ☑ Continues the remote session.
☐ Ends the remote session. **Alias CPERSIST**

CONNECTREMOTE= ○ SAS/CONNECT ○ 7+

session ID The session ID for a remote session.
Alias CREMOTE, REMOTE

CONNECTSTATUS ○ SAS/CONNECT ○ 7+

☑ Displays a status window for a SAS/CONNECT file transfer.   ☐
Alias CSTATUS

CONNECTWAIT ○ SAS/CONNECT ○ 7+

☑ Waits for a remote submit to complete.   ☐ **Alias CWAIT**

CONSOLELOG= ○ 7+

Init.   *physical file name or device*   The location of the console log
(for SAS kernel error messages).

COPIES= ○ 7+

n The number of copies to print.

CPUCOUNT= ○ 9+

n The number of central processors available for use (for thread-
enabled applications).

CPUID

Init. ☑ At the beginning of the SAS session, a note identifying the
hardware is written in the log.   ☐

CSYSRPUTSYNC= ○ SAS/CONNECT ○ 9+

A %SYSRPUT statement in an asynchronous remote session is
executed: YES   Immediately.   NO   At the next synchronization point.
This is the default.

DATASTMTCHK= ⟲ 7+

The DATA statement allows as a one-level SAS dataset name: NONE Any SAS name. COREKEYWORDS Any SAS name except RETAIN, SET, MERGE, or UPDATE. This is the default. ALLKEYWORDS Any SAS name except words that, as keywords, could begin a statement in a data step. Use this option to generate a syntax error when the semicolon is omitted at the end of a DATA statement.

DATE

☑ The date and time are printed in the log and in the title lines of any print file. ☐ The date and time are not printed in title lines.

DBCS

☑ Allows multiple bytes per character. This option is required for double-byte character sets. ☐ Uses one byte per character.

DBCSLANG=

language The double-byte character set (language or writing system).

DBCSTYPE=

method The coding method for the double-byte character set.

DETAILS

☑ SAS data library directory listings contain additional information, such as dataset labels. ☐

DEVICE=

driver The device driver to display graphics output. **Alias DEV**

DFLANG=

'*language*' The language of international date and datetime informats and formats with the EUR prefix:

Afrikaans Catalan Croatian Czech Danish Dutch English Finnish French German Hungarian Italian Macedonian Norwegian Polish Portuguese Russian Slovenian Spanish Swedish Swiss_French Swiss_German
Default English

DKRICOND=

When a DROP=, KEEP=, or RENAME= dataset option for an input SAS dataset uses a variable name incorrectly: ERROR An error condition is generated. WARN WARNING A warning message is generated. NOWARN NOWARNING The incorrect reference is ignored.

DKROCOND=

When a DROP=, KEEP=, or RENAME= dataset option for an output SAS dataset or a DROP, KEEP, or RENAME statement uses a variable name incorrectly: ERROR An error condition is generated. WARN WARNING A warning message is generated. NOWARN NOWARNING The incorrect reference is ignored.

DLDMGACTION= ⊙7+

Action when a catalog or SAS dataset is damaged: FAIL Generates an error condition. This is the default for batch mode. ABORT Ends the SAS session abnormally. REPAIR Attempts to repair the file. Deletes damaged catalog entries. Rebuilds and repairs indexes and integrity constraints for SAS datasets. This is the default for interactive modes. PROMPT Prompts the user for what action to take.

DLTRUNCHK ⊙z

☑ Creates an error condition on opening a SAS data library that is damaged by truncation. ☐

DMR ⊙ SAS/CONNECT

Start ☑ Allows SAS/CONNECT to start a remote session. ☐

DMS

Start ☑ Opens the SAS windowing environment and the programming windows. ☐

DMSEXP ⊙7+

Start ☑ Opens the SAS windowing environment and the Explorer and programming windows. ☐

DMSLOGSIZE= ⊙9.1+

Init. *n* Limits the number of lines in the Log window. *MIN:* 500 *MAX:* 999999 **Default** 99999

DMSOUTSIZE= ⊙9.1+

Init. *n* Limits the number of lines in the Output window. *MIN:* 500 *MAX:* 999999 **Default** 99999

DMSSYNCHK ⊙9+

When multiple steps are submitted in an interactive windowing session and a syntax error or serious semantic error occurs while processing a data step: ☑ SAS enters syntax check mode, in which it checks the syntax of subsequent steps, but does not process observations. ☐ SAS attempts to resume normal execution at the next step.

DSNFERR

When a specified input SAS dataset is not found: ☑ An error message is generated. ☐ A _NULL_ input SAS dataset, with no variables, is used.

DTRESET ⊙9+

When showing date and time on pages of the log and standard print file: ☑ Shows the current time for each page. ☐ Shows the time the SAS session started.

DUPLEX ⊙7+

☑ Prints on both sides of the paper. ☐ Prints on one side.

ECHO= ⟳ W X
Init. '*message*' Displays message while initializing. □

ECHOAUTO
Start ☑ Statements from the autoexec file are written to the log. □

EMAILAUTHPROTOCOL= ⟳ 9+
Init. The e-mail authentication protocol.

EMAILDLG= ⟳ W X
Init. The e-mail dialog: NATIVE SAS

EMAILHOST=
Init. *name* The SMTP server.

EMAILID=
Init. "*user ID*" The e-mail user ID.

EMAILPORT= ⟳ 8.1+
Init. *n* The SMTP port.

EMAILPW=
Init. "*password*" The e-mail password.

EMAILSYS=
Init. *name* The e-mail interface: SMTP MAPI VIM
Start *script file* The e-mail script. ⟳ X

ENCODING= ⟳ 9+
Init. *name* The character set of text in the SAS session. ANYASCII
Does not translate data among ASCII encodings. ANYEBCDIC Does
not translate data among EBCDIC encodings.

ENGINE=
Start *engine* The default engine for SAS data libraries.

ENHANCEDEDITOR ⟳ W 8+
Init. ☑ Makes the Enhanced Editor available. □

ERRORABEND
In most error conditions, the SAS session: ☑ Ends abnormally (abends). □ Handles the error conditions normally. **Alias ERRABEND**

ERRORBYABEND ⟳ 9+
When an error occurs because the sort order indicated in a BY statement is not found in the data, the SAS session: ☑ Immediately ends
abnormally (abends). □ Generates an error condition.

ERRORCHECK=

Init.   When a file error occurs in a LIBNAME, FILENAME, LOCK, or %INCLUDE statement in batch mode: NORMAL   Processing continues.   STRICT   Processing stops. The SAS session ends abnormally if the %INCLUDE statement refers to a file that does not exist.
Alias ERRCHECK

ERRORS=

n   For data errors, the maximum number of observations for which complete error messages are printed.

EXPLORER ↺ 7+

Start   ☑ Opens the SAS windowing environment and the Explorer window.   ☐

FILECC ↺ z

Treat column 1 of a print file as: ☑ Carriage control.   ☐ Text.
Default ☑

FILEEXT= ↺ z

When accessing a member of a fileref, using a member name that has a period and file extension: ASIS   Uses the entire member name. INVALID   Creates an error condition.   VERIFY   Checks the extension against the last level of the physical file name, and creates an error condition if they do not match.   IGNORE   Uses only the part of the member name that comes before the period.   **Default** VERIFY

FILELOCKS= ↺ X

Init.   FAIL   If a file cannot be locked, an attempt to open it results in an error condition.   CONTINUE   If a file cannot be locked for a reason other than because it is being used by another user or process, a warning message is issued.   NONE   File locking is disabled.

FILEMOUNT ↺ z

An attempt to allocate an external file on an off-line volume:
☑ Mounts the volume.   ☐ Generates an error condition.

FILEMSGS ↺ z

A file allocation that fails because the file is in use generates error messages that are: ☑ Detailed and, in an interactive session, displayed on the terminal.   ☐ Less detailed and written in the log.

FILENULL ↺ z

When writing a file, zero-length records are: ☑ Written.
☐ Discarded.

FILEPROMPT ↺ z

When the attempt to allocate a file in an interactive session fails because the file does not exist: ☑ Prompts you with the option to create the file.   ☐ Creates an error condition.

FILTERLIST= ⟳W

" *filter | filter . . .* " A list of filters (file names with wild card characters) for use in file dialogs.

FIRSTOBS=

n The first record or observation to be processed from an input file.

FMTERR

When the format of a variable's format attribute cannot be found:
☑ An error message is generated.   ☐ A default format is used.

FMTSEARCH=

(*libref or catalog . . .*) When an informat or format is used, format catalogs are searched in the order listed. If a one-level name is stated, the catalog FORMATS in that library is searched. The default catalogs WORK.FORMATS and LIBRARY.FORMATS are searched first and second unless you list them in a different position in the search order.

FONT= ⟳W

Init. '*font name*' *options* The monospaced font for text windows.
Options *point size character set* BOLD   NORMAL   ITALIC   REGULAR

FONTALIAS= ⟳W

Init. "*SAS font*" "*operating system font*" Substitutes an operating system font for a SAS font.

FORMCHAR=

"*chars*" Formatting characters that are used in the print output of some procedures. These characters are used mainly for printing tables.
Default "|----|+|---+=|-/\<>*"

FORMDLIM=

'*char*' A character to replace page breaks in print output.   ' ' Actual page breaks are used. This is the default.

FULLSTIMER

☑ Writes detailed measurements of computer resources used for each step.   ☐

GISMAPS= ⟳7+

libref or '*physical file name*' The SAS data library that contains the SAS/GIS U.S. Census Tract maps.

HELPCASE ⟳z 8.1+

Init. ☑ Displays help text in uppercase.   ☐

HELPENCMD ⟳9+

Init. Uses help keywords in: ☑ English.   ☐ The localized language.

HELPEXT= ↺ W 8+

Init. HTML help file type: HTM   CHM

HELPLOC= ↺ 7+

Init. (*path*, . . .) The location of the HTML help facility's text and index files.

HELPREGISTER= ↺ W 8+

Init. :"*menu text*" *path* *options*   Adds a help file to the Help menu.
Options "*description*" *topic* CHM HTML HLP

HONORAPPEARANCE ↺ W 7+

Init. ☑ Uses operating system color and font settings.   ☐

HOSTPRINT ↺ W /+

Init. ☑ Uses the operating system printing interface.   ☐

IBUFSIZE= ↺ 9+

n *n*K   *n*M   The buffer size for indexes of SAS datasets.
☐ Indexes use the default buffer size.

ICON ↺ W

☑ Displays an icon. ☐ Displays the SAS AWS.

IMPLMAC

The macro processor: ☑ Checks every statement to see if it is a statement style macro call. ☐ Does not recognize statement-style macro calls.

INITCMD=

Start '*commands*'   Executes the commands to open an AF application instead of the standard windows. The SAS session terminates automatically when the application ends.

INITSTMT=

Start '*statement(s)*'   These statements are executed at the beginning of the SAS session after statements from the autoexec file and before statements from the SYSIN file. **Alias IS**

INSERT= ↺ W X

Start *system option* '*physical file name*'   Adds the physical file name before any already in the system option. **System option**
CONFIG ECHO HELPLOC MAPS MSG SAMPLOC SASAUTOS
SASHELP MSG SASSCRIPT

INVALIDDATA=

'*char*'   A character that represents the missing value produced by informats for invalid numeric data. **Default** '.'

LABEL

☑ Procedures can use variable labels. ☐ The LABEL option of a procedure is ignored. Procedures do not use labels to identify variables.

LEFTMARGIN= ↺ 7+

size "*size unit*" The size of the left margin. **Unit** IN CM

LINESIZE=

n The length of the line that is used in print files. *MIN*: 64 *MAX*: 256
Alias LS

LOADMEMSIZE= ↺ W X 8.1+

Init. Use of memory when SAS loads executable programs: 0 MIN
MAX Uses any available memory. This is the default. 1 Purges programs from memory as soon as they end. *n* *n*K *n*M *n*G Purges programs from memory if their total size exceeds this size.

LOCALE= ↺ 8.2+

locale Localization (language and cultural aspects of communication) for the SAS System.

LOG= ↺ W X

Start '*physical file name*' *or device* The file to which the log is written, for a batch session. ☐

LOGPARM= ↺ 9+

Start '*suboptions*' Controls details of opening log files.
Suboptions
OPEN= When an existing log file is opened: REPLACE Replaces the existing file. REPLACEOLD Replaces the existing file if it is more than one day old. APPEND Adds text to the end of the file.
ROLLOVER= The log file is closed and a new one opened: NONE
Never. AUTO Only when the value of the LOG= option changes.
SESSION Only at the beginning of the SAS session.
WRITE= Stores new messages in the log file: BUFFERED When a buffer is full. IMMEDIATE Whenever submitted statements generate log messages.

LPTYPE= ↺ X

Selects the routine used to send files to a printer: BSD The lpr command. SYSV The lp command.

MACRO

☑ The macro processor is active; macro language objects can be used.
☐ The macro processor is inactive; macro language references may result in an error condition.

MAPS=

libref or '*physical file name*' . . . Libraries to search for map datasets.

MAUTOLOCDISPLAY ↻ 9+

☑ Writes log notes to identify the source of autocall macros. ☐

MAUTOSOURCE

☑ Macros in autocall libraries can be used. ☐

MCOMPILENOTE= ↻ 9+

Writes log notes to confirm compilation of: ALL   All macros.
NOAUTOCALL   Macros other than autocall macros.   NONE   No
macros.

MEMRPT ↻ z

☑ Records memory statistics from the operating system for each step.
☐

MEMSIZE=

Init. *n*   *n*K   *n*M   *n*G   The maximum amount of memory available
to the SAS System.

MERGENOBY= ↻ 8+

When a MERGE statement has no BY statement: NOWARN   Does
not issue a message.   WARN   Issues a warning message.   ERROR
Generates an error condition. **Default** NOWARN

MERROR

When the macro processor finds an apparent macro reference (a
percent sign followed by a word) that cannot be matched to a macro
keyword or macro name: ☑ It writes a warning message.   ☐ It
ignores the reference.

MFILE ↻ 7+

When the MPRINT option is in effect and the fileref MPRINT is
assigned to a file, output produced by the MPRINT option is routed
to: ☑ The MPRINT fileref.   ☐ The log.

MINDELIMETER= ↻ 9.1+

'*char*'   The character used as the delimiter for the list of values used
with the macro IN operator.

MISSING=

'*char*'   The character that is printed for missing values of numeric
variables. **Default** '.'

MLOGIC

☑ The macro processor traces macro control flow and macro statement execution in the log.   ☐

MLOGICNEST ↻ 9.1+

☑ Identifies in MLOGIC log notes any macro that called the current
macro.   ☐

MPRINT

☑ SAS statements generated by macros are written in the log or the MPRINT file, depending on the MFILE option. ☐

MPRINTNEST ↺ 9+

☑ Adds information about macro nesting to the output of the MPRINT option. ☐

MRECALL

When a macro is called that was not found in a previous search of the autocall libraries: ☑ The macro processor searches the autocall libraries again. ☐ The search is not repeated.

MSG= ↺ 7+

Init. '*storage location*' The location of the SAS message library.
Alias SASMSG

MSGCASE

Init. SAS System messages are printed and displayed in: ☑ All uppercase letters. ☐ Upper- and lowercase letters.

MSGLEVEL=

Generates: I Extra log messages. N The standard log messages.

MSTORED

☑ The macro catalog in the library specified by the SASMSTORE= option is used to store macros compiled with the STORE option and is searched for called macros that are not found in the WORK.SASMACR catalog. ☐ The STORE option is ignored and only the WORK.SASMACR catalog is searched for compiled macros.

MSYMTABMAX=

n *n*K *n*M *n*G MAX The maximum amount of memory used by all macro variables. Any additional macro variables are stored on disk.

MULTENVAPPL

SAS/AF and SAS/FSP applications that are created use: ☑ Portable features. ☐ Environment-specific features.

MVARSIZE=

n *n*K *n*M MAX The maximum size of a macro variable that is kept in memory. Any larger macro variable value is stored on disk.

NETENCRYPT ↺ 7+

☑ Encrypts network communications. ☐

NETENCRYPTALGORITHM= ↺ 7+

"*algorithm*" ("*algorithm*", . . .) Algorithm(s) to encrypt network communications. **Algorithms** DES RC2 RC4 SAS Proprietary Triple DES **Alias NETENCRALG**

NETENCRYPTKEYLEN= ⊙7+

n The key length for encryption of network communications.
Alias NETENCRKEY

NETMAC= ⊙7+

☑ Uses MACs (message authentication codes) from the MD5 one-way hash function to test for integrity of network communications. ☐

NEWS=

Start '*physical file name*' Messages from this file, typically bulletins for SAS users in multi-user installations, are written to the SAS log. ☐

NLSCOMPATMODE ⊙9+

Init. ☑ Provides compatibility with national language support features of previous SAS versions. ☐ Uses standard encoding for national languages.

NOTES

☑ Notes are written to the log. ☐
Alias LNOTES

NUMBER

☑ The page number appears on the first title line of each page of print output. ☐ The page number does not appear in title lines.

NUMKEYS= ⊙W

Init. *n* The number of F-keys.

NUMMOUSEKEYS= ⊙W

Init. *n* The number of mouse buttons. **Note** Mouse buttons have function key names RMB, Shf RMB, MMB, etc.

OBJECTSERVER ⊙7+

Start ☑ The SAS session is a DCOM/CORBA server. ☐

OBS=

n or MAX The last observation or record read from an input file. Subsequent observations or records are ignored.

OPLIST

Init. ☑ Command-line settings of SAS system options are written to the log. ☐

ORIENTATION= ⊙7+

The paper orientation for printing: PORTRAIT REVERSEPORTRAIT LANDSCAPE REVERSELANDSCAPE

OVP

☑ Print files can contain overprinting; the log uses overprinting to underline errors. ☐

PAGEBREAKINITIAL ○9+
Start ☑ Writes a page break at the beginning of the log and standard print file. ☐

PAGENO=
n The page number for the next page of print output. **Alias PAGNO**

PAGESIZE=
n The number of lines per page in print output. *MIN:* 15 *MAX:* 32767
Alias PS

PAPERDEST= ○7+
name The paper destination (bin) of printed pages.

PAPERSIZE= ○7+
name or (width, height) The paper size for printing. Paper size names are defined in the SAS Registry. **Width, height** *size* "*size unit*" **Unit** IN CM **Default** LETTER

PAPERSOURCE= ○7+
name The paper source (tray) for printing.

PAPERTYPE= ○7+
'*name*' The type of paper for printing.

PARM=
'*string*' The parameter string passed to an external program.

PARMCARDS=
fileref Data lines following a PARMCARDS statement are copied to this file. The procedure then reads the data from the file.

PRINT=
Init. '*physical file name*' *or device* The standard print file (in batch mode).

PRINTCMD= ○X
command The operating system command used to send files to a printer (or print spool).

PRINTERPATH= ○8+
'*printer name*' ('*printer name*' *fileref*) Identifies the printer for ODS printing. Printer names are defined in the SAS Registry.

PRINTINIT
Start Initializes the standard print file: ☑ Immediately. ☐ Not at all, or only after print output is generated, depending on the operating system.

PRINTMSGLIST ⊙ 7+

An error condition that generates a list of error messages writes in the log: ☑ The entire list.   ☐ Only the top-level message.

PROC

The PROC statement can invoke: ☑ External programs.   ☐ Only procedures.

PROCLEAVE=

*n   n*K   The amount of memory that is set aside to allow for procedure termination under certain error conditions.

QUOTELENMAX ⊙ 9+

☑ Writes a log message when a quoted string is too long.   ☐

REGISTER= ⊙ W 7+

Init. '*menu item*' '*command*' optional '*working directory*'   Adds an operating system command (or application) to the Tools menu.

REMOTE=

See **CONNECTREMOTE=**.

REPLACE=

YES   NO   ☑   ☐   Equivalent to the dataset option. Does not apply to scratch SAS data libraries.

REP_MGRLOC= ⊙ 7+

libref   The location of the repository manager for common metadata.

REUSE=

YES *or* NO   Equivalent to the dataset option.

RIGHTMARGIN= ⊙ 7+

size   "*size unit*"   The size of the right margin.   **Unit** IN   CM

RSASUSER

Start   Access to the SASUSER library. ☑ Read-only.   ☐ Read-write.

RTRACE=

Init. Makes a list of files used in the session:
ALL   All files accessed.   NONE   None. ⊙ W
ON   All files accessed.   OFF   None. ⊙ X

RTRACELOC= ⊙ W X

Init. '*physical file name*'   The location of the list of files created by the RTRACE option.

S=

n or MAX   The maximum length of lines in a program file.   **Default** MAX

S2=

n or S   The maximum length of lines in a secondary program file.
Default S

S99NOMIG ⟳z

On an attempt to open a migrated file: ☑ Generates an error condition.   ☐ Recalls the file.

SASAUTOS=

('*storage location*', . . .)   The autocall library or libraries.   ☐

SASCMD= ⟲ SAS/CONNECT ⟲ 8+

"*file options*"   Command on the remote computer to start a remote session.

"!sascmd *options*"   Uses the same command that would start a local session.   ⟲ 9+

SASCONTROL= ⟲W

SAS windows have: SYSTEMMENU   A window control menu.
NOSYSTEMMENU   No window control menu.   MINMAX   Minimize/maximize buttons.   NOMINMAX   No minimize/maximize buttons.

SASHELP=

Init. '*physical file name*' . . .   The SAS data library that contains SAS System help files.

SASINITIALFOLDER= ⟲W 8+

directory   The working directory.

SASMSG=

See **MSG**.

SASMSTORE=

libref   The SAS data library that contains the SASMACR catalog of compiled macros used in the session.

SASSCRIPT= ⟲ SAS/CONNECT

('*storage location*' . . .)   The aggregate storage location(s) for SAS/CONNECT scripts.   **Note** Obtain the generated fileref as the system option name **SASFRSCR**.

SASUSER=

Init. '*physical file name*'   The SASUSER library, which contains the user profile catalog.

SEQ=

n   The length of the numeric portion of the sequence-number field in SAS source lines.   *MIN:* 1   *MAX:* 8

SEQENGINE= ⟲7+

engine   The default sequential engine.

SERROR

If an apparent macro variable reference (an ampersand followed by a word) cannot be matched to a macro variable, the macro processor:
☑ Issues a warning message.   ☐ Ignores the reference.

SET=

Init. '*environment variable*' '*value*'   Defines a SAS environment variable (usually a path).

SETINIT

Init. ☑ SAS System site license information can be altered.   ☐

SGIO ↺ W 8+

☑ Uses scatter/gather I/O.   ☐

SHORTFILEEXT ↺ W 7–8

Init. ☑ Uses 3-character file extensions for SAS files. This works only in an environment of 8.3 file names.   ☐

SIGNONWAIT ↺ SAS/CONNECT ↺ 9+

Starts a remote session: ☑ Synchronously.   ☐ Asynchronously.

Alias CONNECTSWAIT, SWAIT

SKIP=

n   The number of lines that are skipped at the top of each page in a print file before the title lines.   *MIN:* 0   *MAX:* 20

SOLUTIONS ↺ 7+

Init. ☑ Displays the Solutions menu item and folder.   ☐

SORTANOM= ↺ X 8+

Host sort options: b   Multi-call mode (for Syncsort).   t   Log statistics.   v   Log commands.

SORTCUT= ↺ X

Selecting the sort program when the option SORTPGM=BEST is in effect: *n*   The host sort program is used when sorting more than this many observations.   0   The host sort program is not used.
Default 0

SORTCUTP= ↺ X z

Selecting the sort program when the option SORTPGM=BEST is in effect: *n*   *n*K   *n*M   The host sort program is used when sorting more than this many bytes.   0   The host sort program is not used.
Default 0

SORTDUP= ↺ 7+

When the SORT procedure option NODUP applies at the same time that a DROP= or KEEP= dataset option removes variables from the SAS dataset, the procedure looks for duplicates of: PHYSICAL   All the variables present, before applying the DROP= or KEEP= dataset option. LOGICAL   Only those variables in use after applying the DROP= or KEEP= dataset option.

SORTEQUALS ↻ 9+

☑ Keeps observations that have equal key values in the same order when sorting.   ☐ Disregards the original order of observations that have equal key values.

SORTPARM= ↻ X z

'*parameters*'   Parameters passed to the host sort program.

SORTPGM=

Sort program: SAS   HOST   BEST

SORTSEQ=

collating sequence   The default collating sequence to use when sorting SAS datasets.   **Collating sequence** ASCII   EBCDIC   REVERSE   NATIONAL   DANISH   FINNISH   ITALIAN   SPANISH   SWEDISH

SORTSIZE=

n   *n*K   *n*M   *n*G   MAX   The maximum amount of memory available to the sort routine when sorting SAS datasets.

SOURCE

☑ SAS source statements are written to the log.   ☐

SOURCE2

☑ Secondary source statements (from files included by %INCLUDE statements) are written to the log.   ☐

SPLASH ↻ W

Init.   ☑ Displays splash window at startup.   ☐

SPLASHLOC= ↻ W

Init.   '*physical file name*'   The splash window image.

SPOOL

SAS program lines are executed and: ☑ Stored in a utility dataset in the WORK library for later use, for example by the RECALL command.   ☐ Discarded.

STARTLIB ↻ 8+

Librefs stored from a previous session are: ☑ Used.   ☐ Ignored.

STATS ↻ z

☑ Performance statistics are written in the log for each step, if available.   ☐

STAX ↻ z

☑ Attention interrupts are handled by the operating system.   ☐ The session ends when the user presses the attention key.

STIMEFMT= ○ W X 8+

Displays system time measurements as: S   SECONDS   Seconds.   M
MINUTES   Minutes and seconds.   H   HOURS   Hours, minutes, and
seconds.

STIMER

☑ Notes performance statistics from the operating system for each
step.   □

SUMSIZE= ○ 7+

*n   n*K   *n*M   *n*G   MAX   The maximum amount of memory available
to the summarization engine used in the SUMMARY, TABULATE,
REPORT, and other procedures.

SYMBOLGEN

☑ The macro processor notes the result of resolving macro variable
references.   □

Alias SGEN

SYNCHIO ○ 8+

Start   ☑ Waits for I/O to complete before starting any other tasks.
□ Executes other tasks at the same time as I/O.

SYNTAXCHECK ○ 9+

When a syntax error or serious semantic error occurs in a noninterac-
tive session while processing a data step: ☑ SAS enters syntax check
mode, in which it checks the syntax of subsequent steps, but does not
process observations.   □ SAS attempts to resume normal execution at
the next step.

SYSIN=

Start   '*physical file name*'   The specified SAS program file is
executed after the autoexec file and INITSTMT= statements.   □

SYSINP= ○ z

Start   *name*   A program that generates the SAS program lines. This
option, if used, overrides the SYSIN= option.

SYSLEAVE=

n   The amount of memory that is set aside to allow for SAS System
termination under certain error conditions.

SYSPARM=

'*string*'   A parameter string. The SYSPARM() function call and the
&SYSPARM macro variable reference can be used to refer to this string.

SYSPRINT=

Init.   *printer*   Selects a printer.   *printer*   '*physical file name*'
Selects a print file.   ○ W 7+

Init.   *printer*   '*printer   print options*'   Selects a default printer.   ○ X

DDname Redirects print output. DUMMY Suppresses print output.
* Ends redirection of print output. ↻ z 7+

SYSPRINTFONT= ↻ 8.2+

Init. '*font name*' *options* The monospaced font for printing.
Options *point size* *character set* BOLD NORMAL ITALIC
REGULAR NAMED *printer* DEFAULT ALL

SYSRPUTSYNC ↻ SAS/CONNECT ↻ 9+

The %SYSRPUT statement changes the local macro variable value:
☑ Immediately (synchronously). ☐ At the next synchronization
point.
Alias CSYSRPUTSYNC

TAPECLOSE=

The position of a tape volume when a SAS data library is closed:
REREAD At the beginning of the file. LEAVE At the end of the file.
REWIND At the beginning of the volume. FREE Unmounted.
DISP As set by operating system. Values vary by operating system.

TBUFSIZE= ↻ 7+

n *n*K *n*M The transmision buffer size. 0 Transmissions use the
default buffer size.

TCPPORTFIRST= ↻ 7+

n The beginning of the range of TCP/IP ports available to connect to
a remote host.

TCPPORTLAST= ↻ 7+

n The end of the range of TCP/IP ports available to connect to a
remote host.

TERMINAL

Start Applies the settings of the BATCH system option: ☑ If no
interactive environment is available. ☐ Regardless of environment.

TERMSTMT= ↻ 9+

'*statement(s)*' Statements to execute at the end of the SAS session.
These statements execute when a batch program ends or when the
ENDSAS statement is executed.

TEXTURELOC= ↻ 9+

'*physical file name*' *or libref* Location for ODS image files.

THREADS

☑ Allows multithreading for increased performance if multiple
processors are available. ☐

TOOLSMENU ↻ 9+

☑ Displays the Tools menu. ☐

TOPMARGIN= ↻ 7+

size "*size unit*" The size of the top margin. **Unit** IN CM

TRANTAB=

(*local-to-transport, transport-to-local, lowercase-to-uppercase, uppercase-to-lowercase, character classification, scanner translation, delta characters, scanner character classification, DBCS system table, DBCS user table*) Names of translation tables (entries) that the SAS System uses to convert text or data from one representation to another.

UNBUFLOG ↻ W X 7+

Init. The log is: ☑ Unbuffered. □ Buffered.

UNIVERSALPRINT ↻ 8.1+

☑ Uses Universal Printing. □

USER=

'*physical file name*' *or libref* One-level SAS file names refer to this SAS data library. The default is USER=WORK, or USER=USER if the USER libref is defined.

UTILLOC=

Init. WORK *or* ('*storage location*' . . .) Locations for utility files for thread-enabled applications.

UUIDCOUNT= ↻ 8.2+

n The number of values the UUID generator provides at one time.

UUIDGENDHOST= ↻ 8.2+

host port The UUID server.

V6CREATEUPDATE= ↻ 9+

Using the V6 engine to create or update SAS datasets results in: IGNORE No mention in the log. NOTE A log note. WARN A warning message. ERROR An error condition This option does not affect the use of the V6 engine to read version 6 SAS datasets.

VALIDFMTNAME= ↻ 9+

Format names longer than 8 characters and informat names longer than 7 characters: LONG Are permitted. WARN Generate a warning message. ERROR Generate an error condition.

VALIDVARNAME= ↻ 7+

Variable names: V7 Are treated as mixed-case. UPCASE Are treated as uppercase. ANY Can contain any combination of characters. V6 Are treated as uppercase and can be no more than 8 characters long.

VECTOR ↻ X z

Init. ☑ Uses vector processing for selected routines, if vector hardware is available. □ Does not use vector processing.

VERBOSE

Init. ☑ Writes a note in the log about system options set at initialization. ☐

VIEWMENU ↺ 9+

☑ Displays the View menu. ☐

VNFERR

When a nonexistent input SAS dataset is required to contain a particular variable: ☑ An error condition results. ☐ The SAS dataset is treated as containing the required variable.

WEBUI ↺ W 8+

Init. ☑ Uses Web user interface variations. ☐

WORK=

Start '*storage location*' The location of the WORK library.

WORKINIT

Start ☑ The WORK library is erased at the beginning of the SAS session. ☐ The WORK library is not erased.

Start ☑ A new directory is created for the WORK library. ☐ The existing directory is used for the WORK library. ↺ X

WORKTERM

☑ The WORK library is erased at the end of the SAS session. ☐ The WORK library is not erased.

XCMD ↺ 7+

☑ The X command is recognized. ☐

XMIN ↺ W 7+

Init. ☑ The X command's display is minimized. ☐

XSYNC ↺ W

An operating system command executes: ☑ Synchronously; in the foreground. ☐ Asynchronously; in the background.

XWAIT ↺ W

After an operating system command executes, control returns to the SAS System: ☑ After you enter the appropriate operating system command. ☐ Immediately.

YEARCUTOFF=

year $1582 \leq year \leq 19900$ The earliest year of the 100-year period that can be referred to as two-digit year numbers by SAS date and SAS datetime informats and functions.

LAST=

SAS dataset Treated as the most recently created SAS dataset.

10

Files

Files are declared in FILENAME and LIBNAME statements and then used in data step and proc step statements.

Devices

In addition to standard physical files, the SAS System's file routines also handle several kinds of devices and access methods, which are identified by device names.

DISK Online direct access storage. TAPE Sequential storage.
PRINTER Printer. PLOTTER Plotter. TERMINAL Line-mode user I/O. DUMMY Nothing.

TEMP A temporary file (with no visible physical file name).
CATALOG A SAS catalog or entry identified by its SAS file name (quoted) but treated as an external file, or a catalog treated as a directory (a catalog or any entry can be read, but only text entry types can be written). NAMEPIPE Named pipe. PIPE Unnamed pipe.

EMAIL E-mail. FTP FTP (File transfer protocol).
SOCKET TCP/IP socket. URL HTTP server.

DRIVEMAP List of available hard disk drives. COMMPORT Communications port. DDE Dynamic Data Exchange. ⊙ W

XPRINTER The default printer. ⊙ X

CART Tape cartridge. HFS An HFS file from Unix System Services.
MVS An MVS file. ⊙ z UPRINTER Universal Printing. ⊙ z 8.2+

File System Options

These options define characteristics of input and output files. Use them in the FILENAME, LIBNAME, FILE, INFILE, and %INCLUDE statements and in some commands that have to do with files.

RECFM= Record format. Values vary by operating system. F Fixed length. V Variable length. U Undefined. D Data sensitive. N No format. P Print format. S370V S370VB S370VBS IBM System/370 file formats. S Stream (for FTP and TCP/IP).

LRECL=*n* Logical record length: the number of characters in a record.

BLKSIZE=*n* BLK=*n* Block size.

DEVICE=*device* Device.

NEW OLD New or replaced output file.

ENCODING= Character set of text file. ↺ 8.2+

HOLD Hold print output until released (in an interactive session).

COMTIMEOUT=EOF *or* WAIT *or* ZERO Response to communications port timeout condition.

For named pipes: BLOCK *or* NOBLOCK BYTE *or* MESSAGE EOFCONNECT RETRY=*time* SERVER *or* CLIENT

For DDE: HOTLINK COMMAND NOTAB

For catalogs: DESC='*label*' MOD LRECL= RECFM=V F P

For TCP/IP: SERVER RECONN=*n* TERMSTR='LF' 'CRLF' 'NULL'

For FTP or HTTP: USER= PASS= DEBUG PROMPT LRECL= RECFM=V F S BLOCKSIZE= For FTP: HOST= CD='*directory*' WD= RCMD='*command*' LIST LS RHELP RSTAT S370V S370VS For HTTP: PROXY=

For e-mail: TO= CC= SUBJECT= ATTACH=

UNBUF Unbuffered. ↺ X

ANSI OEM The character set used in the file. ↺ W

DISP= VOLSER *or* VOL= UNIT= SPACE= DSORG= OPTCD= BUFNO=*n* LABEL= NOMOUNT REUSE WAIT=*minutes* ↺ z

DISP=REP Creates new file or replaces existing file. ↺ z 8.2+

Filerefs

Most filerefs are defined in FILENAME statements. These additional predefined filerefs have special meanings in a SAS program:

DATALINES DATALINES4 CARDS CARDS4 Input to data step from data lines in the program file at the end of the data step.

PARMCARDS Input to selected procedures from parameter lines in the program at the end of the proc step.

LOG Output to the log file.

PRINT Output to the standard print file.

Libraries

A SAS data library is either a physical file or a directory, depending on whether the file system supports directories. A unique name, or libref, identifies each library. The librefs listed below have specific meanings in a SAS session.

SASUSER   Individual user settings and preferences.

WORK   Short-term storage within a SAS session; one-level SAS dataset names refer to this library by default.

USER   One-level SAS dataset names refer to this library if it is defined.

SASHELP   Message text, help windows, and sample data.

LIBRARY   Add-on informats and formats.

DICTIONARY   Table and session characteristics in SQL statements.

The DICTIONARY libref is available only in SQL. It include these tables, which list objects in the SAS environment: CATALOGS CHECK_CONSTRAINTS   COLUMNS   CONSTRAINT_COLUMN_USAGE CONSTRAINT_TABLE_USAGE   DICTIONARIES   ENGINES   EXTFILES FORMATS   GOPTIONS   INDEXES   LIBNAMES   MACROS MEMBERS   OPTIONS   REFERENTIAL_CONSTRAINTS   STYLES TABLE_CONSTRAINTS   TABLES   TITLES   VIEWS

Use a DESCRIBE TABLE statement to view the column definitions.

Example

PROC SQL; DESCRIBE TABLE DICTIONARY.OPTIONS;

Engines

Access to SAS libraries is managed by routines called engines. There is a native engine for each release of the SAS System. There are also transport engines, which store SAS files in an ASCII text format so that they can be moved between SAS implementations, and interface and interface view engines, which create or access files in formats defined by other software systems.

These are some examples of native library engines: BASE   V9   V7 V6   TAPE   V6TAPE   REMOTE   XPORT

These are some interface and interface view engines: XML   ORACLE ODBC   BMDP   OSIRIS   SPSS   CDD   DTIF

The ENGINE= system option determines which native library engine is used by default. The SEQENGINE= system option indicates a default engine for libraries on sequential devices. You can specify the engine for a new or existing SAS data library immediately after the libref in the LIBNAME statement.

XML engine options ○ 9+

XMLDATAFORM=ELEMENT ATTRIBUTE   XMLTYPE=GENERIC ORACLE OIMDBM EXPORT HTML   INDENT=n OIMSTART=n XMLMETA=NO YES   XMDOUBLE=FORMAT PRECISION   CHARSET= ENCODING=   TRANTAB=   TAGSET=   XMLMAP=*file*

SASEDOC engine options ○ 9.1+

Use an ODS path in place of the physical file name.

DOC_SEQNO=n

Member Types

The SAS files that are members of a SAS data library are identified by two-level names of the form *libref.member*. The SAS files can belong to several different member types. Sometimes, within a SAS data library, a member is identified by a two-level name of the form *member.type*, to distinguish members of different types that have the same name.

These are selected member types: DATA   VIEW   SAS dataset. CATALOG   SAS catalog.   PROGRAM   Compiled data step. ACCESS   Access descriptor.   ITEMSTOR   Item store.   ⟳ 7+ MDDB   Multidimensional database (summary).

Entry Types

A SAS catalog contains data structures that are called entries. There are many different entry types, each with a specific purpose. In a SAS program, an entry is usually identified by a four-level name, *libref.catalog.entry.type*. Within a particular catalog, an entry can be identified by a two level name, *entry.type*. In some contexts, the entry type can be omitted, for a three-level or one-level name.

These are selected entry types: AFGO   Identifies the AF entry recently displayed.   AFPGM   Values entered in a program entry window. CATAMS   Text data created by a program.   CBT   AF window with questions and answers.   CPARMS   Window color settings. EDPARMS   SAS/AF editing environment.   FOLDER   Desktop folder. FONT   Font.   FORMAT   Numeric format.   FORMATC   Character format.   FORMULA   Window definition for FSVIEW procedure. FRAME   AF window that displays objects.   GLOBAL   SYMBOL, LEGEND, AXIS, or PATTERN statement.   GOPTIONS   Graphics options.   GRSEG   Graphics output.   HELP   AF window that displays text.   IMAGE   Image file.   INFMT   Numeric informat.   INFMTC Character informat.   KEYS   A set of function key definitions.   LIST A list of values for data validation.   LOG   Text from the LOG window. MACRO   Macro.   MENU   AF window allowing menu selection. MSYMTAB   Values of local macro variables.   OUTPUT   Text from the OUTPUT window.   PMENU   Menu bar.   PROFILE   User charac-teristics.   PROGRAM   AF window that contains an SCL program. QRYPROF   Profile for the QUERY window.   QUERY   Query stored from the QUERY window.   REPT   Report design for REPORT procedure.   SCL   SCL program with no window.   SCREEN   Window definition for FSEDIT procedure.   SLIST   SCL list.   SOURCE   SAS program text.   TITLE   Title line or footnote line.   TOOLBOX   Tool box.   TRANTAB   Translation table.   WSAVE   Window size and location.

Special SAS Dataset Names

These special SAS dataset names can be used in most places where the syntax of a SAS statement or command calls for a SAS dataset name.

ALL   In some contexts, all the SAS datasets in a library.
DATA   The next in the series DATA1, DATA2, DATA3, . . .
LAST   The most recently created SAS dataset.
NULL   No SAS dataset.

Views

A view, or SAS data view, is a SAS dataset that is physically stored in two or more files. Typically, the data description is stored in one or two files, and it refers to data values found in one or more different files.

Views that use data values in SAS datasets can be created in the SQL procedure or in the data step. SQL views are defined using the CREATE VIEW statement of SQL, with an SQL query. Data step views are created by adding the VIEW= option to the DATA statement of a data step. The data values in both SQL views and input data step views are not determined until a later step reads from the view; then the values are put together one observation at a time. To change the data values in a view, you have to change the data values in the files that the view refers to

An input data step view can also create a SAS dataset from data in an input text file or from any other source of data available to the data step. With SAS/ACCESS interfaces, SQL views can access DBMS data. You can edit some SQL views, and the changes are stored in the underlying files. Other views cannot be edited.

Indexes and Integrity Constraints

An index of a SAS data file keeps track of the location of observations in the file based on the values of one or more key variables. An index can let you read individual observations and speed up processing of WHERE clauses. It can allow you to read the file in a different order than it is stored in, and with the UNIQUE index option, it can protect the integrity of the file by preventing you from adding duplicate observations. To create an index, use the INDEX= dataset option. You can also use the DATASETS and SQL procedures to create and manage indexes.

An integrity constraint is designed to maintain the integrity of a SAS data file. It prevents modifications to the data that would violate a rule that you specify. For example, you can require that a variable have values that fall within a certain range, that every observation have a unique value for a variable, or that one variable have a nonmissing value whenever another variable has a nonmissing value. An integrity constraint creates an error condition whenever a user or program attempts to modify data values in a way that would violate its rule. A SAS data file can have several integrity constraints. Integrity constraints may create indexes to speed up their processing. Use the DATASETS procedure to create and manage integrity constraints.

Both indexes and integrity constraints can slow down unrelated processing of the SAS data file, especially for a program that makes many modifications to the data. Such a program may run faster if you delete the indexes and integrity constraints and rebuild them afterward. The output of the CONTENTS procedure includes descriptions of the indexes and integrity constraints of a SAS data file.

Generation Datasets

A generation dataset stores several versions of a SAS dataset under the same name. By default, you read the most recent generation when you read the file and create a new generation when you create a new SAS dataset of that name. Use the GENMAX= and GENNUM= dataset options to create and use generation datasets. Use the DATASETS procedure with these dataset options to manage generation datasets.

The historical generations appear with a number sign and a three-digit generation number appended to the member name. For example, the first generation created of the member name ACT would be ACT#001.

To use indexes or integrity constraints with a generation dataset, you must create the indexes or integrity constraints separately for each new generation.

Audit Files

An audit file is a special SAS data file that records all or selected changes to observations in a SAS data file, including changes that are rejected by indexes or integrity constraints. The association between the SAS data file and its audit file is called an audit trail. Use the AUDIT statement of the DATASETS procedure to create and manage an audit trail. To read, query, print, or copy the audit file of a SAS data file, use the same SAS dataset name, but use the dataset option TYPE=AUDIT.

The audit file generally contains one observation for each change to an observation in the SAS data file. It contains all the variables of the SAS data file, plus these:

ATOBSNO   The observation number of the change (if available).

ATDATETIME   The date and time of day when the change was made.

ATUSERID   The user ID of the user or job that made the change.

ATRETURNCODE   The return code of the change.

ATMESSAGE   The log message, if any, generated by the change.

ATOPCODE   The operation, or kind of change: DA   Added observation.   DD   Deleted observation.   DR   Updated observation (before).   DW   Updated observation (after).   EA   Error attempting to add observation.   ED   Error attempting to delete observation.   EW   Error attempting to update observation.

user variables   Other audit variables defined in the USER_VAR statement. These variables, although stored in the audit file, are accessed as if they were in the SAS data file itself. Values are not stored for these variables if they are entered when deleting an observation.

An audit file is automatically deleted if the SAS data file is deleted, replaced, or sorted in place. It is not copied when the SAS data file is copied. If the SAS data file is renamed, the audit file remains associated with the SAS data file under the new name. If you create a new generation of a generation dataset that has an audit trail, the audit file becomes part of the historical generation, and the audit trail is no longer active. If an audit file becomes damaged or deleted, the SAS data file cannot be read or updated until the audit trail is terminated with the TERMINATE statement of the DATASETS procedure.

Dataset Options

At most places where a SAS dataset is used in a SAS program, dataset options can be used to modify the way the SAS dataset is read or written. Dataset options appear in parentheses after the SAS dataset name:

SAS dataset (*dataset option   dataset option   . . .*)

Dataset options might be valid when a SAS dataset is created **(C)**, modified **(M)**, read **(R)**, or updated **(U)**, as indicated in the entries below. Use the MODIFY statement of the DATASETS procedure to modify dataset options that represent settings that are stored in the SAS dataset. Some dataset options have the same name and purpose as system options. Use the dataset option to override the system option for a specific SAS dataset. Do not use dataset options with SQL views.

ALTER=
password   Assigns a password for alter-protection or accesses an alter-protected SAS file.

BUFNO=
n   Number of buffers to use.

BUFSIZE=   **(C)**
*n   n*K   *n*M   *n*G   *n*X   MAX   The buffer size.

CNTLLEV=   **(MRU)**
LIB   Library control level: the entire library is locked.   ⊙ 7+
MEM   Member control level: the entire SAS dataset is locked.
REC   Record control level: the SAS dataset is locked one observation at a time.

COMPRESS=   **(C)**
YES   CHAR   Observations in the SAS dataset are compressed with a character-compression algorithm (RLE) for storage.

NO Observations are not compressed.

BINARY Observations are compressed with a binary compression algorithm (RDC) for storage. $\circlearrowleft$ 7+

DLDMGACTION= (MR) $\circlearrowleft$ 7+

Action when the SAS dataset is damaged: FAIL Generates an error condition. This is the default for batch mode. ABORT Ends the SAS session abnormally. REPAIR Attempts to repair the file. Rebuilds and repairs indexes and integrity constraints. This is the default for inter-active modes. PROMPT Prompts the user for what action to take.

DROP= (CR)

variables The list of variables to exclude.

ENCODING= $\circlearrowleft$ 9+

Translation of character encoding: ANY Not required. ANYASCII Not required for ASCII encodings. ANYEBCDIC Not required for EBCDIC encodings. *encoding value* From a specified encoding. **Encoding values** "utf-8" latin1 cyrillic arabic *etc.*

ENCRYPT= (C)

YES The SAS data file is encrypted. This option is valid only when creating a password-protected SAS data file. The file's passwords cannot subsequently be modified. NO The SAS data file is not encrypted. This is the default.

FILECLOSE=

The position of a tape volume when a SAS dataset is closed: REREAD At the beginning of the file. LEAVE At the end of the file. REWIND At the beginning of the volume. DISP As set by operating system. Overrides the TAPECLOSE= system option. Supported values vary by operating system.

FILEDISP= $\circlearrowleft$ z

When writing to a sequential library for the first time after opening it: NEW Treats the library as new, and writes at the beginning of the li-brary. OLD Writes at the end of the library, or if the member already exists, overwrites the member (and any members that follow it).

FIRSTOBS= (RU)

n The first observation to process from the input file. Use this option to skip observations at the beginning of a SAS dataset.

GENMAX= $\circlearrowleft$ 7+

n The maximum number of generations for a generation dataset. 0 The SAS dataset is not a generation dataset. This is the default for a new SAS dataset.

GENNUM= $\circlearrowleft$ 7+

n The generation number of the generation dataset. 0 The base (current) generation. *-n* A historical generation, counting back from the base generation. 1000 Generation #000. * All generations. Use this value when renaming all generations of a generation dataset.

IDXNAME= (RU) ⟳7+

index Uses this index for WHERE processing.

IDXWHERE= (RU) ⟳7+

For WHERE processing: YES Uses the best available index.
NO Uses a sequential search.

IN= (RU)

variable Creates a logical variable that shows whether an observation comes from the specified SAS dataset. Use only in SET, MERGE, MODIFY, and UPDATE statements.

INDEX= (C)

(*index definition . . .*) Defines indexes for a SAS dataset.

Index definitions

variable index options A simple index, which uses only one variable. The variable name is also used as the index name.

index=(*variable variable . . .*) *index options* A composite index, which uses two or more variables. The index name cannot be the same as the name of a variable.

Index options /NOMISS Excludes from the index any observation that has missing values for all key variables. /UNIQUE Prevents observations that duplicate existing key values from being added to the SAS dataset.

KEEP= (CR)

variables Variables to be read from or written to the SAS dataset.

LABEL=

'*description*' Descriptive label for the SAS dataset.

OBS= (RU)

n or MAX Processing from an input file stops at the *n*th observation.

OUTREP= (C) ⟳7+

name The requirements vector.

POINTOBS= (C) ⟳8+

The SAS dataset, if compressed, can be accessed with: YES Random access. (This is valid only with REUSE=NO.) NO Sequential access only.

PW=

password Assigns a password to protect a SAS file from being read, written, and altered; or accesses a password-protected SAS file.

PWREQ=

When a required password for the SAS dataset is missing or incorrect in an interactive session: YES   A requestor window appears.   NO   An error condition occurs.

READ=

password   Assigns a password for read-protection or accesses a read-protected SAS file.

RENAME=

(*variable(s)=new name(s) . . .*)   Changes variable names. If you use the KEEP= dataset option for the same SAS dataset, use the old variable names in the KEEP= option. If any renamed variables appear in the WHERE= dataset option, use the old names in the WHERE expression. The numeric suffix style of abbreviated variable list can be used in the RENAME= option, but no other form of abbreviated variable list is allowed.

REPEMPTY=   (C) ↻ 8+

When the SAS dataset being created has no observations and has the same name as an existing SAS dataset: YES   Replaces the existing SAS dataset with the new SAS dataset (depending on the REPLACE= option).   NO   Creates an error condition.

REPLACE=   (C)

When the SAS dataset being created has the same name as an existing SAS dataset: YES   Replaces the existing SAS dataset with the new SAS dataset.   NO   Creates an error condition.

REUSE=   (C)

YES   Allows the space of deleted observations to be reused in a compressed SAS dataset. (This overrides the POINTOBS= option, making the SAS dataset unable to be accessed by random access methods.)   NO   Does not allow the space of deleted observations to be reused in a compressed SAS dataset.

ROLE=   (R) ↻ 9+

Use of the table in a star schema join: FACT   The fact table.   DIMENSION   DIM   A dimension table.

SORTEDBY=

sort order / optional collating sequence   Indicates how observations in the SAS dataset are currently sorted.

NULL   Indicates that observations are not necessarily in sorted order.

SORTSEQ=   ↻ 9+

collating sequence   The collating sequence for sorting character variables in the SAS dataset.

TOBSNO=

n The number of observations per transmission for a remote SAS dataset.

TRANTAB= ○ 9+

translation table A translation table (entry) for translating the characters in the SAS dataset.

TYPE=

SAS dataset type A code for special uses of SAS datasets in certain procedures, as audit trails, etc.

WHERE=

(condition) Selects observations to process.

WHEREUP= (U) ○ 7+

When updating a SAS dataset that has a WHERE clause: YES Applies the WHERE condition when adding and modifying observations. NO Allows modified or added observations that do not meet the WHERE condition.

WRITE=

password Assigns a password for write-protection or accesses a write-protected SAS file.

Passwords

SAS files other than catalogs can be protected by passwords. Operations on SAS files are divided into three levels, ALTER, WRITE, and READ.

You can have separate passwords for different levels of access, or the same password for all access to the file. You can password-protect all levels or only the higher levels; for example, an alter-protected file can be written and read without a password. Higher-level passwords can be used in place of lower-level passwords: an ALTER password can be used to write or read a file, or a WRITE password can be used to read a file.

For SAS datasets, passwords are mainly implemented using dataset options. The READ=, WRITE=, and ALTER= dataset options are used for different levels of password protection, or the PW= dataset option for a single password. Use the dataset option to assign the password when you create the SAS file. Later, use the same password when you read, write, or alter the SAS dataset. You can change, add, or remove passwords for existing SAS datasets using the DATASETS procedure.

For compiled data steps, passwords are used with options, which look like dataset options, after the PGM= option in the DATA statement.

If you do not supply a password or supply an incorrect password for a protected file in an interactive session, a requestor window prompts you for the correct password.

When you create a file, you can assign the same password for all three levels using the PW= option. You can then use the PW= option or one of the other password options when accessing that file. The PW= option can also be used with the appropriate password when accessing an file that has different passwords for different levels.

When you create a password-protected SAS data file, you can encrypt it with the ENCRYPT=YES dataset option. Encryption makes it difficult for an external program to read any of the data in the file. The passwords of an encrypted SAS data file cannot subsequently be changed. To use a different password, you have to create a new copy of the file.

Passwords are used with these syntax rules:

password option=password . . .   Assigns passwords when creating a file.

password option=password   Accesses a protected file.

password option=/password   Adds a password to an existing file.

password option=password/   ALTER=*password password option=/* WRITE=*password* READ=/   Removes a password.

password option=old password/new password ALTER=*password password option=/new password* WRITE=*password* READ=/*new password* Changes a password.

Passwords and encryption are also applied to a SAS data file's indexes and audit files. The password protection of a view does not extend to data in other files that the view refers to.

The password is required when a new SAS dataset replaces an existing password-protected SAS dataset. If you use passwords for a generation dataset, use the same passwords for each generation.

11

ODS Drivers

ODS, the Output Delivery System, provides endless flexibility in the use of the output that procedures generate. With its drivers, ODS can direct the output objects from proc steps to any of various types of files, or destination formats. As it does so, it can apply style definitions to the output data to control its overall appearance.

ODS output is controlled primarily through the ODS statement, a global statement described in chapter 4. This chapter lists options for specific drivers and components for style definitions. A few procedures also have statement options for details of ODS output. Terms in data step statements can also create output objects for ODS; see the FILE and PUT statements in chapter 5.

SAS versions 7 and 8 include ODS in a more primitive form with fewer destinations, options, and attributes.

Drivers

Each ODS driver creates a different kind of output and uses a set of options appropriate to the approach it takes. The options appear in the ODS statement with this form:

ODS *driver options*;   Applies settings or actions to the indicated destination format.

Drivers open and close files using forms of these options:

FILE='*file*' (*file options*)   Opens an output file.
CLOSE   Closes the output file(s).

The Markup and Printer drivers can produce various destination formats. You can indicate the destination format name in an option for the driver or by using it as an alias for the driver. For example, HTML is an alias for Markup that indicates the HTML destination format. A driver can write multiple destinations at the same time. To do this, use aliases, or use the ID= option in the ODS statement to name or number each destination so that you can set options for each destination separately.

An ODS statement with a destination name and no action option opens the destination for output. Most drivers require an option to identify the destination file. To avoid creating unnecessary output, close any destination you are not using before any SAS step that creates output.

Listing

The Listing driver produces the familiar text-only print output that SAS has always produced. The output can be displayed in the Output window of the SAS windowing environment or printed on any printer. The Listing destination is open by default.

Driver option

DATAPANEL= Number of observations per panel when writing a table that is too wide for the page: *n* *n* observations. DATA A number of observations selected for fastest performance. PAGE As many rows as will fit on a page.

Document

The Document driver saves an ODS document for subsequent browsing or conversion to other destination formats.

Driver options

NAME=*document* (*access option*) A SAS file name for the ODS document.

DIR=(*location*) Location for ODS output: PATH=*path* (*access option*) LABEL='*label*' CATALOG=*catalog* (*access option*)

CATALOG=*catalog* Copies image files to this catalog.
CATALOG=_NULL_ Does not copy image files. This is the default.

Access options UPDATE Adds to any existing contents of the location. This is the default. WRITE Deletes any existing entries.

Output

The purpose of the Output destination is to create a SAS data file from an output object, especially a table object. The table columns provide values and names for the output variables.

Driver options

object (*object options*)=*SAS dataset* Directs the output object(s) to the SAS dataset. **Object options** MATCH_ALL Creates a separate SAS dataset for each object. MATCH_ALL=*macro variable name* Creates a separate SAS dataset for each object and assigns a list of the SAS dataset names to a macro variable. PERSIST=PROC Maintains the selection list for subsequent steps (but only if the MATCH_ALL option is in effect). PERSIST=RUN Closes the SAS datasets and resets the selection list at the end of the step.

CLEAR   Sets the exclusion list to EXCLUDE ALL.

Markup

The Markup driver adds tags to data to write web pages and other visual or symbolic documents that are not treated as a sequence of pages.

Destination formats

Tagsets provides the tag syntax for the markup file. SAS provides tagsets for several markup languages and other file formats. To create other tagsets, use the TEMPLATE procedure.

XML   Ordinary XML.

HTMLCSS   HTML with CSS.

HTML4   HTML 4 with embedded stylesheets.

CHTML   Compact minimal HTML without style information.

PHTML   Plain HTML with a small set of style elements.

SASXMOH   Very simple HTML.

SASXMOG   XML with some features of Oracle8i XML.

SASXMOR   XML compatible with Oracle8i XML.

SASIOXML   Generic XML.

DOCBOOK   DocBook XML.

SASXMOIM   XML for the Open Information Model (OIM).

WML   WMLOLIST   Wireless Markup Language.

EVENT_MAP   SHORT_MAP   XML that labels tagset event and variable names. This can help you identify tags for use in a new tagset.

SASFMT   XML with format markup tags.

SASXMISS   XML with alternate missing value text.

SASXMNSP   XML with alternate no-space value text.

CSV   CSVALL   CSVBYLINE   CSV (comma separated values) data file.

IMODE   HTML for NTT.

Driver options

TAGSET=*tagset*   The tagset, which determines the destination format. **Alias** TYPE **Default** XML

page='*file*' (*page options*) . . .   Opens an output file to hold the page.

STYLE=*style definition*   The style definition.

BASE='http://*path*'   The prefix for link addresses.

ANCHOR='*name*'   The prefix for anchor names. Anchors identify objects and locations in a markup file. If you write output from more than one step to the same file, use a different anchor prefix for each step so that every anchor name in the file is unique.

CHARSET=*name*   The character set declaration.

ENCODING=*character encoding*   Converts text to a different character encoding.   TRANTAB='*name*'   Translation table for character translation of the markup text.

NEWFILE=   Creates new output files for each: PROC   Step.   BYGROUP   BY group.   PAGE   Output page.   OUTPUT   TABLE   Output object.

NONE   Puts all output in the same output file.   Names for the new output files are formed with numeric suffixes.   **Default** NONE

PATH=*location* (*path option*)   The directory or storage location for generated files.   GPATH=*location* (*path option*)   A storage location for generated picture files.   **Location** catalog   directory fileref '*physical directory name*'   **Path option** URL=*path*   The URL path for links to the files.   URL=NONE   Links to the files do not use a path.

Displays title and footnote lines for graphics as: GTITLE GFOOTNOTE   Graphics.   NOGTITLE   NOGFOOTNOTE   Styled text.

HEADTEXT='*objects*'   METATEXT='*objects*'   Markup code added to the header.

RECORD_SEPARATOR=*string*   Record-separator character(s). Specify control characters as a character hexadecimal constant. RECORD_SEPARATOR=NONE   Writes native line breaks. **Alias** RECSEP   RS

Pages

BODY   FILE   The output. This page is required.

CONTENTS   A table of contents.

PAGE   A list of output pages with descriptions and links.

FRAME   A frame set for BODY, CONTENTS, and PAGE.

STYLESHEET   Style sheet.

CODE   Style definitions such as XSL.

Page options

NO_BOTTOM_MATTER   NOBOT   Omits the concluding tags from the file. Use this option if you will append subsequent output to the file.

NO_TOP_MATTER   NOTOP   Omits the head and opening body tags from the file.   Use this option to append output to a file to which you have written output in a previous step.

URL=*url*   An url to use instead of the file name for links to the file.

DYNAMIC   Sends output directly to a web server instead of a local file.

RTF options

KEEPN   Keeps a table on a single page when possible.   NOKEEPN Splits a table between pages.

DECIMAL_ALIGN=   Align numeric columns at: YES   Decimal point. NO   Right.

TITLE='*text*'   AUTHOR='*text*'   OPERATOR='*text*'   Document descriptor information.   SASDATE   Uses the time of the SAS session as the creation date of the document.

COLUMNS=*n*   Divides a page into *n* columns.

TEXT='*text*'   Adds a text note to the output.

Printer

The Printer driver prepares output for destinations that are based on pages, such as printers. In addition to the available ODS options, the ODSPRINT group of system options control many general qualities of output to printers, such as margin widths and paper type.

Destination formats

Page description language:

POSTSCRIPT PS Generic PostScript.

PDF Portable Document Format (PDF).

PDFMARK PostScript with PDF tags for creating a PDF file.

PCL PCL.

Default PS

Driver options

PRINTER="*name*" Selects a printer from the SAS Registry. **Alias** PRT

HOST Uses operating system printer drivers.

SAS Uses SAS printer drivers instead of operating system printer drivers. ○ W

TEXT='*text*' Adds a text note to the output.

STYLE=*style definition* The style definition.

COLOR= Applies color information for: YES Everything. FULL Text and graphics. GRAY GREY Text and graphics in grayscale. MONO BW Neither text nor graphics; shows them in monochrome. NO Nothing; shows everything in monochrome.

BACKGROUND=YES BACKGROUND Uses background colors with text. BACKGROUND=NO NOBACKGROUND Disregards background colors for text.

COLUMNS=*n* Divides a page into *n* columns.

FONTSCALE A relative font size scaling factor **Default** 100

UNIFORM Uses uniform column widths for all pages of a table.

STARTPAGE= Page breaks. YES ON NO OFF NOW NEVER

CONTENTS=YES CONTENTS Generates a table of contents. CONTENTS=NO NOCONTENTS Does not generate a table of contents.

PDF options

Use these options with the PDF and PDFMark destinations to control details of the generated PDF file.

BASE='http://*path*' The prefix for link addresses.

ANCHOR='*prefix*' The prefix for anchor names. TITLE='*text*' AUTHOR='*text*' SUBJECT='*text*' KEYWORDS="*word . . .*" Document descriptor information.

PDFNOTE Generates object descriptions according to FLYOVER= attributes in the style definition. NOPDFNOTE Disregards FLYOVER= attributes.

Options for bookmarks: BOOKMARKGEN=YES BOOKMARKGEN=ON BOOKMARKGEN Generates bookmarks. BOOKMARKGEN=NO BOOKMARKGEN=OFF NOBOOKMARKGEN Does not generate bookmarks. BOOKMARKLIST=SHOW BOOKMARKLIST=YES BOOKMARKLIST=ON BOOKMARKLIST Creates and displays a bookmark list. BOOKMARKLIST=HIDE Creates a bookmark list, but hides it. BOOKMARKLIST=NO BOOKMARKLIST=OFF NOBOOKMARKLIST Does not create a bookmark list.

NOTOC Omits the table of contents.

Style

ODS style determines such characteristics of the appearance of output as fonts, colors, and spacing. Style applies only to those destination formats that allow control over appearance. Destination formats that have a fixed appearance, such as Listing and Output, are not affected by style options.

Style Definitions

A style definition encompasses all aspects of the appearance of output. It is stored in a template store, a kind of item store used for ODS definitions. Style definitions are used especially for the HTML and Printer output destination.

Statements in the TEMPLATE procedure create style definitions. The DEFINE STYLE statement names the style definition, and the STYLE and REPLACE statements create the style elements that make up the style definition.

To apply a style definition to output, name the style definition in the STYLE= option of the ODS statement. Style definitions use one-level names. ODS searches the active template stores to find the style definition you indicate.

Base SAS includes several style definitions in the template store SASHELP.TEMPLMST. These are selected style definitions:

Default The standard look, especially for HTML output.

Beige   Brick   Brown   Color variations.

Printer   sansPrinter   serifPrinter   Using laser printer fonts.

Sasweb   HTML enhancements.

Statdoc   Streamlined for clarity of presentation.

Minimal   A simplified style definition with a more uniform look.

Style Elements

A style element determines the style of a part of the output. The purpose of style elements is to build a style definition.

STYLE and REPLACE statements in the TEMPLATE procedure create style elements. A style element can be completely defined in a single statement, or it can be defined as a modification of an existing style element.

Each style element is a set of style attributes. You can read the style definitions in SASHELP.TEMPLMST to see what style elements they contain and what style attributes make up those style elements.

Style Attributes

A style attribute represents a single quality. For example, the thickness of a rule could be indicated by one style attribute and the color of the rule by another style attribute. Style attributes are used in defining style elements, and they can also be indicated individually in the STYLE= option of a few procedures. Not all style attributes are used in all destinations. For example, the Output driver ignores all style attributes that indicate visual formatting.

The STYLE= option can indicate a style element, a style element modified by one or more style attributes, or just a list of style attributes. The syntax for a style attribute is one of the following:

attribute=value   Provides a value for the attribute.

attribute=ON   Turns the attribute on.

attribute=OFF   Turns the attribute off.

attribute   Another way of writing *attribute*=ON.

The following are size units that may be used in size values for visual destinations.

PX   Pixels.   PT   Points.   MM   Millimeters.   CM   Centimeters. IN   Inches.   EM   Width equal to font height, typically the width of a capital M.   EX   X-height, the height of a lowercase x.   %   Relative size (of cell, table, etc.).

Color values in style attributes can be written in any of the various color name forms used in SAS. In addition, they can be written as Internet-style RGB values, with six hexadecimal digits preceded by #, for example, #FF0000.

Visual Attributes

LEFTMARGIN=*size*   RIGHTMARGIN=*size*   TOPMARGIN=*size* BOTTOMMARGIN=*size*   Document margins.

OUTPUTWIDTH=*size*   OUTPUTHEIGHT=*size*   CELLWIDTH=*size* CELLHEIGHT=*size*   The dimensions of an object.

JUST=   Justification of contents: LEFT   L   Left.   CENTER   C   Center. RIGHT   R   Right.   DEC   D   At decimal point of numeric value.

VJUST=   Vertical alignment: TOP   MIDDLE   BOTTOM

BORDERWIDTH=*size*   Width of table border.

CELLPADDING=*size*   The distance between the edge of a cell and its contents.   CELLSPACING=*size*   The spacing between adjacent cells.

RULES=   Location of rules in a table: ROWS   Between rows.   COLS Between columns.   ALL   Between rows and columns.   GROUP   At the header or footer.   NONE   None.

FOREGROUND=*color*   The color for text and other foreground objects.   LINKCOLOR=*color*   VISITEDLINKCOLOR=*color* ACTIVELINKCOLOR=*color*   Colors for link text.

BORDERCOLOR=*color*   Border color.

BACKGROUND=*color*   Background color of object.

BACKGROUNDIMAGE="*address*"   Image file for object background. WATERMARK=ON   Prevents scrolling of document's background image.   WATERMARK=OFF   Background image scrolls with document.

FONT=(*font face(s), font size, font style(s)*)   The font for a cell or for the other text of a table.

Treatment of spaces and line breaks: ASIS=ON   As literal text.
ASIS=OFF   As separators.   NOBREAKSPACE=ON   Does not add line
breaks.   NOBREAKSPACE=OFF   Adds line breaks at spaces where
needed.

PROTECTSPECIALCHARACTERS=   Treatment of the special characters <, >, and &: ON   As literal text.   OFF   As HTML code.   AUTO   As
a markup tag when a text string begins with < and ends with >.

BULLETS=   List item mark: 'disc' 'circle' 'square' 'upper-alpha'
'upper-roman' 'lower-alpha' 'lower-roman' 'decimal' 'none'

URL="*address*"   Creates a link.   HREFTARGET=   Window to activate
for link: _SELF   _TOP   _PARENT   _BLANK   "*name*"

PREIMAGE="*address*"   POSTIMAGE="*address*"   Adds an image before
and after the object.   PRETEXT="*text*"   POSTTEXT="*text*"   Adds text
before and after the object.

Options for the table of contents entry: LISTENTRYANCHOR=YES
Makes it a link.   LISTENTRYANCHOR=NO   Shows it without a link.
LISTENTRYDBLSPACE=YES   Double-spaces.
LISTENTRYDBLSPACE=NO   Single-spaces.

FLYOVER="*text*"   Mouseover or contextual text to describe the cell.

Markup Attributes

HTMLCONTENTTYPE="*type*"   Content type declaration for the
markup file.   HTMLDOCTYPE='<!DOCTYPE *type* >'   Document type
declaration for the markup file.

HTMLCLASS="*name*"   Applies a class name to the object (usually the
name of a class defined in the style sheet).   HTMLID="*name*"   Applies
an ID (a unique name) to the object.   HTMLSTYLE="*style*"   Applies a
style (usually CSS code) to the object.

INDENT=*n*   Indents the object markup by *n* spaces.

TAGATTR='*code*'   Adds markup code to the cell.

PREHTML='*code*'   POSTHTML='*code*'   Places markup code before
and after the object.

PAGEBREAKHTML='*code*'   Markup code for page breaks.

ABSTRACT=ON   Excludes styles from generated style sheet files.
ABSTRACT=OFF   Includes styles in generated style sheet files.

Table Attributes

Use table attributes in a PROC TEMPLATE step to create a table definition, which adds details of shape and structure to a table. In addition
to the indicated values for each attribute, you can use a variable name
in order to compute a value in statements in the PROC TEMPLATE
step. Attributes may apply to the table as a whole or to its columns,
headers, and footers.

These Boolean attributes have values of ON and OFF. GENERIC=   Treats
the definition as a generic column or header.   PRINT_HEADERS=
PRINT_FOOTERS=   Print headers and footers.   JUSTIFY=   Justifies
the value instead of the format field.   PRINT=   Prints the column or
header.   MAXIMIZE=   Divides text evenly among lines.

WIDTH=*n*   Column width.   JUST=   Justification of format field or
header text: LEFT   L   CENTER   C   RIGHT   R   VJUST=   Vertical
justification: TOP   T   CENTER   C   BOTTOM   B

ALT="*text*" Alternate text, a short description that may be displayed in place of the object. LONGDESC="*text*" A description of the object.

STYLE=*style* Style to apply to the object. PARENT=*path* Inherit attributes from this object.

For tables

These Boolean attributes have values of ON and OFF. BALANCE= Places approximately the same number of columns in each panel. BYLINE= Writes BY values before each BY group. CENTER= Centers each panel independently. CLASSLEVELS= Displays a BLANK_DUPS column value whenever a preceding BLANK_DUPS column value is displayed. CONTENTS= Places the object in the table of contents. DOUBLE_SPACE= Double-spaces. DATA_FORMAT_OVERRIDE= Allows the data component to override the format of a column definition. EVEN= Divides extra space evenly among columns. NEWPAGE= Puts the table on a new page. ORDER_DATA= Orders columns according to their order in the data component. SPLIT_STACK= Allows a value to split between pages. USE_NAME= Allows column names to be used as column headers. WRAP= Wraps columns of wide tables. WRAP_SPACE= Adds blank line between rows when wrapping columns.

LABEL="*text*" *or variable* Object label. CONTENTS_LABEL="*text*" Table of contents text.

COL_SPACE_MIN=*n* COL_SPACE_MAX=*n* The minimum and maximum spacing between columns.

HEADER_SPACE= FOOTER_SPACE= Space between data lines and header or footer: 0 1 2

PANELS=*n* Divides the width of the page into *n* panels. PANELSPACE=*n* Spacing between panels.

REQUIRED_SPACE=*n* Data lines required for table on page.

TYPE=*type* SAS dataset type for output SAS dataset.

For columns

These Boolean attributes have values of ON and OFF. DROP= Omits the column from the output. OPTIONAL= Omits column if there is insufficient space. FLOW= Applies text wrap. BLANK_INTERNAL_DUPS= BLANK_DUPS= Blanks repeated values ID= Repeats the column on every panel. PRE_MERGE= Merges with the previous column. MERGE= Merges with the next column.

DATANAME=*column* Selects a column from the data component.

WIDTH_MAX=*n* Maximum width if the header is wider than the column. FUZZ=*x* Threshold for small values converted to 0. FORMAT=*format* FORMAT_WIDTH=*n* FORMAT_NDEC=*n* Applies a format to the column.

PRE_SPACE=*n* Space before the column. SPACE=*n* Space after the column. GLUE=*n* The relative importance of keeping a column together with the next column.

HEADER= Header text: "*text*" *header definition* _LABEL_

VARNAME=*name* LABEL='*label*' Output variable attributes.

SEPARATOR='*char*' Writes a separator character after the formatted value. TEXT_SPLIT='*char*' This character in a formatted value
indicates a line break.

For headers and footers

These Boolean attributes have values of ON and OFF. REPEAT=
Repeats the header text to fill its allocated space. EXPAND_PAGE= Extends the header to the edge of the page. FORCE= Expands the column width to the longest word in the header text. SPILL_MARGIN=
Extends into the margin. SPILL_ADJ= Extends into the adjacent
header space. TRUNCATE= Starts a new line in the middle of a word
if necessary. FIRST_PANEL= Limits a spanning header to the first
panel. LAST_PANEL= Limits a spanning footer to the last panel.

SPLIT='*char*' This character in a text value indicates a line break.

ABBR='*text*' An abbreviation. ACRONYM='*text*' An acronym.

START=*column* END=*column* Indicates the location of a spanning
header. EXPAND='*character*' Repeats this character to extend the
header to fill its space.

SPACE=*n* Blank lines between header lines or footer lines.

Tagset Attributes

Tagsets contain the tags that define a markup language for the Markup
driver. Tagset attributes are coding and identifying attributes that
apply to a tagset as a whole. Write them in a PROC TEMPLATE step in
attribute statements associated with the DEFINE TAGSET statement.

PARENT=*tagset* Inherit attributes from this tagset.

OUTPUT_TYPE='*type*' Markup language or file standard: XML
HTML WML CSV LATEX

EMBEDDED_STYLESHEET= Allows stylesheets to be embedded in the
headers of page files: YES ON NO OFF

STACKED_COLUMNS= When there are a large number of columns:
YES ON Stacks columns to fit the available width. NO OFF
Places all columns side by side.

SPLIT='*string*' Code string that stands for a line break.

NOBREAKSPACE='*string*' Code string that stands for a nonbreaking
space. **Example** NOBREAKSPACE=' ';

MAP='*characters*' Special characters that require translation.

MAPSUB='*string/string/...*' Code strings that substitute for the
special characters in the MAP= attribute.

COPYRIGHT="(*text*)" Text of copyright statement.

TRADEMARK="(*text*)" Text of trademark statement.

INDENT=*n* Indents all generated markup by *n* spaces.

DEFAULT_EVENT='*name*' The event to execute when a requested
event is not found in the tagset; the error-handling event.

LOG_NOTE='*message*' Message written to the SAS log when the
tagset is used.

12

Descriptive Statistics

Any number that is calculated from a statistical sample or population can be called a statistic. The SAS System has special support for a group of descriptive statistics. For the most part, these are simple, general statistics that can be used to describe any set of numerical data.

Statistics Programming

The descriptive statistics can be calculated in a data step or in various procedures. In a data step, you can use a set of variables as a population to calculate a statistic. Use a function call in which the name of the statistic is the function name and the variables are arguments.

In a procedure that supports descriptive statistics, you can calculate a statistic on all the values of a single variable in a SAS dataset or, with the BY or CLASS statement, for groups of observations. Name the statistic and variables in the PROC, OUTPUT, or other statement, according to the syntax rules of the procedure. PROC statement options and the optional FREQ and WEIGHT statements affect the way the procedure calculates the statistics.

PROC Statement Options

VARDEF=   Controls the way statistics are calculated based on the variance divisor: N   Population statistics.   DF   Sample statistics.   WGT WEIGHT   Weighted population statistics.   WDF   Weighted sample statistics. See D in the statistic formulas for details.

EXCLNPWGT   Disregards observations that do not have a positive weight value. (Many procedures do this by default.) ⊘ 7+

PCTLDEF=   The method for determining quantiles after the observations are put in sequence:

1   Linear interpolation between the two closest observations.

2   The value of the closest observation. For a quantile that falls halfway between two observations, it uses the value of the even-numbered observation.

3   The actual value if the quantile falls on an observation. The value of the next higher observation if the quantile falls between two observations.

4   Linear interpolation, based on one more observation than is actually present.

5   The average of the actual value and the value of the next higher observation if the quantile falls on an observation. The value of the next higher observation if the quantile falls between two observations.

WEIGHT

WEIGHT *variable*;   Names the weight variable. A weight variable indicates the relative importance, or weight, of each observation. Fractional values are allowed for the weight variable.

By default, there is no weight variable. In this case, each observation is equally important. The weight for each observation is 1.

All procedures disregard observations that have a missing value for the weight variable (beginning with version 7). Procedures may use only observations whose weight is positive. Some procedures do this by default; for others, you can use the EXCLNPWGT option to create the same effect. In any case, procedures do not use negative weights. If a procedure considers observations that have nonpositive values of the weight variable, it counts them with a weight of 0.

FREQ

FREQ *variable*;   Names the frequency variable. A frequency variable indicates the number of times to use an observation. For example, if the value of the frequency variable is 25 in an observation in the SAS dataset, that observation is counted as 25 observations with identical values.

By default, there is no frequency variable, and each observation is counted once.

Statistics

Some of the more complicated descriptive statistics, marked **S** in the entries below, are not implemented as functions and are available only in selected procedures.

Many statistics are meaningful only for certain kinds of samples. The specific requirements are noted in the entries below.

You can also calculate statistics directly from the sample values or from other statistics. The formulas are shown in the entries that follow. These additional symbols are used in the formulas:

D   The variance divisor:
           N, if VARDEF=N
           N − 1, if VARDEF=DF or for a function

SUMWGT, if VARDEF=WGT
SUMWGT − 1, if VARDEF=WDF

x	Each of the values in the sample
w	Each of the weights (1, if unweighted)
Σ	Summation over the values in the sample
SC	$\sum x^3$
SF	$\sum x^4$
MEAN2	MEAN*MEAN
MEAN3	MEAN*MEAN*MEAN
VAR2	VAR*VAR

CSS

Corrected sum of squares. Sum of squares, corrected for the mean.
Formula USS − MEAN*SUM   **Requires** N ≥ 1

CV

Percent coefficient of variation.   **Formula** 100*STD/MEAN   **Requires** N ≥ 2, MEAN ≠ 0

KURTOSIS

Kurtosis. A measurement of the importance of the extreme areas (tail thickness) of the distribution.   **Formula** (SF − 4*MEAN*SC + 6*MEAN2*USS − 3*MEAN3*SUM)/(VAR2)*N*(N + 1)/
((N − 1)*(N − 2)*(N − 3)) − 3*(N − 1)*(N − 1)/((N − 2)*(N − 3))
Requires N ≥ 4, STD > 0, unweighted   **Alias KURT**

MAX

Maximum. The highest value.

MEAN

Mean. The arithmetic average of the values.   **Formula** SUM/SUMWGT

MIN

Minimum. The lowest value.

MODE

S Mode. The most common value.

N

Sample size; number of nonmissing values.

NMISS

Number of missing values.

PRT/PROBT

S The two-tailed probability value for T.   **Formula** 2*PROBT(−ABS(T), N − 1)   **Requires** N ≥ 2, STD > 0, VARDEF=DF

Quantiles

Values that are selected so that a certain relative frequency is above the value and a certain relative frequency is below.

MEDIAN   The middle value, with half the values above it and half below it (equivalent to P50).

P1, P5, P10, P90, P95, P99   Percentiles, with a certain percent of values below them.

Q1, Q3   Quartiles, equivalent to P25, P75.

RANGE

Range. The difference between the maximum and minimum. **Formula** MAX - MIN

SKEWNESS

Skewness. A measurement of the sidedness of the distribution. **Formula** (SC - 3*MEAN*USS + 2*MEAN2*SUM)/(VAR*STD) * N/((N - 1)*(N - 2))   **Requires** N ≥ 3, STD > 0, unweighted

STD

Standard deviation. The square root of the variance. A measure of dispersion. **Formula** SQRT(VAR) **Requires** N ≥ 2

STDERR

Standard error of the mean. **Formula** SQRT(VAR/N) **Requires** N ≥ 2, VARDEF=DF **Alias STDMEAN**

SUM

Sum. Total. **Formula** Σwx

SUMWGT

S Sum of weights. In an unweighted sample, N.   **Formula** Σw

T

S Student's *t* statistic, used to test the null hypothesis that the mean of the population that the sample represents is 0. **Formula** MEAN/STDERR **Requires** N ≥ 2, STD > 0, VARDEF=DF

USS

Uncorrected sum of squares. **Formula** Σwx^2

VAR

Variance. **Formula** CSS/D **Requires** N ≥ 2, D > 0

13

Display Manager

Display manager is at the heart of the SAS interactive windowing environment. With the programming windows of display manager, you can edit and run SAS programs and view the results. You can also work with SAS files, creating, editing, and managing them.

You have several choices of ways to work with display manager windows. You can enter commands on a command line, press function keys that are programmed with commands, or select menu items from the menus in the menu bar. To execute commands from within a SAS program, use the DM statement.

Many of the windows display lists. In a text-mode environment, there is a selection field next to each item in the list, and you can take actions on the items by entering short selection codes in the selection fields. Enter a question mark as a selection code to get a list of the available actions. In a graphical environment, you can act on list items by selecting actions from a popup menu.

Windows

Each window has a one-word SAS name. Commands use the SAS name to refer to the window. For example, PROGRAM is the SAS name of the Program Editor window. Use the SAS name of a window as a command to activate the window. Some of the window-name commands have optional or required terms that determine the data that is displayed in the window.

Several windows have their own commands that you can use only in those windows. Those commands are listed in this section.

Display Manager Windows

CATALOG   Lists entries of a catalog. **Option** *catalog* **Alias** CAT

DIR   Lists members of a library. **Options** *libref libref.member type*

DSINFO   Describes a file. **Options** *libref   fileref 'physical file name'* ⏎ z

FILENAME   Lists all defined filerefs and their physical file names. **Alias** FILEN

FNAME   Lists librefs and filerefs. ⏎ z

FOOTNOTES   Displays footnote lines for editing. **Alias** FOOT, FOOTNOTE

FSLIST   Displays a text file for browsing. **Option** *file*

KEYS   Displays function key definitions for editing.

LIBNAME   Lists librefs and their properties. **Alias** LIB

LISTING   Output. Displays the standard print file, with print output from the session. **Options** ON   OFF   HIDE   **Alias** LIST, OUTPUT

LOG   Displays the log. **Options** ON   OFF

MANAGER   Output manager. Lists the print output of the standard print file by step. **Options** ON   OFF   **Alias** MAN, MGR, OUTPUT

MEMLIST   Lists members of a PDS. **Option** *file* ⏎ z

NOTEPAD   Displays text of an entry for editing. **Option** *entry* **Alias** NOTE

OPTIONS   Displays system options for editing. **Alias** OPTION

OUTPUT   An alias for either LISTING or MANAGER.

PROGRAM   Program Editor. A text editor window for editing and submitting SAS programs. **Options** ON   OFF   **Alias** PGM, PROG

TITLES   Displays title lines for editing. **Alias** TITLE

VAR   Lists the variables of a SAS dataset with attributes. You can change the name, informat, format, and label attributes of the variables. **Option** *SAS dataset*

WEDIT   Enhanced Editor. A file-oriented text editor window. **Options** *file*   USE   NOUSE ⏎ 8+

FOOTNOTES, OPTIONS, and TITLES window commands

CANCEL   Closes the window and restores previous settings.

END   Closes the window and saves new settings.

KEYS window commands

COPY   Recalls function key definitions from the user profile.

COPY *entry*   Recalls function key definitions from the KEYS entry.

PURGE   Removes special function keys from list.

SAVE   Saves changes in the user profile.

SAVE *entry*   Saves changes in a KEYS entry.

CANCEL   Closes the window and restores the previously saved or default function key definitions.

END   Closes the window and saves any changes in the user profile.

LISTING window commands

AUTOSCROLL   Displays the window's scrolling increment.

AUTOSCROLL *distance*   Sets the window's automatic scrolling increment.   AUTOSCROLL 0   Turns off automatic scrolling.

LINESIZE   Displays the standard print file's line size.

LINESIZE *n*   Sets the standard print file's line size.

PAGE *toggle*   Displays paged or unpaged text.

PAGESIZE   Displays the standard print file's page size.

PAGESIZE *n*   Sets the standard print file's line size.

LOG window commands

AUTOSCROLL   Displays the window's automatic scrolling increment.

AUTOSCROLL *distance*   Sets the window's automatic scrolling increment.   AUTOSCROLL 0   Turns off automatic scrolling.

LINESIZE   Displays the log's line size.

LINESIZE *n*   Sets the log's line size.

NOTEPAD window commands

DESCRIPTION   Displays the entry's description.

DESCRIPTION '*description*'   Changes the entry's description.

NTITLE '*description*'   Changes the window's title.

CANCEL   Closes the window and discards changes.

END   Closes the window and saves changes.

PROGRAM window commands

RECALL   RECALL *n*   Retrieves a previously submitted block of lines.

SUBMIT   SUB   END   Submits the contents of the window to be executed as SAS statements. (If text is selected in the window, only the selected text is submitted.)

SUBMIT '*statements*'   Submits the specified string to be executed.

SUBMIT BUF=*buffer*   Submits a named paste buffer.

SUBTOP   SUBTOP *n*   Submits the first line or first lines from the window to be executed.

Applications

These applications in the interactive environment also have window names, even though they are not necessarily contained in a single window.

AF   An AF application. **Options** C=*entry* The AF entry. FRAME=*name or number*   A frame of a CBT entry. *n*   A selection from a MENU entry.

AFA   An AF application displayed in its own window. **Options** See AF, above. **Alias** AFAPPL

DESKTOP   Displays applications, files, and other objects arranged in folders.

EXPLORER   Displays files and other objects arranged in a hierarchy.

FONTLIST   Displays a list of available fonts. ⟳ 8.1+

HELP   Online help. **Option** *topic*

QUERY   Assembles SQL queries. **Alias** Q

SASCOLOR   Displays color settings for editing.

SYNCONFIG   Syntax color scheme. ↻ 8.2+

VIEWTABLE   Displays a SAS dataset for browsing or editing.
Alias VIEWT

Commands

There are display manager commands, which can be used in display manager windows generally, and text editor commands, for text editor windows such as the Program Editor and Notepad windows. Both kinds of commands are listed here.

Mode-Toggle Commands

Mode-toggle commands turn modes on and off.

mode ON   Turns the mode on.

mode OFF   Turns the mode off.

mode   Switches the mode between on and off.

Modes

AUTOADD   On: displays blank lines when you scroll past the bottom of the text in a text editor window. Off: displays END OF TEXT at the bottom of the text in a text editor window.

AUTOFLOW   On: flows text imported with the INCLUDE, COPY, or PASTE command.

AUTOSPLIT   Controls what happens when you press the enter key in the middle of a line of text in a text editor window. On: splits the line of text into two lines. Off: moves the cursor to the beginning of the next line.

AUTOWRAP   Controls what happens when data that is wider than the window is imported with the INCLUDE or COPY command or when data is stored with the FILE command to a file that is narrower than the data. On: wraps text. Off: truncates text.

CAPS   On: converts any lowercase letters you type to uppercase.

CLOCK   On: displays the time in the bottom line of the screen. ↻ z

COMMAND   On: displays a menu bar or a command line in the window, depending on the PMENU mode. Off: displays a command line in the window. **Alias** COM

ICON   On: shrinks the window to an icon.

INDENT   Text flow results. On: keeps lines indented. Off: left-aligns.

NULLS   On: trailing spaces in fields are converted to nulls to make inserting text easier. ↻ z

NUMBERS   On: displays line numbers at the left side of a text editor window. **Alias** NUM, NUMS, NUMBER

PMENU   On: displays menu bars or command lines in windows. Off: displays only command lines. **Alias** PM

RALIGN   Text flow results. On: fully justified. Off: left-aligned.

STATUS   On: displays status information in the upper right corner of active primary windows.

SCROLLBAR   On: displays scroll bars. **Alias** SBAR

SEQUENCE   On: removes line numbers from text files. **Alias** SEQ

SYNCOLOR   On: shows syntax color coding in the text editor window. ⊙ 8.2+

TOOLTIPS   On: shows tool tips. ⊙ W X

WMENUPOP   On: displays popup menus with the right mouse button. ⊙ W

ZOOM   On: makes the window as large as possible. **Alias** Z

Scrolling Commands

When the content of a window is larger than its displayed area, scrolling commands move the content to display other parts of it. You can also use scroll bars for scrolling.

direction   *direction distance*   Scrolls in the indicated direction.
Direction BACKWARD BAC UP FORWARD FORW DOWN DO
LEFT RIGHT **Distance** *n* A specific number of lines or columns.
CURSOR CUR CU To the cursor location. HALF H Half the height or width of the window. MAX M To the end of the data.
PAGE PA The height or width of the window.

BOTTOM   Scrolls down to the bottom.

TOP   Scrolls up to the top.

n   Scrolls to the indicated line.

HSCROLL *distance*   Sets the default horizontal distance. **Alias** HS

VSCROLL *distance*   Sets the default vertical distance. **Alias** VS

:

:*line command*   Executes the line command on the line where the cursor is located.

?

See **PREVCMD**.

BFIND

BFIND '*string*' *part option*   Searches backward for a string. Equivalent to the FIND command with the PREV option.

BOUNDS

BOUNDS   Indicates the current left and right boundaries in a text editor window. The boundaries control text flow and alignment.

BOUNDS *left right*   Sets new left and right boundaries.

BYE

BYE   Ends the SAS session. **Alias ENDSAS**

CANCEL

CANCEL   Closes a window immediately. In some windows, this discards or undoes changes. **Alias CAN**

CASCADE

CASCADE   Cascades all open windows so that the names are visible.

CHANGE

CHANGE '*string*' '*string*' *options*   Searches for the first string and replaces it with the second string.

CHANGE   Repeats the search and replacement of the most recent CHANGE command.

Options The same as those used in the FIND command. **Alias C**

Example CHANGE '¬' '∧' ALL

CLEAR

CLEAR   CLEAR *window*   Clears the data area of the window.

CLEAR *part*   Clears the indicated part of the window.

Parts TEXT   MASK   TABS

CLEAR RECALL   Clears the recall buffer so that previously submitted lines cannot be recalled.

Alias CLE

COLOR

COLOR *part color optional video attribute*   Sets the color and video attribute of a part of the window.

Parts BACKGROUND   BAC   BANNER   BAN   BORDER   BO
BYLINE   COMMAND   COM   DATA   DA   ERROR   E   FOOTNOTE
MENU   MENUBORDER   MENUB   MESSAGE   MES   MSG   MTEXT
MT   NOTES   NO   NUMBERS   NUMB   SOURCE   SO   TEXT   TE
TITLE   WARNING   WA

Colors RED   R   GREEN   G   BLUE   B   CYAN   C   MAGENTA   M
YELLOW   Y   BLACK   K   GRAY   GREY   A   WHITE   W   NEXT

Video attributes REVERSE   R   BLINK   B   HIGHLIGHT   H
UNDERLINE   U

COLOR SYNTAX;   Applies syntax color coding in the text editor window. (Also see the SYNCOLOR mode-toggle command.) ○ 8.2+

COPY

COPY *entry options*   Copies the catalog entry into the window.

COPY *entry entry*   Duplicates an entry.

Options When copying into a text editor window, all the options of the INCLUDE command apply.

CURPOS

CURPOS   Reports the cursor position.

CURPOS *line optional column*   Moves the cursor.

CURSOR

CURSOR   Moves the cursor to the command line.

CUT

CUT *options*   Cuts marked text from the window and copies it to a paste buffer. **Options** The same as in the STORE command.

DELETE

DELETE *entry*   Deletes a catalog entry. **Alias DEL**

DMOPTLOAD ○ 8.2

DMOPTLOAD *SAS dataset or "registry key"*   Loads a stored set of system option settings.

DMOPTLOAD   Loads system option settings from SASUSER.MYOPTS.

DMOPTSAVE ○ 8.2

DMOPTSAVE *SAS dataset or "registry key"*   Stores system option settings.

DMOPTSAVE   Stores system option settings in SASUSER.MYOPTS.

END

END   Closes a window normally.
Alias SUBMIT, **SUB**

ENDSAS

See **BYE**.

EXPLODE ○ z

EXPLODE   Displays the full length of truncated text fields.

FILE

FILE *file options*   Stores the window's text data in a text file.

FILE   Stores the window's text data in the text file most recently used in a FILE or INCLUDE statement.

Options

APPEND A Appends to the file. REPLACE R Replaces the previous contents of the file.

TABS T Compresses the file by replacing blanks with tabs.

ATTR Also stores attributes along with the text.

FILL

FILL   FILL '*character*' and/or *n*   Inserts *n* fill characters at the cursor location, if the cursor is in a blank area of a text field in a text editor window. **Example** FILL '-' 80

FIND

FIND '*string*' *options*   Searches for the string.

FIND   Repeats the most recent text search.

Options

Where: NEXT N Forward from the cursor location. FIRST F Forward from the beginning of text. PREV Backward from the cursor location. LAST L Backward from the end of text. ALL A All occurrences in the text.

Part: PREFIX PREF At beginning of word. SUFFIX SUF At end of word. WORD W As entire word.

ICASE   Ignores case: treats uppercase and lowercase letters as matching.
Alias F

GSUBMIT

GSUBMIT *'string'* or BUF=*buffer*   Submits SAS statements for execution. **Alias GSUB**

HOME

HOME   Moves the cursor to the command line. **Alias HO**

INCLUDE

INCLUDE *fileref or 'physical file name'* *options*   Copies the text file into the text editor window.

INCLUDE   Copies the text file most recently used in a FILE or INCLUDE command into the text editor window.

Options

NOATTR   Does not copy attributes that are stored in the text file.

NOTABS   Converts tabs to blanks.

REPLACE   R   Replaces the contents of the window.

Alias INC

LOCK

Equivalent to the LOCK statement.

MARK

MARK   MARK CHAR   Marks the beginning or end of a text selection in the active window. The marked text can then be used by the CUT and STORE commands or searched by the FIND and CHANGE commands.

MARK BLOCK   Marks the beginning or end of a block selection in the active window.

MZOOM

MZOOM   Displays the message line in a dialog box. Use this command when a message is too long to display completely. **Alias MZ**

NEXT

NEXT   NEXT *window*   Activates a different open window.

PASTE

PASTE *options*   Copies a paste buffer into the window at the cursor location.

Options

BLOCK   Copies text as a block.   CHAR   Copies text as a string.

BUFFER=*buffer*   Uses a named paste buffer.

PCLEAR

PCLEAR   PCLEAR BUFFER=*buffer*   Clears a paste buffer.

PLIST

PLIST   Writes a list of paste buffers in the log.

PREVCMD

PREVCMD   Restores the previously entered command line.
Alias ?

PREVWIND

PREVWIND   PREVWIND *window*   Activates a different open window.

RCHANGE

RCHANGE   Repeats the search and replacement of the most recent CHANGE command.

RESET

RESET   Cancels all pending line commands and hides special lines.

RESHOW

RESHOW   Redisplays the window.

RESIZE

RESIZE   Returns cascaded or tiled windows to their previous sizes and locations.

RFIND

RFIND   Repeats the most recent text search.

RFIND ICASE   Repeats the most recent text search, ignoring case.

RSUBMIT ○ SAS/CONNECT

RSUBMIT *options*   Submits the contents of the window to a remote session for execution. Equivalent to the RSUBMIT/ENDRSUBMIT statements. **Alias RSUB**

SAVE

SAVE   SAVE *entry options*   Stores the window's data in a catalog entry. **Options** For a window that displays text, the options of the FILE command apply. **Alias SAV**

SIGNON/SIGNOFF ○ SAS/CONNECT

Equivalent to the SIGNON/SIGNOFF statements.

SMARK

SMARK   Marks the beginning or end of a rectangular block of text on the screen.

STARTSAS ○ 8+

STARTSAS   Displays a dialog to set options for a new SAS process.

STORE

STORE *options*   Copies marked text to a paste buffer.

Options

ALL   Copies all marked text.   LAST   Copies the most recently marked text. This is the default.

APPEND   Appends to, rather than replaces, the paste buffer.

BUFFER=*buffer*   Uses a named paste buffer.

SUBMIT

SUBMIT   Submits the contents of the window for execution.

Alias SUB, END

SUBTOP

SUBTOP   SUBTOP *n*   Submits the first *n* lines in the window for execution.

TILE

TILE   Tiles all open windows so that they do not overlap.

UNDO

UNDO   Undoes the most recent action in the text editor window, if it was editing or typing.

UNMARK

UNMARK   Unmarks the one marked area that is displayed in the window or the marked area at the cursor location.

UNMARK ALL   Unmarks all marked text in the window. You can then use the FIND and CHANGE commands to search all the text in the window.

WDEF

WDEF *top left height width*   Sets the location and size of the window.

WPOPUP

WPOPUP   Displays a popup menu for the cursor location.

WSAVE

WSAVE   Saves the location, size, colors, and video attributes of the window in the user profile.

WSAVE ALL   Saves attributes of all open windows.

X

Equivalent to the X statement.

Line/Block Commands

Line commands are normally entered in the line number fields of a text editor window. They can also be entered on the command line or in a function key, prefixed by a colon (:).

A block command is a line command that affects a block of lines. Enter the block command on the first and last lines of the block. Block commands can be identified by their repeated characters. For example, CC is the block command form of the C line command.

An argument for a line command should immediately follow the line command code, with no spaces in between. Type a space after a line command, if necessary, to separate it from characters of the line number. The arguments are optional, with a default of 1, except as indicated. The argument for a block command only needs to be entered on one of the two lines that define the block.

$(n$ $((n$ Shifts left n columns, deleting the first n characters.

$)n$ $))n$ Shifts right n columns.

$<n$ $<<n$ Shifts left n columns, but does not delete nonblank characters.

$>n$ $>>n$ Shifts right n columns, but does not delete nonblank characters.

A   Indicates that text is to be copied after this line.

B   Indicates that text is to be copied before this line.

Cn CC   Copies lines to the location indicated by the A, B, or O line command.

CLn CCL   Changes letters to lowercase. **Alias** LC LLC

COLS   Displays a ruler. **Alias** CO

CUn CCU   Changes letters to uppercase. **Alias** UC UUC

Dn DD   Deletes lines.

In IAn Inserts lines after the current line.

IBn Inserts lines before the current line.

JC   JJC   Centers the line between the left and right boundaries.

JCn JJCn Centers the line around the nth column.

JL   JJL   Left-aligns the line at the left boundary.

JLn JJLn Left-aligns the line at the nth column.

JR   JJR   Right-aligns the line at the right boundary.

JRn JJRn Right-aligns the line at the nth column.

Mn MM   Moves lines to the location of the A, B, or O line command.

MASK   Displays a mask line. The mask line is the initial value of inserted lines. **Alias** MA

MCL   Changes selected text to lowercase.

MCU   Changes selected text to uppercase.

O   Indicates that text being copied is to be overlaid over this line, or beginning at this line. When text is overlaid, any spaces present in the line are replaced by characters in the text being copied.

Rn RRn Repeats a line or block a number of times.

TABS   Displays a tabs line. Each T in the tabs line represents a tab stop. **Alias** TAB, TA

TABSn Displays a tabs line and sets tab stops every n positions.

TC   Connects the line with the following line.

TF   Flows text up to the next blank line.

TF*n*   Flows text up to the next blank line, using the indicated right margin.

TFA   Flows text to the end of the data.

TFA*n*   Flows text to the end of the data, using the indicated right margin.

TS*n*   Splits the line at the cursor location and inserts lines.

14

Informats

Informats convert text data, such as data from an input text file, to SAS character or numeric values. Informats are most commonly used to read a value for a variable; the type of the informat, character or numeric, must correspond to the type of the variable.

When an informat is specified, the informat name is followed by a period. Depending on the informat, there can be two optional whole number arguments, before and after the period.

In user-entry windows, each field should have a compatible informat and format. Informats marked ✪ in the entries below have a compatible or mostly compatible format with the same name.

To create an expression from an informat, use the INPUT, INPUTC, or INPUTN function. To create informats for a specific purpose, use the FORMAT procedure.

Character Informats

Character informats use an optional width argument, shown as w, which can be between 1 and 32767. The default width is usually 1 or the width of a variable or a window field.

$ASCII ✪
$ASCII$w$. Reads ASCII text.

$BINARY ✪
$BINARY$w$. Character binary: converts each 8 input binary digit characters to one character.

$CHAR ✪
$CHAR$w$. Reads text or any data unchanged.

$CHARZB

$CHARZB*w*.   Treats nulls (zero bytes) as blanks.

$EBCDIC ✪

$EBCDIC*w*.   Reads EBCDIC text.

$F ✪

$F*w*.   Standard character informat: discards leading spaces; treats period as missing.

Alias $ A width argument is required when using this alias.

$HEX ✪

$HEX*w*.   Character hexadecimal: converts each pair of hexadecimal digits to one character.

$KANJI ✪ ↻ 7+

$KANJI*w*.   Removes shift codes from DBCS data.

$KANJIX ✪ ↻ 7+

$KANJIX*w*.   Adds shift codes to DBCS data.

$OCTAL ✪

$OCTAL*w*.   Character octal: converts each 3 octal digits to one character.

$PHEX

$PHEX*w*.   Character packed hexadecimal: converts each input byte to two characters, discarding the last half byte.

$QUOTE ✪

$QUOTE*w*.   Removes leading and trailing quote marks.

$REVERJ ✪

$REVERJ*w*.   Reversed; right to left.

$REVERS ✪

$REVERS*w*.   Reversed, with leading spaces removed.

$UCS2B ✪ ↻ 8.2+

$UCS2B*w*.   Reads big-endian 16-bit UCS2 Unicode without a byte-order mark.

$UCS2L ✪ ↻ 8.2+

$UCS2L*w*.   Reads little-endian 16-bit UCS2 Unicode without a byte-order mark.

$UCS2X ✪ ↻ 8.2+

$UCS2X*w*.   Reads 16-bit UCS2 Unicode.

$UPCASE ✪

$UPCASE*w*.   Converts lowercase letters to uppercase.

$UTF8X ✪ ⊙ 8.2+

$UTF8X*w*. Reads 8-bit UCS2 Unicode.

$VARYING

$VARYING*w*. *length variable* Varying length. Use only in the INPUT statement.

Numeric Informats

Numeric informats use optional width and decimal arguments, shown as *w* and *d*. The decimal argument indicates the location of the decimal point, if the input data does not actually contain a period. For binary informats, it indicates that the value is divided by the indicated power of 10 after being read. The default *d* value is 0. Except as noted, the arguments are subject to these restrictions: $1 \leq w \leq 32$; $0 \leq d \leq 31$. The decimal argument is not required to be less than the width argument. For binary informats, the restriction is $0 \leq d \leq 10$.

Most numeric informats treat fields that contain blanks or a period as standard missing values. Numeric informats that read decimal digits can also treat letters as special missing values if you use the MISSING statement.

BINARY ✪

BINARY*w.d* $w \leq 64$ Reads binary integers

BITS

BITS*w.d* $d + w \leq 64$ Skips *d* bits, then reads *w* bits as a binary integer.

BZ

BZ*w.d* Treats blanks as zeros.

COMMA ✪

COMMA*w.d* Ignores commas, dollar signs, blanks, percent signs, hyphens, and parentheses. Treats a leading left parenthesis (or hyphen) as a minus sign.

Alias DOLLAR ✪ NEGPAREN ✪

COMMAX ✪

COMMAX*w.d* The same as COMMA, but with periods and commas interchanged.

Alias DOLLARX ✪

EUR... ✪ ⊙ 8.1+

EURO*w.d* $w \geq 2$ Similar to COMMA, but also handles euro symbols.

EUROX*w.d* $w \geq 2$ Similar to COMMAX, but also handles euro symbols.

F ✪

F*w.d* *w.d* Standard numeric informat: ordinary numeric data and scientific notation.

Alias BEST ✪ D ✪ E ✪

FLOAT ✪

FLOAT*w.d* *w* = 4 Single-precision floating point.

HEX✪

HEX*w.* *w* < 16 Reads hexadecimal integers.

HEX*w.* *w* = 16 Reads the hexadecimal representation of an 8-byte floating point value.

IB✪

IB*w.d* *w* ≤ 8 Signed integer binary.

IBR ✪ ⟳ 7+

IBR*w.d* *w* ≤ 8 Signed integer binary with little-endian byte ordering.

IEEE ✪

IEEE*w.d* 3 ≤ *w* ≤ 4 IEEE single-precision floating point.

IEEE*w.d* 5 ≤ *w* ≤ 8 IEEE double-precision floating point.

MRB ✪

MRB*w.d* 2 ≤ *w* ≤ 8 Microsoft real binary (floating point).

NUMX ✪

NUMX*w.d* The same as the standard numeric informat, but with the decimal point written as a comma.

OCTAL ✪

OCTAL*w.d* *w* ≤ 24 Reads octal integers.

PD ✪

PD*w.d* *w* ≤ 16 Packed decimal.

PERCENT ✪

PERCENT*w.d* *d* ≤ 2 The same as COMMA, except that if a percent sign follows the value, the value is divided by 100.

PIB ✪

PIB*w.d* *w* ≤ 8 Unsigned (positive) integer binary.

PIBR ✪ ⟳ 7+

PIBR*w.d* *w* ≤ 8 Unsigned (positive) integer binary with little-endian byte ordering.

PK ✪

PK*w.d* *w* ≤ 16 Unsigned packed decimal.

RB

RB*w.d* $2 \leq w \leq 8$ Real binary; floating point.

S370F...

Informats for compatibility with native IBM mainframe (System/370) data formats.

S370FF*w.d*   EBCDIC numeric. ❂ ⟳ 7+

S370FHEX*w.d*   EBCDIC hexadecimal. ❂ ⟳ 8.2+

S370FIB*w.d* $w \leq 8$ Signed integer binary with big-endian byte ordering. ❂

S370FPD*w.d* $w \leq 16$ IBM mainframe packed decimal. ❂

S370FPDU*w.d* $w \leq 16$ IBM mainframe packed decimal for positive values only (creating an error condition for negative values).

S370FPIB*w.d* $w \leq 8$ Unsigned (positive) integer binary with big endian byte ordering. ❂ **Alias** S370FIBU ❂

S370FRB*w.d* $2 \leq w \leq 8$ IBM mainframe real binary. ❂

S370FZD*w.d*   IBM mainframe (EBCDIC) zoned decimal. ❂

S370FZDL*w.d*   IBM mainframe zoned decimal leading sign. EBCDIC zoned decimal with the sign bit in the first byte. ❂

S370FZDS*w.d* $w \geq 2$ IBM System/370 zoned decimal separate leading sign: EBCDIC numeric digits with the first character blank or a minus sign. ❂

S370FZDT*w.d* $w \geq 2$ IBM System/370 zoned decimal separate trailing sign: EBCDIC numeric digits with the last character blank or a minus sign. ❂

S370FZDU*w.d*   IBM System/370 unsigned zoned decimal. The same as S370FZD, but not valid for negative numbers. ❂

YEN ⊙

YEN*w.d*   *d:* 0, 2   Ignores commas, periods, blanks, and yen signs (ASCII \, U.S. EBCDIC $).

ZD ⊙

ZD*w.d*   Zoned decimal.

ZDB

ZDB*w.*   Zoned decimal with blanks treated as zeros.

ZDV

ZDV*w.d*   Zoned decimal, applied strictly.

Time Informats

The informats in this section convert text data to SAS date, SAS date-time, and SAS time values. Entries indicate the most useful widths; these are not necessarily the only widths allowed for these informats.

Informats marked ✦ have international equivalents. See the entry for **...DF...** for details.

...DF... ✪

*prefix*DF*suffix w.* International date and datetime informats. The prefix of the informat name indicates the language. The suffix identifies the equivalent informat.

Prefixes and Languages

AFR   Afrikaans   CAT   Catalan   CRO   Croatian   CSY   Czech
DAN   Danish   DES   Swiss_German   DEU   German   ENG   English
ESP   Spanish   EUR   Selected in the DFLANG= system option
FIN   Finnish   FRA   French   FRS   Swiss_French   HUN   Hungarian
ITA   Italian   MAC   Macedonian   NLD   Dutch   NOR   Norwegian
POL   Polish   PTG   Portuguese   RUS   Russian   SLO   Slovenian
SVE   Swedish

Suffixes and Equivalent Informats

DE   DATE   DT   DATETIME   MY   MONYY

Examples

ESPDFDE is the Spanish-language version of the DATE informat.

SVEDFMY is the Swedish-language version of the MONYY informat.

ANYDT... ↺ 9.1+

These informats read an input field according to the DATE, DATETIME, DDMMYY, JULIAN, MMDDYY, MONYY, TIME, or YYQ informat. When an input field does not indicate the date or the time of day, the informat uses 0 as the respective default value.

ANYDTDTE*w.*   Extracts a SAS date value.

ANYDTDTM*w.*   Extracts a SAS datetime value.

ANYDTTME*w.*   Extracts a SAS time value.

DATE ✪ ✈

DATE*w.*   *w* ≥ 7   Reads a day, three-letter month abbreviation, and two- or four-digit year as a SAS date value.

DATETIME ✪ ✈

DATETIME*w.*   13 ≤ *w* ≤ 40   Reads a combined DATE and TIME format as a SAS datetime value.

DDMMYY ✪

DDMMYY*w.*   *w* ≥ 6   Reads a day, month, and year as a SAS date value.

JDATEYMD ↺ 8+

JDATEYMD*w.*   *w* ≥ 12   Reads date values in the form yymmmdd or yyyymmmdd in Japanese kanji DBCS text.

JNENGO ↺ 8+

JNENGO*w.*   *w* ≥ 16   Reads date values in the form yymmdd in Japanese kanji DBCS text.

JULIAN ✪

JULIAN*w.*   *w* ≥ 5   Reads a year and three-digit day of year as a SAS date value.

MINGUO ✪

MINGUO*w*. 6 ≤ *w* ≤ 10   Reads a Taiwan-era year (1=1912), month, and day as a SAS date value.

MMDDYY ✪

MMDDYY*w*. *w* ≥ 6   Reads a month, day, and year as a SAS date value.

MONYY ✪ ⇢

MONYY*w*. *w* ≥ 5   Reads a three-letter month abbreviation and year as a SAS date value.

MSEC

MSEC*w*. *w* = 8   Reads an IBM System/370 time-of-day clock value as a SAS time value.

NENGO ✪

NENGO*w*. *w* ≥ 7   Reads a Japanese era (M, T, S, or H), year, month, and day as a SAS date value.

PDJULG

PDJULG*w*. *w* = 4   Reads a packed decimal year and day of year ('*YYYYDDD*F'X) as a SAS date value.

PDTIME

PDTIME*w*. *w* = 4   Reads a packed decimal hour, minute, and second ('0*HHMMSS*F'X) as a SAS time value.

RMFDUR

RMFDUR*w*. *w* = 4   Reads an RMF measurement interval field (packed decimal minutes, seconds, milliseconds) as a number of seconds.

RMFSTAMP

RMFSTAMP*w*. *w* = 8   Reads an RMF time and date field as a SAS datetime value.

SHRSTAMP ◌7+

SHRSTAMP*w*. *w* = 8   Reads an SHR date and time field as a SAS datetime value.

SMFSTAMP

SMFSTAMP*w*. *w* = 8   Reads an SMF time-date field as a SAS datetime value.

STIMER ◌9+

STIMER*w*.   Reads elapsed time. The time can be written in seconds, minutes and seconds, or hours, minutes, and seconds, with a colon between each time unit. For example, 1:00 is 1 minute, while 1:00:00 is 1 hour. This informat reads the time measurements that the STIMER system option generates.

TIME ✪

TIME*w*. *w* ≥ 5 Reads hours, minutes, and optionally seconds and fractions of seconds as a SAS time value. Also reads 12-hour clock times with the suffix AM or PM.

TODSTAMP

TODSTAMP*w*. *w* = 8 Reads an IBM System/370 time-of-day clock value as a SAS datetime value.

TU

TU*w*. *w* = 4 Reads an unsigned binary field that contains timer units as a SAS time value. A timer unit is $\frac{1}{38,400}$ second.

YYMMDD ✪

YYMMDD*w*. *w* ≥ 6 Reads a year, month, and day as a SAS date value.

YYMMN ✪ ⟳ 7+

YYMMN*w*. *w*: 4, 6 Reads a year and month (with no punctuation) as a SAS date value.

YYQ ✪

YYQ*w*. *w* ≥ 4 Reads a year, the letter Q, and a quarter (1–4) as a SAS date value.

15

Formats

A format converts a character or numeric value to a text string in order to display or print the value. The use and syntax of formats parallels that of informats. However, the decimal argument is more important for formats than for informats. For most numeric formats, it determines the number of decimal places that are produced.

To create an expression from a format, use the PUT, PUTC, or PUTN function. To create formats for a specific purpose, use the FORMAT procedure.

Character Formats

Character formats use an optional width argument, shown as w, which can be between 1 and 32767. Character formats left-align when the output they produce is shorter than the width of the format.

$ASCII

$ASCII$w$.   Writes ASCII text.

$BIDI ◌ 9+

$BIDI$w$.   Writes a visually oriented string.

$BINARY

$BINARY$w$.   Character binary: converts each character to 8 output binary digit characters.

$CHAR

$CHAR$w$.   Writes a character value unchanged. Same as the standard character format.

$EBCDIC

$EBCDIC$w$.   Writes EBCDIC text.

$F

$F*w*. Standard character format. Writes a character value unchanged.
Alias $ A width argument is required when using this alias.

$HEX

$HEX*w*. Character hexadecimal: writes each character as two hexadecimal digits.

$KANJI ⟳ 7+

$KANJI*w*. Adds shift codes to DBCS data.

$KANJIX ⟳ 7+

$KANJIX*w*. Removes shift codes from DBCS data.

$MSGCASE

$MSGCASE*w*. Converts letters to uppercase if the system option MSGCASE is on.

$OCTAL

$OCTAL*w*. Character octal: writes each character as 3 octal digits.

$QUOTE

$QUOTE*w*. $w \geq 3$ Writes a string surrounded by double quotes ("*string*").

$REVERJ

$REVERJ*w*. Reversed; right to left.

$REVERS

$REVERS*w*. Reversed, with leading spaces removed.

$UCS2B ⟳ 8.2+

$UCS2B*w*. Writes big-endian 16-bit UCS2 without a byte-order mark.

$UCS2L ⟳ 8.2+

$UCS2L*w*. Writes little-endian 16-bit UCS2 without a byte-order mark.

$UCS2X ⟳ 8.2+

$UCS2X*w*. Writes 16-bit UCS2 in native byte sequence without a byte-order mark.

$UPCASE

$UPCASE*w*. Converts lowercase letters to uppercase.

$UTF8X ⟳ 8.2+

$UTF8X*w*. Writes UTF-8, 8-bit Unicode.

$VARYING

$VARYING*w*. *length variable* Varying-length. Use only in the PUT statement.

Numeric Formats

Numeric formats use an optional width argument, *w*, which can range from 1 to 32. Most also use an optional decimal argument, *d*, which can range from 0 to 31. For formats that print decimal points, *d* must be less than *w*. In binary formats, which cannot contain a decimal point, the *d* argument tells the format to multiply the number by that power of 10 before formatting. In these binary formats, *d* can be no more than 31, but it does not have to be less than *w*.

Some binary formats can write only positive values; if you use such a format to write a negative value, it writes it as positive. Many formats can write only integer values; they truncate fractional values. Most numeric formats right-align when they produce output that is shorter than the width of the format, but formats that produce words or output that begins with a letter usually left-align.

BEST

BEST*w*. Writes a number as precisely as possible in the width.

BINARY

BINARY*w*. *w* ≤ 64 Writes binary integers.

COMMA

COMMA*w.d* *w* ≥ 2 Commas separate every three digits.

COMMAX

COMMAX*w.d* *w* ≥ 2 The same as COMMA, but with periods and commas interchanged.

D

D*w.s* *s* < *w*, *s* ≤ 16 Writes numbers with at least *s* significant digits using, within certain ranges, the same number of decimal places.

DOLLAR

DOLLAR*w.d* *w* ≥ 2 The same as COMMA, but preceded by a dollar sign.

DOLLARX

DOLLARX*w.d* *w* ≥ 2 The same as DOLLAR, but with periods and commas interchanged.

E

E*w*. *w* ≥ 7 Scientific (exponential) notation using E.

Example
```
1.25E+10
```

EUR... ◌ 8.1+

EURFR*currency w.d* $w \geq 2$ Converts currencies to euros.

EURTO*currency w.d* $w \geq 2$ Converts euros to other currencies. See the EUROCURR function for the three-letter currency codes.

EURO*w.d* $w \geq 2$ Similar to DOLLAR, but with a euro symbol.

EUROX*w.d* $w \geq 2$ Similar to DOLLARX, but with a euro symbol.

F

F*w.d*   *w.d*   Standard numeric format. Writes a decimal point and a fixed number of decimal places if $d > 0$.

FLOAT

FLOAT*w.d* $w = 4$ Single-precision floating point.

FRACT

FRACT*w.* $w \geq 4$ Writes fractions in reduced form.

HEX

HEX*w.* $w < 16$ Writes hexadecimal integers.

HEX*w.* $w = 16$ Writes the hexadecimal representation of an 8-byte floating point value.

IB

IB*w.d* $w \leq 8$ Signed integer binary.

IBR ◌ 7+

IBR*w.d* $w \leq 8$ Signed integer binary with little-endian byte ordering.

IEEE

IEEE*w.d* $3 \leq w \leq 4$ IEEE single-precision floating point.

IEEE*w.d* $5 \leq w \leq 8$ IEEE double-precision floating point.

MRB

MRB*w.d* $2 \leq w \leq 8$ Microsoft real binary (floating point).

NEGPAREN

NEGPAREN*w.d* $d \leq 2$ Commas separate every three digits; negative numbers are in parentheses.

NUMX

NUMX*w.d*   The same as the standard numeric format, but with the decimal point written as a comma.

OCTAL

OCTAL*w.* $w \leq 24$ Writes octal integers.

PD

PD*w.d* $w \leq 16$ Packed decimal.

PERCENT

PERCENT*w.d* $w \geq 4$, $d \leq 2$ Writes numbers as percents, followed by a percent sign, with negative values enclosed in parentheses.

PIB

PIB*w.d* $w \leq 8$ Unsigned (positive) integer binary.

PIBR ⊙ 7+

PIBR*w.d* $w \leq 8$ Unsigned (positive) integer binary with little-endian byte ordering.

PK

PK*w.d* $w \leq 16$ Unsigned packed decimal.

RB

RB*w.d* $2 \leq w \leq 8$, $d \leq 10$ Real binary; floating point.

ROMAN

ROMAN*w.* $w \geq 2$ Writes Roman numerals using capital letters.

S370F...

Formats for compatibility with native IBM mainframe (System/370) data formats.

S370FF*w.d*   EBCDIC numeric. ⊙ 7+

S370FHEX*w.d*   EBCDIC hexadecimal. ⊙ 8.2+

S370FIB*w.d* $w \leq 8$ Signed integer binary with big-endian byte ordering.

S370FIBU*w.d* $w \leq 8$ Unsigned integer binary (absolute value) with big-endian byte ordering.

S370FPD*w.d* $w \leq 16$ IBM mainframe packed decimal.

S370FPDU*w.d* $w \leq 16$ IBM mainframe unsigned packed decimal (absolute value).

S370FPIB*w.d* $w \leq 8$ Unsigned (positive) integer binary with big-endian byte ordering. Writes negative values as 'FF'X.

S370FRB*w.d* $2 \leq w \leq 8$ IBM mainframe real binary.

S370FZD*w.d*   IBM mainframe zoned decimal.

S370FZDL*w.d*   IBM mainframe zoned decimal leading sign: EBCDIC zoned decimal with the sign bit in the first byte.

S370FZDS*w.d* $w \geq 2$ IBM mainframe zoned decimal separate leading sign: EBCDIC numeric digits with the first character blank or a minus sign.

S370FZDT*w.d* $w \geq 2$ IBM mainframe zoned decimal separate trailing sign: EBCDIC numeric digits with the last character blank or a minus sign.

S370FZDU*w.d*   IBM System/370 unsigned zoned decimal. The same as S370FZD, but writes the absolute value.

SSN

SSN*w*.   *w* = 11   Nine-digit number with hyphens after the third and fifth digits.

WORDF

WORDF*w*.   5 ≤ *w* ≤ 32767   Writes number in words, with hundredths written as a fraction.

WORDS

WORDS*w*.   5 ≤ *w* ≤ 32767   Writes number in words, with hundredths written in words.

YEN

YEN*w.d*   *w* ≥ 2, *d*: 0, 2   The same as COMMA, but preceded by a yen sign.

Z

Z*w.d*   Writes number with leading zeros.

ZD

ZD*w.d*   *d* ≤ 10   Zoned decimal.

Time Formats

Time formats are numeric formats that write SAS date, SAS time, and SAS datetime values. Widths up to 32 are often allowed, but the useful widths are shown in the entries. Instead of detailed descriptions, examples show the output that each format produces.

Formats marked ✦ have international equivalents. See the entry for **...DF...** for details. The symbol + in a format name indicates an optional suffix to change the symbol that the format writes as a delimiter. Symbol suffixes are:

B   space (blank)
C   :   colon
D   –   hyphen (dash)
N   none (the format width is smaller)
P   .   period
S   /   slash

...DF...

*prefix*DF*suffix w*.   International date and datetime formats. The prefix of the format name indicates the language. The suffix identifies the equivalent format.

Prefixes and Languages

AFR   Afrikaans   CAT   Catalan   CRO   Croatian   CSY   Czech
DAN   Danish   DES   Swiss_German   DEU   German   ENG   English
ESP   Spanish   EUR   Selected in the DFLANG= system option
FIN   Finnish   FRA   French   FRS   Swiss_French   HUN   Hungarian
ITA   Italian   MAC   Macedonian   NLD   Dutch   NOR   Norwegian

POL Polish PTG Portuguese RUS Russian SLO Slovenian
SVE Swedish

Suffixes and Equivalent Formats

DD DDMMYY   DE DATE   DN WEEKDAY
DT DATETIME   DWN DOWNAME   MN MONNAME
MY MONYY   WDX WORDDATX   WKX WEEKDATX

Example FINDFMN writes month names in Finnish.

DATE ✈

DATE*w*. *w*: 5, 7, 9 Writes a SAS date value: 06SEP   06SEP93
06SEP1993

DATEAMPM

DATEAMPM*w.d* *w*: 7, 10, 13, 16, 19, *d* + 20 Writes a SAS datetime
value using a 12-hour clock (for *w* ≥ 13): 01JAN60   01JAN60:10
01JAN60:10 AM   01JAN60:10:00 AM   01JAN60:10:00:08 AM

DATETIME ✈

DATETIME*w.d* *w*: 7, 10, 13, 16, *d* + 17 Writes a SAS datetime value:
06SEP93   06SEP93:14   06SEP93:14:03   06SEP93:14:03:17

DAY

DAY*w*. *w* = 2 Writes the day of the month of a SAS date value.

DDMMYY+ ✈

DDMMYY*w*. *w*: 2, 4, 5, 6, 8, 10 Writes a SAS date value: 06   0609
06/09   060993   06/09/93   06/09/1993

DDMMYYB*w*.   06 09   06 09 93   06 09 1993 ↻ 7+

DDMMYYC*w*.   06:09   06:09:93   06:09:1993 ↻ 7+

DDMMYYD*w*.   06-09   06-09-93   06-09-1993 ↻ 7+

DDMMYYN*w*. *w*: 2, 4, 6, 8 060993   06091993 ↻ 7+

DDMMYYP*w*.   06.09   06.09.93   06.09.1993 ↻ 7+

DDMMYYS*w*.   06/09   06/09/93   06/09/1993 ↻ 7+

DOWNAME ✈

DOWNAME*w* *w*: 1, 2, 3, 9 Writes the name of the day of the week of
a SAS date value: M   Mo   Mon   Monday

DT...

DTDATE*w*. *w*: 5, 7, 9 Writes the date of a SAS datetime value: 06SEP
06SEP93   06SEP1993 ↻ 8.1+

DTMONYY*w*. *w*: 5, 7 Writes the month and year of a SAS datetime
value: APR11   APR2011 ↻ 8.2+

DTWKDATX*w*. Writes the date of a SAS datetime value, similar to the
WEEKDATX format. ↻ 8.2+

DTYEAR*w*. *w*: 2, 4 Writes the year of a SAS datetime value: 07
2007 ↻ 8.2+

DTYYQC*w*. *w*: 4, 6 Writes the year and quarter of a SAS datetime
value: 00:4   2000:4 ↻ 8.2+

HHMM

HHMM*w.d*   *w*: 2, 4, 5, *d* + 6   Writes a SAS time value: 15   1547
15:47

HOUR

HOUR*w.d*   2 ≤ *w* ≤ 20, *d* < *w* – 2   Writes the hour of a SAS time value.

JULDAY

JULDAY*w.*   *w* = 3   Writes the day of the year of a SAS date value.

JULIAN

JULIAN*w.*   *w*: 5, 7   Writes the year and day of the year of a SAS date
value.

MINGUO

MINGUO*w.*   *w*: 6–7, 8–10   Writes a SAS date value as a Taiwan-era
date (year 1 = 1912): 840922   0084/09/22

MMDDYY+

MMDDYY*w.*   *w*: 2, 4, 5, 6, 8, 10   Writes a SAS date value: 08   0827
08/27   082799   08/27/99   08/27/1999

MMDDYYB*w.*   08 27   08 27 99   08 27 1999   ↻7+

MMDDYYC*w.*   08:27   08:27:99   08:27:1999   ↻7+

MMDDYYD*w.*   08-27   08-27-99   08-27-1999   ↻7+

MMDDYYN*w.*   *w*: 2, 4, 6, 8   082799   08271999   ↻7+

MMDDYYP*w.*   08.27   08.27.99   08.27.1999   ↻7+

MMDDYYS*w.*   08/27   08/27/99   08/27/1999   ↻7+

MMSS

MMSS*w.d*   *w*: 2, 5, 7–20, *d* = *w* – 6   Writes a SAS time value or a
number of seconds as minutes and seconds, or writes a number of
minutes as hours and minutes: 24:10

MMYY+

MMYY*w.*   *w*: 5, 7   Writes the month and year of a SAS date value:
08M99   08M1999

MMYYC*w.*   08:99   08:1999

MMYYD*w.*   08-99   08-1999

MMYYN*w.*   *w*: 4, 6   0899   081999

MMYYP*w.*   08.99   08.1999

MMYYS*w.*   08/99   08/1999

MONNAME ✈

MONNAME*w.*   *w*: 1, 3, 9   Writes the name of the month of a SAS date
value: S   Sep   September

MONTH

MONTH*w.*   *w* = 2   Writes the month number of a SAS date value.

MONYY ✈

MONYY*w.*   *w:* 5, 7   Writes the month and year of a SAS date value:
APR11   APR2011

NENGO

NENGO*w.*   2 ≤ *w* ≤ 10   Writes the Japanese era (M, T, S, or H), year,
month, and day of a SAS date value.

QTR

QTR*w.*   *w* = 1   Writes the quarter number of a SAS date value.

QTRR

QTRR*w.*   *w* = 3   Writes the quarter number of a SAS date value as a
Roman numeral.

TIME

TIME*w.d*   *w:* 2, 5, 8, 10–20, *d* = *w* – 9   Writes a SAS time value as
hours and optional minutes, seconds, and fractional seconds: 5
  5:15   5:15:00   5:15:00.00

TIMEAMPM

TIMEAMPM*w.d*   *w:* 2, 5, 8, 11, 13–20, *d* = *w* – 12   Writes a SAS time
value or the time of day of a SAS datetime value using a 12-hour
clock: AM   10 AM   10:00 AM   10:00:08 AM

TOD

TOD*w.d*   *w:* 2, 5, 8, 10–20, *d* = *w* – 9   Writes the time of day of a SAS
datetime value or a SAS time value as hours and optional minutes,
seconds, and fractional seconds (similar to the way the TIME format
writes the corresponding SAS time values, but with leading zeros).

WEEKDATE

WEEKDATE*w.*   *w:* 3, 9, 15, 17, 23, 29   Writes a SAS date value:
Mon   Monday   Mon, Oct 12, 92   Mon, Oct 12, 1992
Monday, Oct 12, 1992   Monday, October 12, 1992

WEEKDATX ·)

WEEKDATX*w.*   *w:* 3, 9, 15, 17, 23, 29   Writes a SAS date value:
Mon   Monday   Mon, 12 Oct 92   Mon, 12 Oct 1992
Monday, 12 Oct 1992   Monday, 12 October 1992

WEEKDAY ✈

WEEKDAY*w.*   *w* = 1   Writes the number of the day of the week of a
SAS date value, with Sunday=1, Saturday=7.

WORDDATE

WORDDATE*w.*   *w:* 3, 9, 12, 18   Writes a SAS date value: Oct
October   Oct 12, 1992   October 12, 1992

WORDDATX ✈

WORDDATX*w.*   *w:* 3, 9, 12, 18   Writes a SAS date value: Oct

October   12 Oct 1992   12 October 1992

YEAR

YEAR*w.*   *w:* 2, 4   Writes the year of a SAS date value: 07   2007

YYMM+

YYMM*w.*   *w:* 5, 7   Writes the year and month of a SAS date value:
93M09   1993M09

YYMMC*w.*   93:09   1993:09

YYMMD*w.*   93-09   1993-09

YYMMN*w.*   *w:* 4, 6   9309   199309

YYMMP*w.*   93.09   1993.09

YYMMS*w.*   93/09   1993/09

YYMMDD+

YYMMDD*w.*   *w:* 2, 4, 5, 6, 8, 10   Writes the year, month, and day
of a SAS date value: 99   9908   99-08   990827   99-08-27
1999-08-27

YYMMDDB*w.*   99 08   99 08 27   1999 08 27   ◔7+

YYMMDDC*w.*   99:08   99:08:27   1999:08:27   ◔7+

YYMMDDD*w.*   99-08   99-08-27   1999-08-27   ◔7+

YYMMDDN*w.*   *w:* 2, 4, 6, 8   990827   19990827   ◔7+

YYMMDDP*w.*   99.08   99.08.27   1999.08.27   ◔7+

YYMMDDS*w.*   99/08   99/08/27   1999/08/27   ◔7+

YYMON

YYMON*w.*   *w:* 5, 7   Writes the year and month of a SAS date value:
93SEP   1993SEP

YYQ+

YYQ*w.*   *w:* 4, 6   Writes the year and quarter of a SAS date value: 00Q4
2000Q4

YYQC*w.*   00:4   2000:4

YYQD*w.*   00-4   2000-4

YYQN*w.*   *w:* 3, 5   004   20004

YYQP*w.*   00.4   2000.4

YYQS*w.*   00/4   2000/4

YYQR+

YYQR*w.*   *w:* 6, 8   Writes the year and quarter of a SAS date value:
00QIV   2000QIV

YYQRC*w.*   00:IV   2000:IV

YYQRD*w.*   00-IV   2000-IV

YYQRN*w.*   w = 5, 7   00IV   2000IV

YYQRP*w.*   00.IV   2000.IV

YYQRS*w.*   00/IV   2000/IV

16

Functions

Functions are used mainly in data step programming. A function call can be used as an expression or as part of an expression, including a WHERE expression or SQL expression.

Most functions can also be used in macro expressions. The syntax of the function call is slightly different. See the %SYSFUNC macro function for details. Functions that cannot be used in a macro expression are marked with the symbol ¬%

Return Values

A function returns either character or numeric values and is classed as a character function or a numeric function. The INPUT function is an exception that can return either a character value or a numeric value, depending on its arguments. (See "Arguments" on the next page.)

The length of the value returned by a character function is measured in two ways. The length of the value when it is used in an expression may vary depending on the argument values. Nevertheless, a fixed amount of memory is used to hold the value, and this memory length is usually at least 200. Some functions derive their memory length from the memory length of one of the arguments. If you assign the result of a character function call to a variable, declare the variable as a character variable with an appropriate length (typically in a LENGTH statement) before the assignment statement that contains the function call. If a variable appears first as the target variable of a character function call, the target variable length is 200 or the memory length of the function, which may be shorter or longer than you want the variable to be.

The entries that follow show the data type for each function and, for character functions, an indication of the length. Numeric functions are identified by the symbol **N**. For character functions, the symbol is **$**, followed by the length of the function. A range might be shown for the expression length; the memory length is the longest length indicated.

Functions that have a primary string argument may return the same memory length and expression length as the argument. Where no length is indicated, the memory length is 200 characters or more, and the expression length can be any length up to that maximum length.

Arguments

A function call consists of the function name followed by a list of arguments in parentheses:

function(argument, argument, . . .)

Arguments are expressions whose values are used by the function. Each argument should be of a particular type. Most arguments are numeric values. The numeric arguments of many functions are limited to a particular range of values. If a numeric value outside that range is used as an argument, the function returns a missing value or generates an error condition.

Character values are also common arguments. A few functions require variables, arrays, or other types of arguments. These symbols indicate specific kinds of arguments:

x	Number.
n	Whole number.
θ	Angle measurement in radians.
X	Random variate, in the range of a probability distribution.
P	Probability, between 0 and 1.
string	Character value that represents a string.
char	Single character.
chars	Character value that represents a set of characters.
code	Character code value that is defined by the function.
sample	A set of numbers for statistical analysis.
nc	Optional noncentrality parameter.

OF

When you use several variables to provide arguments to a function, you can list the arguments in an alternate way. Instead of separating the arguments with commas, you can use the keyword OF and a variable list. In a variable list, variable names are separated by spaces:

function(OF variable variable . . .)

You can use abbreviated variable lists; they are especially useful for statistic functions. An array reference with the special subscript * represents the variable list that was used to define the array. A prefix followed by a colon indicates a list of all available variables whose names start with the prefix.

Example

MEAN(OF X1-X10) computes the mean of the variables X1 to X10.

ABS

ABS(*x*)   **N**   *Math.* Returns the absolute value.

ADDR ○7+

ADDR(*variable*)   **N**   Returns the address (the location in memory) of the argument. Valid only in 32-bit environments.

ADDRLONG

ADDRLONG(*variable*)   **$**   Returns the address (the location in memory) of the argument as a binary value.

AIRY

AIRY(*x*)   **N**   *Math.* The airy function.

ANY... ○9+

ANY*class*(*string*)   ANY*class*(*string, n*)   **N**   Searches the string for the first character that belongs to the character class. Returns the location if the search item is found, or 0 if it is not found.

Character classes

ALNUM   Alphanumeric character.

ALPHA   Letter.

CNTRL   Control character.

DIGIT   Digit.

FIRST   Letter or underscore (SAS name first character).

GRAPH   Graphical (visible) character.

LOWER   Lowercase letter.

NAME   Letter, underscore, or digit (SAS name character).

PRINT   Printable (visible or whitespace) character.

PUNCT   Punctuation character.

SPACE   Whitespace character (space, tab, etc.).

UPPER   Uppercase letter.

XDIGIT   Hexadecimal digit (0–9, A–F, a–f).

Search start and direction

The optional second argument *n* indicates the starting point and direction of the search. If *n* is positive, the search starts at that character location and proceeds to the right. If *n* is negative, the search starts at the location of the absolute value of *n* and proceeds to the left. If *n* is negative and its absolute value is greater than the length of the string, the search starts at the last character of the string. If *n* is 0, no characters are searched and the function returns 0. The default value for *n* is 1; if the second argument is omitted, the search begins at the first character and proceeds to the right.

Examples

ANYLOWER('Most') is 2.

ANYSPACE('Most') is 0.

ANYNAME('Most', -1) is 4.

ARCOS

ARCOS(*x*)   −1 ≤ *x* ≤ 1   **N**   *Trig.* Returns the arc cosine. The inverse of the cosine function.

ARSIN

ARSIN(*x*) $-1 \leq x \leq 1$ **N** *Trig.* Returns the arc sine. The inverse of the sine function.

ATAN

ATAN(*x*) **N** *Trig.* Returns the arc tangent. The inverse of the tangent function.

ATAN2 ⊙ 9.1+

ATAN2(*x, x*) **N** *Trig.* The relative arc tangent.

ATTRC/ATTRN

ATTRC(*dataset ID, attribute name*) **$** ATTRN(*dataset ID, attribute name*) **N** *I/O.* Returns the value of an attribute of a SAS dataset.

Character attributes

CHARSET The character set of the sort order: ASCII EBCDIC ANSI OEM Returns blank if not sorted.

ENCRYPT Whether the SAS dataset is encrypted: YES NO ⊙ 7+

ENGINE The name of the engine.

LABEL The dataset label.

LIB The libref.

MEM The member name.

MODE The access mode (set in the OPEN function).

MTYPE The member type.

SORTEDBY The sort order clause (as it would appear in the BY statement). Returns blank if not sorted.

SORTLVL A code indicating how the dataset was sorted: WEAK A sort order was claimed by the user. STRONG A sort order resulted from SAS processing. Returns blank if not sorted.

SORTSEQ The name of the alternate collating sequence used to sort the file. Returns blank if not sorted or if sorted with the native collating sequence. ⊙ 7+

TYPE The dataset type.

Numeric attributes

ALTERPW Whether alter-protected.

ANOBS Whether the number of observations is known.

ANY A code indicating the presence of variables and observations: -1 = no variables, 0 = no observations, 1 = observations and variables **Alias** VAROBS

ARAND Whether random access is supported. **Alias** RANDOM

ARWU Whether the engine can write to files.

CRDTE Creation datetime.

ICONST Integrity constraints are: 0 = none, 1 = general, 2 = referential, 3 = both. ⊙ 7+

INDEX Whether indexing is possible.

ISINDEX Whether indexes exist.

ISSUBSET   Whether a WHERE clause is in effect.

LRECL   Logical record length.

LRID   Record ID length. ↻ 7+

MAXGEN   Maximum number of generations. ↻ 7+

MODTE   Modification datetime.

NDEL   The number of deleted observations (still physically present in the dataset).

NEXTGEN   Next generation number. ↻ 7+

NLOBS   The number of logical observations (that is, observations that have not been deleted). Returns –1 if the number is unknown.

NLOBSF   The number of observations available after applying FISTOBS= and OBS= options and WHERE clauses. Determining this may require reading the entire dataset. ↻ 7+

NOBS   The number of physical observations. Returns –1 if the number is unknown.

NVARS   The number of variables.

PW   Whether password-protected.

RADIX   Whether accessible by observation number.

READPW   Whether read-protected.

TAPE   Whether a sequential file.

WHSTMT   The type of WHERE clause in effect: 0 = none, 1 = permanent, 2 = temporary, 3 = both kinds.

WRITEPW   Whether write-protected.

BAND

BAND(*n*, *n*) $0 \leq n < 2^{32}$ **N**   *Bitwise*. Returns the bitwise logical AND operation on the two whole numbers.

BETA ↻ 9+

BETA(α, β)   **N**   *Math*. The beta function.

BETAINV

BETAINV(P, α, β)   **N**   *Probability*. The inverse distribution function of the beta distribution with the parameters α and β.

BLSHIFT

BLSHIFT(*n*, *distance*) $0 \leq n < 2^{32}$, $0 \leq distance \leq 31$ **N**   *Bitwise*. Returns the whole number shifted left by the indicated distance.

Example BLSHIFT(15, 3) is 120.

BNOT

BNOT(*n*) $0 \leq n < 2^{32}$ **N**   *Bitwise*. Returns the bitwise logical NOT operation on the whole number.

BOR

BOR(*n*, *n*) $0 \leq n < 2^{32}$ **N**   *Bitwise*. Returns the bitwise logical OR operation on the two whole numbers.

BRSHIFT

BRSHIFT(*n, distance*) $0 \le n < 2^{32}, 0 \le distance \le 31$ **N** *Bitwise.*
Returns the whole number shifted right by the indicated distance.

Example BRSHIFT(15, 3) is 1.

BXOR

BXOR(*n, n*) $0 \le n < 2^{32}$ **N** *Bitwise.* Returns the bitwise logical exclusive OR operation on the two whole numbers.

BYTE

BYTE(*n*) **$** 1 $0 \le n \le 255$ Returns a character from the standard character set (ASCII or EBCDIC, depending on the computer).

CAT ↻ 9+

CAT(*string, . . .*) **$** Concatenates the strings and returns the result.
Overflow If the length of the concatenated string is greater than the length of the target variable, the function generates an error condition. If this occurs in a data step or SQL, the function returns a blank value.

CATS ↻ 9+

CATS(*string, . . .*) **$** Concatenates the strings after removing leading and trailing spaces and returns the result. **Overflow** See **CAT**.

CATT ↻ 9+

CATT(*string, . . .*) **$** Concatenates the strings after removing trailing spaces and returns the result. For a numeric argument, the function removes all spaces from the formatted value. **Overflow** See **CAT**.

CATX ↻ 9+

CATX(*delimiter, string, . . .*) **$** Removes leading and trailing spaces, concatenates the strings with the delimiter between them, and returns the result. **Overflow** See **CAT**.

CDF

CDF(*distribution, X, distribution parameters*) **N** *Probability.* A distribution function. The distribution parameters vary by distribution. The distribution can be abbreviated to four characters.

CDF('BERNOULLI', *X, P*) Bernoulli.

CDF('BETA', *X, α, β, optional left location, right location*) Beta.

CDF('BINOMIAL', *X, P, n*) Binomial.

CDF('CAUCHY', *X, optional α, β*) Cauchy.

CDF('CHISQUARED', *X, d.f., nc*) Chi-squared.

CDF('EXPONENTIAL', *X, optional λ*) Exponential.

CDF('F', X, *n.d.f., d.d.f., nc*) F.

CDF('GAMMA', *X, α, optional β*) Gamma.

CDF('GEOMETRIC', *X, P*) Geometric.

CDF('HYPERGEOMETRIC', *X, population size, category size, sample size, optional odds ratio*)   Hypergeometric.

CDF('LAPLACE', *X, optional* θ, λ)   Laplace.

CDF('LOGISTIC', *X, optional* θ, λ)   Logistic.

CDF('LOGNORMAL', *X, optional* θ, λ)   Lognormal.

CDF('NEGBINOMIAL', *X, P, n*)   Negative binomial.

CDF('NORMAL' *or* 'GAUSS', *X, optional* θ, λ)   Normal.

CDF('PARETO', *X, a, optional k*)   Pareto.

CDF('POISSON', *X*, λ)   Poisson.

CDF('T', *X, d.f., nc*)   T.

CDF('UNIFORM', *X, optional left location, right location*)   Uniform.

CDF('WALD' *or* 'IGAUSS', *X, d*)   Wald (Inverse Gaussian).

CDF('WEIBULL', *X, a, optional* λ)   Weibull.

CEIL

CEIL(*x*)   **N**   *Rounding.* Returns the smallest integer greater than or equal to the argument. Returns the integer if the argument is within 10^{-12} of an integer.

CEILZ ↺ 9+

CEILZ(*x*)   **N**   *Rounding.* Returns the smallest integer greater than or equal to the argument.

CEXIST

CEXIST(*catalog name*)   CEXIST(*entry name*)   **N**   *I/O.* Returns 1 if the catalog or entry exists, 0 if it does not.

CEXIST(*catalog name*, 'U')   CEXIST(*entry name*, 'U')   **N**   Returns 1 if the catalog or entry can be updated, 0 if it cannot.

CHOOSEC/CHOOSEN ↺ 9.1+

CHOOSEC(*n, value, value, . . .*)   **$**   CHOOSEN(*n, value, value, . . .*)   **N**   Returns the *n*th value listed. If *n* is negative, it counts backward from the end of the list. Use CHOOSEC for character values, CHOOSEN for numeric values.

CINV

CINV(*P, d.f.*)   CINV(*P, d.f., nc*)   **N**   *Probability.* The inverse distribution function of the chi-squared distribution with the indicated parameters.

CLOSE

CLOSE(*dataset ID*)   **N**   *I/O.* Closes the SAS dataset and returns an error code.

CNONCT

CNONCT(*x, d.f., P*)   **N**   *Probability.* Returns the nonnegative noncentrality parameter for a noncentral chi-square distribution with the indicated parameters.

COALESCE/COALESCEC ↻ 9.1+

COALESCE(*x, x, . . .*)   **N**   COALESCEC(*string, string, . . .*)   **$**
Returns the first nonmissing argument.

COLLATE

COLLATE(n_1, n_2)   COLLATE(n_1, , *length*)   COLLATE(n_1)   **$**
Returns a segment of the standard character set (ASCII or EBCDIC,
depending on the computer). The segment begins with character
number n_1 and includes consecutive characters that continue to
character number n_2, to the indicated length, or to the end of the
character set.

COMB ↻ 8+

COMB(*n, r*)   **N**   *Math.* Returns the number of combinations of *n*
elements selected *r* at a time. This is computed as:
FACT(N)/(FACT(R)*FACT(N - R))

COMPARE ↻ 9+

COMPARE(*string, string, optional modifiers*)   **N**   Compares the
two strings and returns a value that indicates the location of the first
character that differs between them, or 0 if the strings match. The
absolute value of the return value is the character position of the
first character that differs. The return value is negative if the first
string is a lower value, positive if the second string is a lower value.
Modifier action codes I Ignore case. L Remove leading spaces.
N Interpret name literals. : Truncate to the length of the shorter
string.

COMPBL

COMPBL(*string*)   **$** 1–same   Returns the string with any consecutive
spaces converted to single spaces.

COMPGED ↻ 9+

COMPGED(*base string, test string, optional cutoff, modifiers*)   **N**
Text analysis. Returns the generalized edit distance, a score computed
from the differences between the two strings. The scoring for edit
operations is determined by the CALL COMPCOST routine. However,
the function does not return a value greater than the cutoff value. See
COMPARE for modifiers.

COMPLEV ↻ 9+

COMPLEV(*string, string, optional cutoff, modifiers*)   **N**   *Text
analysis.* Returns the Levenshtein edit distance, a count of the number
of character changes between the two strings. However, the function
does not return a value greater than the cutoff value. See **COMPARE**
for modifiers.

COMPOUND

COMPOUND(*a, f, r, n*)   **N**   *Financial.* Compound interest is
described by an initial amount (*a*), a final amount (*f*), an interest rate

(r), and a length of time (n). Provide any three of these values, and the function calculates the remaining value.

Example COMPOUND(1, 2, .07, .) calculates how many years it takes for money to double at 7% annual interest.

COMPRESS

COMPRESS(*string, chars, optional modifiers*)   COMPRESS(*string*)
\$ ≤same   Returns the string with the indicated characters (or spaces) removed.

Modifiers

Adds to the list of characters: A   Letters.   C   Control characters.
D   Digits.   F   Letters and underscore.   G   Visible (graphic) characters.   L   Lowercase letters.   N   Letters, underscore, and digits.
P   Punctuation.   S   Whitespace.   U   Uppercase letters.   W   Printable characters.   X   Hexadecimal characters (digits and A-F).

T   Removes trailing spaces from the arguments.   I   Ignores case.
K   Removes all characters other than the listed characters from the
string.   O   Look at character and modifier arguments only on the
initial call to the function.

CONSTANT ↺ 8+

CONSTANT(*name, optional argument*)   *Math.* Returns any of various mathematical and system numerics constants.

CONSTANT('E') e, the base of the exponential function.

CONSTANT('EULER')   Euler's constant.

CONSTANT('PI')   Pi (π).

CONSTANT('EXACTINT', *optional length*)   The largest integer in
the range of integers that can be represented exactly in the indicated
length of a numeric variable (or a length of 8).

CONSTANT('BIG')   The largest numeric value.

CONSTANT('LOGBIG', *optional base*)   The log of the largest numeric
value. The default base is e.

CONSTANT('SQRTBIG')   The square root of the largest numeric value.

CONSTANT('SMALL')   The smallest positive numeric value.

CONSTANT('LOGSMALL', *optional base*)   The log of the smallest
positive numeric value. The default base is e.

CONSTANT('SQRTSMALL')   The square root of the smallest positive
numeric value.

CONSTANT('MACEPS')   The difference between 1 and the next larger
numeric value.

CONSTANT('LOGMACEPS', *optional base*)   The log of the difference
between 1 and the next larger numeric value. The default base is e.

CONSTANT('SQRTMACEPS')   The square root of the difference
between 1 and the next larger numeric value.

CONVX ↺ 8+

CONVX(*effective yield, frequency, a_1, a_2, . . .*)   **N**   *Financial.*
Returns the convexity.

CONVXP ↺ 8+

CONVXP(*par value, nominal paid interest rate, interest payment frequency, number of payments remaining, time till next payment, nominal yield to maturity*)   **N**   *Financial.* Returns the convexity for a bond or other periodic loan.

COS

COS(*θ*)   **N**   *Trig.* Returns the cosine of the angle.
Example COS(CONSTANT('PI')) is –1.

COSH

COSH(*θ*)   **N**   *Trig.* Returns the hyperbolic cosine of the angle.

COUNT ↺ 9+

COUNT(*string, substring, optional modifiers*)   **N**   Counts the number of times the substring occurs in the string.
Modifiers I   Ignore case.   T   Remove trailing spaces.

COUNTC ↺ 9+

COUNTC(*string, chars, optional modifiers*)   **N**   Counts the number of the indicated characters in the string.
Modifiers I   Ignore case.   T   Remove trailing spaces.   V   Count characters other than the ones listed.   O   Look at character and modifier arguments only on the initial call to the function.

CSS

CSS(*sample*)   **N**   *Statistic.* The corrected sum of squares.

CUROBS

CUROBS(*dataset ID*)   **N**   *I/O.* Returns the observation number of the current observation in the SAS dataset.

CV

CV(*sample*)   **N**   *Statistic.* The coefficient of variation.

DACC...

DACC...(*age, value, parameters*)   **N**   *Depreciation.* Accumulated depreciation: how much the value of an asset has depreciated, using a particular depreciation method.

DACCDB(*age, value, recovery period, rate*)   The declining balance method.

DACCDBSL(*age, value, recovery period, rate*)   The declining balance method switching to the straight-line method.

DACCSL(*age, value, recovery period*)   The straight-line method.

DACCSYD(*age, value, recovery period*)   The sum-of-years-digits method.

DACCTAB(*age, value, rate1, rate2, . . .*)   Using the rates provided.

DAIRY

DAIRY(*x*)   **N**   The derivative of the airy function.

DATDIF

DATDIF(*date, date, calendar code*)   **N**   Returns the number of days from the first date to the second date. **Calendar code** 'Actual' 'Act/Act'   Calculates the actual number of days.   '360'   '30/360' Calculates based on 30-day months.   ○ 7+

DATE

DATE()   **N**   Returns the current date.

DATEPART

DATEPART(*SAS datetime*)   **N**   Returns a SAS date.

DATETIME

DATETIME()   **N**   Returns the current date and time.

DAY

DAY(*SAS date*)   **N**   Returns day of month.

DCLOSE

DCLOSE(*directory ID*)   **N**   I/O. Closes the directory and returns an error code.

DEP...

DEP...(*age, value, parameters*)   **N**   *Depreciation.* Current-period depreciation: how much the value of an asset depreciates in a year, ending at the indicated age, using a particular depreciation method.

DEPDB(*age, value, recovery period, rate*)   The declining balance method.

DEPDBSL(*age, value, recovery period, rate*)   The declining balance method switching to the straight-line method.

DEPSL(*age, value, recovery period*)   The straight-line method.

DEPSYD(*age, value, recovery period*)   The sum-of-years-digits method.

DEPTAB(*age, value, rate1, rate2, . . .*)   Using the rates provided.

DEQUOTE

DEQUOTE(*string*)   **$** ≤same   Returns the string with quotes removed and quoted quotes reduced.

Example DEQUOTE("'Don''t'") is Don't.

DEVIANCE ○ 8+

DEVIANCE(*distribution name, X, parameters, optional ε*)   **N** *Probability.* Returns the deviance for a particular distribution.

DEVIANCE('BERNOULLI', *X, P, optional ε*)   Bernoulli.

DEVIANCE('BINOMIAL', *X, μ, n, optional ε*)   Binomial.

DEVIANCE('GAMMA', *X, μ, optional ε*)   Gamma.

DEVIANCE('NORMAL' *or* 'GAUSSIAN', *X, μ*)   Normal.

DEVIANCE('POISSON', *X, μ, optional ε*)   Poisson.

DEVIANCE('WALD' *or* 'IGAUSS', *X, μ, optional ε*)   Wald (Inverse Gaussian).

DHMS

DHMS(*SAS date, hour, minute, second*)   **N**   Returns a SAS datetime.

DIF

DIF(*value*)   DIF*n*(*value*)   **N ¬%**   Returns the result of subtracting from the argument the value supplied in the *n*th previous execution of the function call. Returns a standard missing value the first *n* times.

DIGAMMA

DIGAMMA(*x*)   **N**   *Math.* The derivative of the log gamma function.

DIM

DIM(*array*)   **N ¬%**   Returns the size of a one-dimensional array.

DIM(*array, n*)   DIM*n*(*array*)   **N ¬%**   Returns the size of dimension *n* of an array.

DINFO

DINFO(*directory ID, information item name*)   **$**   *I/O.* Returns the information item for the directory. Available information items vary by operating system.

DNUM

DNUM(*directory ID*)   **N**   *I/O.* Returns the number of members (files) in the directory.

DOPEN

DOPEN(*fileref*)   **N**   *I/O.* Opens the directory and returns a directory ID.

DOPTNAME

DOPTNAME(*directory ID, n*)   **$**   *I/O.* Returns the name of the *n*th information item for the directory.

DOPTNUM

DOPTNUM(*directory ID*)   **N**   *I/O.* Returns the number of information items for the directory.

DREAD

DREAD(*directory ID, n*)   **$**   *I/O.* Returns the name of the *n*th member (file) in the directory.

DROPNOTE

DROPNOTE(*dataset ID or file ID, note ID*)   **N**   *I/O.* Forgets the previously noted location in the file and returns an error code.

DSNAME

DSNAME(*dataset ID*)   **$**   *I/O.* Returns the name of the SAS dataset.

DUR ↻ 8+

DUR(*effective yield, frequency, a1, a2, . . .*)   **N**   *Financial.* Returns the modified duration.

DURP ↻ 8+

DURP(*par value, nominal paid interest rate, interest payment frequency, number of payments remaining, time till next payment, nominal yield to maturity*)   **N**   *Financial.* Returns the modified duration for a bond or other periodic loan.

ERF

ERF(*x*)   **N**   The error function.

ERFC

ERFC(*x*)   **N**   The complement of the error function. Returns 1 - ERF(X).

EUROCURR ↻ 8.2+

EUROCURR(*amount,* "*currency*", "*target currency*")   **N**   Converts between currencies based on fixed conversion rates.

Currencies

ATS   Austrian schilling.   BEF   Belgian franc.   CHF   Swiss franc.
CZK   Czech koruna.   DEM   Deutschmark.   DKK   Danish krone.
ESP   Spanish peseta.   EUR *or blank*   Euro.   FIM   Finnish markka.
FRF   French franc.   GBP   British pound sterling.
GRD   Greek drachma.   HUF   Hungarian forint.   IEP   Irish pound.
ITL   Italian lira.   LUF   Luxembourg franc.   NLG   Dutch guilder.
NOK   Norwegian krone.   PLZ   Polish zloty.   PTE   Portuguese escudo.
ROL   Romanian leu.   RUR   Russian ruble.   SEK   Swedish krona.
SIT   Slovenian tolar.   TRL   Turkish lira.   YUD   Yugoslavian dinar.

EXIST

EXIST(*SAS file name, optional member type, optional generation*)   **N**   *I/O.* Returns 1 if the SAS file exists, 0 if it does not. The default member type is 'DATA'.

EXP

EXP(*x*)   **N**   Exponential function: returns e^x.

FACT ↻ 8+

FACT(*n*)   **N**   *Math.* Returns the factorial, defined as $n! = 1 \times 2 \times \ldots \times n$.

FAPPEND

FAPPEND(*file ID, optional carriage-control character*)   **N**   *I/O.* Writes the contents of the file data buffer at the end of the file and returns an error code.

Carriage-control characters *space* 0 – 1 + P =

FCLOSE

FCLOSE(*file ID*)   **N**   *I/O.* Closes the file and returns an error code.

FCOL
FCOL(*file ID*)   **N**   *I/O*. Returns the column pointer position.

FDELETE
FDELETE(*fileref*)   **N**   *I/O*. Deletes the file (or the empty directory) and returns an error code.

FETCH
FETCH(*dataset ID*, *option*)   **N**   *I/O*. Reads the next observation from the SAS dataset and returns an error code, or –1 for end of file. **Option** 'NOSET'   Does not assign values to program variables even if the SET routine is in effect.

FETCHOBS
FETCHOBS(*dataset ID*, *n*, *options*)   **N**   *I/O*. Reads the *n*th observation from the SAS dataset and returns an error code, or –1 for end of file. **Options** 'NOSET'   Does not assign values to program variables even if the SET routine is in effect.   'ABS'   Uses physical (absolute) observation numbers.

FEXIST
FEXIST(*fileref*)   **N**   *I/O*. Returns 1 if the file exists, 0 if it does not.

FGET
FGET(*file ID*, *character variable*, *n*)   **N**   *I/O*. Retrieves the next *n* characters from the file data buffer into the character variable and returns an error code, or –1 for end of buffer.

FGET(*file ID*, *character variable*)   **N**   Retrieves the next word or field from the file data buffer into the character variable and returns an error code, or –1 for end of buffer.

FILEEXIST
FILEEXIST(*physical file name*)   **N**   *I/O*. Returns 1 if the file exists, 0 if it does not.

FILENAME
FILENAME(*fileref*, *physical file name*, *optional device*, *host options*, *optional directory fileref*)   **N**   *I/O*. Assigns the fileref to the file or directory and returns an error code. If *fileref* is a blank variable, it generates a fileref. If *physical file name* is blank, it deassigns the fileref.

FILEREF
FILEREF(*fileref*)   **N**   *I/O*. Returns 0 if the file exists, a negative value if the fileref is assigned and the file does not exist, a positive value if the fileref is not assigned.

FIND ↻ 9+
FIND(*string*, *chars*, *optional modifiers*, *optional n*)   FIND(*string*, *chars*, *optional n*, *optional modifiers*)   **N**   Returns the location of the substring in the string, or 0 if the substring is not found. See

ANY... for a description of the optional *n* argument. **Modifiers** I Ignore case. T Remove trailing spaces.

FINDC ⟳ 9+

FINDC(*string, chars, optional modifiers, optional n*)
FINDC(*string, chars, optional n, optional modifiers*) **N** Returns the first location in the string of any of the characters, or 0 if the string does not contain any of the characters. See **ANY...** for a description of the optional *n* argument. **Modifiers** I Ignore case. T Remove trailing spaces. V Search for characters other than the ones listed. O Look at character and modifier arguments only on the initial call to the function.

FINFO

FINFO(*file ID, information item name*) **$** *I/O.* Returns the information item for the file. Available information items vary by operating system.

FINV

FINV(*P, n.d.f., d.d.f., nc*) **N** *Probability.* The inverse distribution function of the F distribution with the indicated parameters.

FLOOR

FLOOR(*x*) **N** *Rounding.* Returns the largest integer that is less than or equal to the argument. Returns the integer if the argument is within 10^{-17} of an integer.
Example FLOOR(101.25) is 101.

FLOORZ ⟳ 9+

FLOORZ(*x*) **N** *Rounding.* Returns the largest integer less than or equal to the argument.

FNONCT

FNONCT(*x, n.d.f., d.d.f., P*) **N** *Probability.* Returns the nonnegative noncentrality parameter for a noncentral F distribution with the indicated parameters.

FNOTE

FNOTE(*file ID*) **N** *I/O.* Notes the current record in the file and returns a note ID for that location.

FOPEN

FOPEN(*fileref, optional access mode, optional record length, optional record format*) **N** *I/O.* Opens the file identified by the fileref and returns the file ID, or 0 if unsuccessful. **Access modes** I Input (the default). O Output. A Append. U Update. S Sequential input. W Sequential update. **Record formats** D Default. F Fixed length. V Variable length. P Print. E Editable. B Binary.

FOPTNAME

FOPTNAME(*file ID, n*) **$** *I/O.* Returns the name of the *n*th information item for the file.

FOPTNUM

FOPTNUM(*file ID*) **N** *I/O.* Returns the number of information items for the file.

FPOINT

FPOINT(*file ID, note ID*) **N** *I/O.* Moves the file pointer to read the record previously noted with the FNOTE function.

FPOS

FPOS(*file ID, n*) **N** *I/O.* Moves the pointer to the indicated column in the file data buffer.

FPUT

FPUT(*file ID, string*) **N** *I/O.* Copies the string to the file data buffer.

FREAD

FREAD(*file ID*) **N** *I/O.* Reads the next record from the file and returns an error code, or –1 for end of file.

FREWIND

FREWIND(*file ID*) **N** *I/O.* Moves the file pointer to read the beginning of the file and returns an error code.

FRLEN

FRLEN(*file ID*) **N** *I/O.* Returns the size of the current record (in the file data buffer).

FSEP

FSEP(*file ID, chars*) **N** *I/O.* Sets the field delimiter characters used by the FGET function. The default delimiter is a space.

FUZZ

FUZZ(*x*) **N** *Rounding.* Returns the integer if the argument is within 10^{-12} of an integer; otherwise, it returns the argument.

FWRITE

FWRITE(*file ID, optional carriage-control character*) **N** *I/O.* Writes the next record to the file and returns an error code.
Carriage-control characters *blank* 0 – 1 + P =

GAMINV

GAMINV(*P, a*) **N** *Probability.* The inverse distribution function of the gamma distribution with the indicated *a* parameter and $b = 1$.

GAMMA

GAMMA(*x*) **N** *Math.* The gamma function: $\Gamma(x)$. For positive integers, GAMMA(X) returns the same value as FACT(X - 1).

GEOMEAN/GEOMEANZ ↻ 9.1+

GEOMEAN(*sample*) GEOMEANZ(*sample*) **N** *Statistic.* Returns the geometric mean. Returns 0 if any argument is 0. GEOMEAN returns 0 if any argument is within 10^{-12} of 0. Negative arguments are invalid.

GETOPTION

GETOPTION(*system option name, options*) **$** Returns the value of the system option. **Options** KEYWORD   CM   IN

GETVARC/GETVARN

GETVARC(*dataset ID, n*)   **$**   GETVARN(*dataset ID, n*)   **N**
I/O. Returns the value of the *n*th variable in the SAS dataset. Use GETVARC for character variables, GETVARN for numeric variables.

HARMEAN/HARMEANZ ⟳ 9.1+

HARMEAN(*sample*)   HARMEANZ(*sample*)   **N**   *Statistic.* Returns the harmonic mean. Returns 0 if any argument is 0. HARMEAN returns 0 if any argument is within 10^{-12} of 0. Negative arguments are invalid.

HBOUND

HBOUND(*array*)   **N** ¬**%**   Returns the upper bound of a one-dimensional array.

HBOUND(*array, n*)   HBOUND*n*(*array*)   **N** ¬**%**   Returns the upper bound of dimension *n* of an array.

HMS

HMS(*hour, minute, second*)   **N**   Returns a SAS time value, or a duration of time in seconds.

HOUR

HOUR(*SAS time or SAS datetime*)   **N**   Returns the hour of the day.
Example HOUR('15:25:00'T) is 15.

HTMLDECODE ⟳ 8+

HTMLDECODE(*string*)   **$**   Decodes HTML text.
Example HTMLDECODE('B&O') is B&O.

HTMLENCODE ⟳ 8+

HTMLENCODE(*string*)   **$**   Encodes a string as HTML text.
Example HTMLENCODE('S<AV') is S<AV.

IFC/IFN ⟳ 9.1+

IFC(*condition, value for true, value for false*)   IFC(*condition, value for true, value for 0, value for missing*)   **$**   IFN(*condition, value for true, value for false*)   IFN(*condition, value for true, value for 0, value for missing*)   **N**   Returns the corresponding value depending on whether the condition is true, false, 0, or missing. Use IFC for character values, IFN for numeric values.

INDEX

INDEX(*string, substring*)   **N**   Returns the first location of the substring in the string, or 0 if the substring is not found.

INDEXC

INDEXC(*string*, *chars*, . . .)   **N**   Returns the first location of any of the characters in the string, or 0 if none of the characters are found.

INDEXW

INDEXW(*string*, *substring*, *optional delimiter*)   **N**   Returns the first location of the substring as a word (or sequence of words) in the string. Otherwise, it returns 0.

INPUT

INPUT(*text*, *optional error control   character informat reference*)
$ informat width ¬**%**   Applies the informat to the text.

INPUT(*text*, *optional error control   numeric informat reference*)
N ¬**%**   Applies the informat to the text.

The informat argument is a literal value, not a character constant or an expression.

Error controls For invalid data: ?   Suppresses log messages.   ??   Also prevents the automatic variable _ERROR_ from being set to 1.

Example INPUT('444', F3.2) is 4.44.

INPUTC/INPUTN

INPUTC(*text*, *character informat reference*, *optional width*)   **$**
INPUTN(*text*, *character informat reference*, *optional width*,
optional decimal)   **N**   Applies the informat to the text.

Example INPUTN('444', 'F3.2') is 4.44.

INT

INT(*x*)   **N**   *Rounding*. Removes the fractional part of the number, returning the integer part. Returns the integer if the argument is within 10^{-12} of an integer.

INTCK

INTCK(*interval code*, *SAS date*, *SAS date*)   **N**   Returns the number of intervals from the first SAS date to the second SAS date.

INTCK(*interval code*, *SAS datetime*, *SAS datetime*)   **N**   Returns the number of intervals from the first SAS datetime to the second SAS datetime.

INTCK(*interval code*, *SAS time*, *SAS time*)   **N**   Returns the number of intervals from the first SAS time to the second SAS time.

Interval codes

For SAS dates:

DAY   Day.   DAY*m*   *m* days.   DAY*m.s*   *m* days with the interval shifted to start on day *s*.

WEEKDAY   Days except for days of the week 1 and 7.
WEEKDAYd_1d_2...W   Days except for days of the week d_1, d_2, . . .

WEEK   Week, starting on Sunday.   WEEK.*s*   Week, shifted to start on day of the week *s*.   WEEK*m*   WEEK*m.s*   *m* weeks.

TENDAY   Ten-day period starting on days 1, 11, and 21 of each month.

SEMIMONTH   Semimonth period starting on day 1 and 16 of each month.

MONTH   Month, starting on day 1 of each month.

QTR   Quarter, starting on Jan 1, Apr 1, Jul 1, Oct 1.

SEMIYEAR   Half year, starting on Jan 1, Jul 1.

YEAR   Year, starting on Jan 1.

DAYm WEEKDAYm WEEKDAY$d_1 d_2$...Wm WEEKm TENDAYm
SEMIMONTHm MONTHm QTRm SEMIYEARm YEARm
m periods.

DAY$m.s$ WEEKDAY$m.s$ WEEKDAY$d_1 d_2$...W$m.s$ WEEK$m.s$
TENDAY$m.s$ SEMIMONTH$m.s$ MONTH$m.s$ m periods with the interval shifted to start on period s.

QTR.s SEMIYEAR.s YEAR.s Period shifted to start at month s.

QTR$m.s$ SEMIYEAR$m.s$ YEAR$m.s$ m periods with the interval shifted to start at month s.

For SAS datetimes: DTDAY   DTWEEKDAY   DTWEEK   DTTENDAY
DTSEMIMONTH   DTMONTH   DTQTR   DTSEMIYEAR   DTYEAR

For SAS times or datetimes:

SECOND   Second.

MINUTE   Minute.

HOUR   Hour.

SECONDm MINUTEm HOURm m periods.

SECOND$m.s$ MINUTE$m.s$ HOUR$m.s$ m periods with the interval shifted to start at month s.

INTNX

INTNX(*interval code, SAS date, n, optional alignment code*)
INTNX(*interval code, SAS datetime, n, optional alignment code*)
INTNX(*interval code, SAS time, n, optional alignment code*)   **N**
Returns the value advanced by the indicated number of intervals. See interval codes above under INTCK.

Alignment code The returned value is: 'BEGINNING' 'B' At the beginning of the interval. This is the default. 'MIDDLE' 'M' At the middle of the interval. 'END' 'E' At the end of the interval.

INTRR

INTRR(*number of payment periods per year, amount 1, amount 2, . . .*)   **N**   *Financial.* Returns the internal rate of return.

INTZ ⊘ 9+

INTZ(*x*)   **N**   *Rounding.* Removes the fractional part of the number, returning the integer part.

IORCMSG ⊘ 7+

IORCMSG()   **$ ¬%**   Returns the text of the error message of the current value of the automatic variable _IORC_.

IQR ⊙ 9+

IQR(*sample*)   **N**   *Statistic.* The interquartile range; the 3rd quartile minus the 1st quartile.

IRR

IRR(*number of payment periods per year, amount 1, amount 2, . . .*)   **N**   *Financial.* Returns the internal rate of return as a percent.

K... ⊙ 7+

Functions for character operations on DBCS text.

KCOMPARE(*string 1, optional start, optional length, string 2*)   **N**
Compares two strings. Use the start argument or start and length arguments to compare only part of the strings; these arguments are measured in bytes. Returns 0 if the two strings are equal, 1 if string 1 is less than string 2, –1 if string 2 is less than string 1.

KCOMPRESS(*string, chars*)   KCOMPRESS(*string*)   **$**   Returns the string with the indicated characters (or spaces) removed.

KCOUNT(*string*)   **N**   Returns the number of characters.

KCVT(*string, type, new type, options*)   **N**   Converts the string from one encoding to another. ⊙ 9+

KINDEX(*string, substring*)   **N**   Returns the first location of the substring in the string.

KINDEXC(*string, chars, . . .*)   **N**   Returns the first location of any of the characters in the string.

KLEFT(*string*)   **$**   Left-aligns: converts leading spaces to trailing spaces.

KLENGTH(*string*)   **N**   Returns the length of the string, not counting trailing spaces. Returns 1 for a null string.

KLOWCASE(*string*)   **$**   Converts uppercase letters to lowercase.

KREVERSE(*string*)   **$**   Reverses the order of characters in the string.

KRIGHT(*string*)   **$**   Right-aligns: converts trailing spaces to leading spaces.

KSCAN(*string, n, optional delimiters*)   **$**   Returns the *n*th token from the string. If *n* < 0, it scans from the end of the string.

KSTRCAT(*string, string, . . .*)   **$**   Concatenates the strings, removing unnecessary SO/SI pairs between them.

KSUBSTR(*string, start*)   KSUBSTR(*string, start, length*)   **$** ≤same
Returns the substring.

KSUBSTRB(*string, start*)   KSUBSTRB(*string, start, length*)   **$** ≤same
Returns the substring. Express start and length arguments in bytes.

KTRANSLATE(*string, replacement chars, chars, . . .*)   **$**   Returns the string with all occurrences of the characters replaced by the corresponding replacement characters.

KTRIM(*string*)   **$**   Returns the string with trailing spaces removed. For a blank argument, it returns a single space.

KUPCASE(*string*)   **$**   Converts lowercase letters to uppercase.

KUPDATE(*character variable, start, optional length, replacement string*) **\$** Changes part of a character variable to the value of the replacement string.

KUPDATE(*character variable, start, length*) **\$** Erases part of a character variable.

KUPDATEB(*character variable, start, optional length, replacement string*) **\$** Changes part of a character variable to the value of the replacement string. Express start and length arguments in bytes.

KUPDATEB(*character variable, start, length*) **\$** Erases part of a character variable. Express start and length arguments in bytes.

KVERIFY(*string, chars, . . .*) **N** Returns the location of the first character in the string that is not one of the characters listed. Otherwise, it returns 0.

KURTOSIS

KURTOSIS(*sample*) **N** *Statistic.* The kurtosis.

LAG

LAG(*numeric value*) LAG*n*(*numeric value*) **N ¬%** Returns the value that was supplied in the *n*th previous execution of the function call. Returns a standard missing value the first *n* times.

LAG(*character value*) LAG*n*(*character value*) **\$ ¬%** Returns the value that was supplied in the *n*th previous execution of the function call. Returns a blank value the first *n* times.

LARGEST ↺ 9+

LARGEST(*n, sample*) **N** *Statistic.* The *n*th largest value.

LBOUND

LBOUND(*array*) **N ¬%** Returns the lower bound of a one-dimensional array.

LBOUND(*array, n*) LBOUND*n*(*array*) **N ¬%** Returns the lower bound of dimension *n* of an array.

LEFT

LEFT(*string*) **\$ same** Left-aligns: converts leading spaces to trailing spaces.

LENGTH

LENGTH(*string*) **N** Returns the length of the string, not counting trailing spaces. Returns 1 for a null or blank string.

Example LENGTH('fire') is 4.

LENGTHC ↺ 9+

LENGTHC(*string*) **N** Returns the length of the string, counting trailing spaces. Returns 0 for a null string.

LENGTHM ↺ 9+

LENGTHM(*string*) **N** Returns the memory length.

LENGTHN ↻ 9+

LENGTHN(*string*)   **N**   Returns the length of the string, not counting trailing spaces. Returns 0 for a null or blank string.

LGAMMA

LGAMMA(*x*)   **N**   *Math.* The log gamma function. Returns LOG(GAMMA(X)).

LIBNAME

LIBNAME(*libref, physical file name, optional engine, engine options*)   **N**   *I/O.* Assigns the libref to the physical file name and returns an error code. If *physical file name* is blank, it deassigns the libref.

LIBREF

LIBREF(*libref*)   **N**   *I/O.* Returns 0 if the libref is assigned, a nonzero number if it is not.

LOG

LOG(*x*)   **N**   *Math.* The natural logarithm function. Returns the base *e* logarithm of the number. The inverse of the EXP function.

LOG2

LOG2(*x*)   **N**   *Math.* Returns the base 2 logarithm of the number.

LOG10

LOG10(*x*)   **N**   *Math.* Returns the base 10 (common) logarithm of the number.
Example LOG10(1000) is 3.

LOGBETA ↻ 9+

LOGBETA(α, β)   **N**   *Math.* The natural logarithm of the beta function.

LOGCDF ↻ 9.1+

LOGCDF(*distribution, X, distribution parameters*)   **N**   *Probability.* The logarithm of a distribution function. Arguments are the same as for the CDF function.

LOGPDF

LOGPDF(*distribution, X, distribution parameters*)   **N**   *Probability.* The logarithm of a probability density function. Arguments are the same as for the CDF function. **Alias LOGPMF**

LOGSDF

LOGSDF(*distribution, X, distribution parameters*)   **N**   *Probability.* The logarithm of a survival function. Arguments are the same as for the CDF function.

LOWCASE

LOWCASE(*string*)   **$ same**   Converts uppercase letters to lowercase.

MAD ○ 9+

MAD(*sample*)　**N**　*Statistic.* The median absolute deviation from the median.

MAX

MAX(*sample*)　**N**　*Statistic.* The maximum.

MDY

MDY(*month, day, year*)　**N**　Returns the SAS date.

MEAN

MEAN(*sample*)　**N**　*Statistic.* The mean; average.

MEDIAN ○ 9+

MEDIAN(*sample*)　**N**　*Statistic.* The median.

MIN

MIN(*sample*)　**N**　*Statistic.* The minimum.

MINUTE

MINUTE(*SAS time or SAS datetime*)　**N**　Returns the minute.

MISSING

MISSING(*numeric or character expression*)　**N ¬%**　Returns 1 if the argument is a missing value, 0 otherwise. ○ 7 i

MOD

MOD(*x, modulus*)　**N**　*Math.* Returns the remainder that results from dividing *x* by *modulus*. Returns 0 if the result is within 10^{-17} of *modulus* or 0.

MODZ ○ 9+

MODZ(*x, modulus*)　**N**　*Math.* Returns the remainder that results from dividing *x* by *modulus*.

MONTH

MONTH(*SAS date*)　**N**　Returns the month.

MOPEN

MOPEN(*directory ID, member name, optional access mode, optional record length, optional record format*)　**N**　*I/O.* Opens the file identified by the directory ID and member name and returns the file ID, or 0 if unsuccessful. See the FOPEN function for details of arguments.

MORT

MORT(*a, p, r, n*)　**N**　*Financial.* A simple loan can be described by an amount *a*, a payment amount *p*, a periodic interest rate *r*, and a length of time *n*. Provide any three of these values, and the function calculates the remaining value.

N

N(*sample*)   **N**   *Statistic.* The number of nonmissing arguments.

NETPV

NETPV(*interest rate, number of payment periods per year, amount 1, amount 2, . . .*)   **N**   *Financial.* Returns the net present value.

NLITERAL ↻ 9+

NLITERAL(*string*)   **$**   Converts the string to a name literal and returns the result.

NMISS

NMISS(*sample*)   **N**   *Statistic.* The number of missing arguments.

NORMAL

NORMAL(*seed*)   **N**   Returns a random number from a normal distribution with $\mu = 0$ and $\sigma = 1$.

NOT... ↻ 9+

NOT*class*(*string*)   NOT*class*(*string, n*)   **N**   Searches the string for the first character that does not belong to the character class. Returns the location if the search item is found, or 0 if it is not found. See **ANY...** for a description of the character classes and the search start and direction.

NOTE

NOTE(*dataset ID*)   **N**   *I/O.* Notes the current observation in the SAS dataset and returns a note ID.

NPV

NPV(*percentage interest rate, number of payment periods per year, amount 1, amount 2, . . .*)   **N**   *Financial.* Returns the net present value.

NVALID ↻ 9+

NVALID(*string*, "*rule*")   **N**   Returns 1 if the string is a valid SAS name, 0 if not. The function disregards trailing spaces. **Rules** NLITERAL   Allows SAS words and name literals.   V7   Allows SAS words only.   ANY   Allows any characters.   In any case, the name is limited to 32 characters in length. The default rule depends on the VALIDVARNAME= system option.

OPEN

OPEN(SAS *dataset, optional access mode*)   **N**   Opens the SAS dataset (SAS data file or SAS SQL view) and returns the dataset ID, or 0 if unsuccessful. Dataset options (other than FIRSTOBS= and OBS=) can be used to affect the way the SAS dataset is read. By default, the SAS dataset is opened with record control level. **Access modes** I   IN   IS

ORDINAL

ORDINAL(*n, sample*)   **N**   Returns the *n*th lowest value in the sample.

PATHNAME

PATHNAME(*fileref or libref*, '*optional type code*') **$** *I/O*. Returns the physical file name. **Type code** L Libref. F Fileref. ⟳ 8.2+

PATHNAME(*SAS file*) **$** *I/O*. Returns the physical file name.

PCTL ⟳ 9+

PCTL*n*(*percent, sample*) **N** *Statistic*. Returns the percentile. The suffix *n* indicates the percentile definition. See chapter 12, "Descriptive Statistics."

PDF

PDF(*distribution, X, distribution parameters*) **N** *Probability*. A probability density function. Arguments are the same as for the CDF function. **Alias PMF**

PEEK ⟳ 7+

PEEK(*address, optional length*) $2 \le length \le 8$ **N** Returns the value from the indicated address in memory. The function retrieves a 4-byte integer value unless you indicate a different data length. Valid only in 32-bit environments.

PEEKC ⟳ 7+

PEEKC(*address, optional length*) **$** Returns data from the indicated address in memory. Valid only in 32-bit environments.

PEEKCLONG ⟳ 8.2+

PEEKCLONG(*address, optional length*) **$** Returns data from the indicated address in memory.

PEEKLONG ⟳ 8.2+

PEEKLONG(*address, optional length*) $2 \le length \le 8$ **N** Returns the value from the indicated address in memory. The function retrieves a 4-byte integer value unless you indicate a different data length.

PERM ⟳ 8+

PERM(*n, r*) **N** *Math*. Returns the number of permutations of *n* items selected *r* at a time. This is computed as FACT(N)/FACT(N - R).

POINT

POINT(*dataset ID, note ID*) **N** *I/O*. Moves to the observation previously noted by the NOTE function and returns an error code.

POISSON

POISSON(λ, *X*) **N** *Probability*. The Poisson distribution function.

POKE ⟳ 7+

POKE(*value, address, optional length*) **N** The same as POKELONG, but valid only in 32-bit environments.

POKELONG ↺ 8.2+

POKELONG(*value, address, optional length*)   **N**   Writes the value at the indicated address in memory and returns an error code. If a length is indicated, the value is written in that many bytes. Otherwise, the entire character value is written or the numeric value is converted to an integer and written using the same number of bytes that a pointer takes up.

PROBBETA

PROBBETA(*X*, α, β)   **N**   *Probability.* The beta distribution function.

PROBBNML

PROBBNML(*P*, *n*, *X*)   **N**   *Probability.* The binomial distribution function.

PROBBNRM

PROBBNRM(*X*, *Y*, *correlation*) $-1 \le correlation \le 1$ **N**   *Probability.* The bivariate normal distribution function with $\mu = 0$ and $\sigma = 1$.

PROBCHI

PROBCHI(*X*, *d.f.*, *nc*)   **N**   *Probability.* The chi-squared distribution function.

PROBF

PROBF(*X*, *n.d.f.*, *d.d.f.*, *nc*)   **N**   *Probability.* The F distribution function.

PROBGAM

PROBGAM(*X*, α)   **N**   *Probability.* The gamma distribution function with $\beta = 1$.

PROBHYPR

PROBHYPR(*population size, category size, sample size, X, optional odds ratio*)   **N**   *Probability.* The hypergeometric distribution function.

PROBIT

PROBIT(*P*)   **N**   *Probability.* The inverse distribution function of the normal distribution with $\mu = 0$ and $\sigma = 1$.

PROBMC

PROBMC(*distribution, quantile, ., d.f., n, optional sample size parameters*)   **N**   *Probability.* Returns the probability.

PROBMC(*distribution, ., P, d.f., n, optional sample size parameters*)   **N**   *Probability.* Returns the quantile.

Distributions

Distributions for multiple comparisons of means.

DUNNETT1   DUNNETT2   Dunnett, one- or two-sided.

RANGE   Studentized range.

MAXMOD   Maximum modulus.

WILLIAMS   Williams.

PROBNEGB

PROBNEGB(*P*, *n*, *X*)   **N**   *Probability*. The negative binomial distribution function.

PROBNORM

PROBNORM(*X*)   **N**   *Probability*. The normal distribution function with $\mu = 0$ and $\sigma = 1$.

PROBT

PROBT(*X*, *d.f.*, *nc*)   **N**   *Probability*. The *t* distribution function.

PROPCASE ○ 9.1+

PROPCASE(*string, optional delimiters*)   **$**   Returns the string converted to proper case (title case). Letters following delimiters are treated as the first letter of a word and are converted to uppercase; subsequent letters are converted to lowercase. The default delimiters are " /-(" and the tab character.

PRXCHANGE ○ 9+

PRXCHANGE(*PRX, n, source string*)   **N**   *PRX*. Returns the string modified *n* times by the search and replace action indicated in the Perl regular expression.

PRXMATCH ○ 9+

PRXMATCH(*PRX, source string*)   **N**   *PRX*. Searches the source string for a pattern and returns the position, or 0 if the pattern is not found.

PRXPAREN ○ 9+

PRXPAREN(*pattern ID*)   **N**   *PRX*. Returns the number of the last submatch, equivalent to $+ in Perl.

PRXPARSE ○ 9+

PRXPARSE(*regular expression*)   **N**   *PRX*. Parses a Perl (5.6.1, with modifications) regular expression (PRX) and returns a pattern ID. Use the pattern ID to represent the regular expression in other PRX functions and CALL routines.

PRXPOSN ○ 9+

PRXPOSN(*PRX, n, source string*)   **N**   *PRX*. Locates the *n*th submatch.

PTRLONGADD ○ 8.2+

PTRLONGADD(*address, optional length*)   **$**   Returns the pointer to the indicated address in memory as a character value.

PUT

PUT(*character value, character format reference alignment option*)   PUT(*numeric value, numeric format reference alignment option*)   **$** format width ¬**%**   Applies the format to the value. The format argument is a literal value, not a character constant or an expression.

Alignment options -L Left.   -C Center.   -R Right. ↺ 8+

Example PUT(4, Z5.) is 00004.

PUTC/PUTN

PUTC(*character value, character format reference, optional width*)
PUTN(*numeric value, numeric format reference, optional width, optional decimal*) **\$**   Applies the format to the value.

Example PUTN(4, 'Z5.') is 00004.

PVP ↺ 8+

PVP(*par value, nominal paid interest rate, interest payment frequency, number of payments remaining, time till next payment, nominal yield to maturity*) **N**   *Financial*. Returns the present value.

QTR

QTR(*SAS date*) **N**   Returns the quarter.

QUANTILE ↺ 9.1+

QUANTILE(*distribution, P, distribution parameters*) **N**
Probability. Returns the quantile from a distribution. Distribution and parameter arguments are the same as for the CDF function.

QUOTE

QUOTE(*string*) **\$**   Produces a quoted string from the argument: encloses it in double quotes and doubles any double quotes it contains.

RANBIN

RANBIN(*seed, n, P*) **N**   *Random number*. Returns a random number from a binomial distribution.

RANCAU

RANCAU(*seed*) **N**   *Random number*. Returns a random number from a Cauchy distribution with $\alpha = 1$ and $\beta = 1$.

RAND ↺ 8.1+

RAND(*distribution, distribution parameters*) **N**   *Random number*. Returns random numbers from the probability distribution. Use the CALL STREAMINIT routine to provide a seed value.

RANEXP

RANEXP(*seed*) **N**   *Random number*. Returns a random number from an exponential distribution with $\lambda = 1$.

RANGAM

RANGAM(*seed, α*) **N**   *Random number*. Returns a random number from a gamma distribution with $\beta = 1$.

RANGE

RANGE(*sample*) **N**   *Statistic*. The range.

RANK

RANK(*char*) **N** Returns the character's number in the standard character set.

RANNOR

RANNOR(*seed*) **N** *Random number.* Returns a random number from a normal distribution with $\mu = 0$ and $\sigma = 1$.

RANPOI

RANPOI(*seed*, λ) **N** *Random number.* Returns a random number from a Poisson distribution.

RANTBL

RANTBL(*seed*, *f(1)*, *f(2)*, . . .) **N** *Random number.* Returns a random counting number from the indicated distribution table.

RANTRI

RANTRI(*seed*, *hypotenuse*) **N** *Random number.* Returns a random number from a triangular distribution on the interval [0, 1].

RANUNI

RANUNI(*seed*) **N** *Random number.* Returns a random number from the uniform distribution on the interval [0, 1].

REPEAT

REPEAT(*string*, *n*) **$** Returns the string repeated $n + 1$ times.

RESOLVE

RESOLVE(*text*) **$ ¬%** Resolves the macro expression that is contained in the character argument and returns the resolved macro expression.

REVERSE

REVERSE(*string*) **$ same** Reverses the order of characters in the string.

Example REVERSE('forward') is drawrof.

REWIND

REWIND(*dataset ID*) **N** *I/O.* Positions the SAS dataset at its first observation and returns an error code.

RIGHT

RIGHT(*string*) **$ same** Right-aligns: converts trailing spaces to leading spaces.

ROUND

ROUND(*x*) **N** *Rounding.* Rounds *x* to the nearest integer.

ROUND(*x*, *unit*) **N** Rounds *x* to the nearest multiple of *unit*. If *unit* is the reciprocal of an integer, the function computes its results by dividing so that integer results will be exact.

Example ROUND(17, 3) is 18.

ROUNDE ○ 9+

ROUNDE(*x*)   **N**   *Rounding.* Rounds *x* to the nearest integer. Rounds to an even integer if *x* is midway between two integers.

ROUNDE(*x, unit*)   **N**   Rounds *x* to the nearest multiple of *unit*. Rounds to an even multiple if *x* is midway between two multiples.

ROUNDZ ○ 9+

ROUNDZ(*x*)   **N**   *Rounding.* Rounds *x* to the nearest integer.

ROUNDZ(*x, unit*)   **N**   Rounds *x* to the nearest multiple of *unit*. The function computes its results by multiplying. If *unit* is a fraction, integer results might not be exact integers.

RXMATCH ○ 7+

RXMATCH(*RX ID, source string*)   **N**   *Regular expression.* Searches the source string for a pattern and returns the position, or 0 if the pattern is not found. Use the RXPARSE function to generate the RX ID that indicates the pattern search.

RXPARSE ○ 7+

RXPARSE(*pattern*)   **N**   *Regular expression.* Returns an RX ID for a pattern. Use the RX ID to represent the pattern in other regular expression functions and CALL routines.

SAVING

SAVING(*f, p, r, n*)   **N**   *Financial.* A series of payments can be described by a final value *f*, a payment amount *p*, a periodic interest rate *r*, and a length of time *n*. Provide any three of these values, and the function calculates the remaining value.

SCAN

SCAN(*string, n, delimiters*)   **$**   Returns the *n*th token from the string. If *n* < 0, it scans backward from the end of the string.

SCANQ ○ 9+

SCANQ(*string, n, delimiters*)   **$**   Returns the *n*th token from the string, not counting delimiters inside quoted strings. If *n* < 0, it scans backward from the end of the string.

SDF

SDF(*distribution, X, distribution parameters*)   **N**   *Probability.* A survival function. Arguments are the same as for the CDF function.

SECOND

SECOND(*SAS time or SAS datetime*)   **N**   Returns the second.

SIGN

SIGN(*x*)   **N**   *Math.* Returns –1 if *x* is negative, 0 if *x* is 0, 1 if *x* is positive.

SIN

SIN(θ)   **N**   *Trig.* Returns the sine of the angle.

Example SIN(.5*CONSTANT('PI')) is 1.

SINH

SINH(θ)   **N**   *Trig.* Returns the hyperbolic sine of the angle.

SKEWNESS

SKEWNESS(*sample*)   **N**   *Statistic.* The skewness.

SLEEP

SLEEP(*n*)   **N**   Suspends execution and displays a dialog box for *n* seconds. Returns the number of seconds execution was suspended.

SMALLEST ↺ 9+

SMALLEST(*n, sample*)   **N**   *Statistic.* The *n*th smallest nonmissing value.

SOUNDEX

SOUNDEX(*word*)   **$** ≤same   *Text analysis.* Encodes a word according to the Soundex algorithm: discards some letters and converts consonants to digits.

Example SOUNDEX('cardboard') is C63163.

SPEDIS

SPEDIS(*user word, dictionary word*)   **N**   *Text analysis.* Returns the spelling distance from the dictionary word to the user word. The spelling distance estimates the likelihood that the dictionary word could accidentally be represented as the user word.

SQRT

SQRT(*x*) $x \geq 0$ **N**   *Math.* Returns the square root.

STD

STD(*sample*)   **N**   *Statistic.* The standard deviation.

STDERR

STDERR(*sample*)   **N**   *Statistic.* The standard error of the mean.

STNAME

STNAME(*2-letter postal code for state*)   **$** 20   Returns the state name in uppercase letters, padded with trailing spaces.

STNAMEL

STNAMEL(*2-letter postal code for state*)   **$** 20   Returns the state name, padded with trailing spaces.

STRIP ↺ 9+

STRIP(*string*)   **$**   Removes leading and trailing spaces and returns the result. This is the same effect as TRIMN(LEFT(STRING)).

Example STRIP(STNAMEL('NE')) is Nebraska.

SUBPAD ↻ 9+

SUBPAD(*string, start*)   SUBPAD(*string, start, length*)   **$**   Returns the substring, padding with trailing spaces if necessary to return the indicated length. Returns a null string if *length* = 0.

SUBSTR

SUBSTR(*string, start*)   SUBSTR(*string, start, length*)   **$**   Returns the substring.

SUBSTRN ↻ 9+

SUBSTRN(*string, start*)   SUBSTRN(*string, start, length*)   **$**
Returns the substring. Returns a null string if the start and length arguments do not select any part of the string.

SUM

SUM(*sample*)   **N**   *Statistic.* The sum.

SYMGET

SYMGET(*macro variable name*)   **$ ¬%**   Returns the value of the macro variable.

SYSGET

SYSGET(*environment variable name*)   **$**   Returns the value of the environment variable.

SYSMSG

SYSMSG()   **$**   *I/O.* Returns a file system error message.

SYSPARM

SYSPARM()   **$**   Returns the parameter string of the SYSPARM= system option.

SYSPROCESSID ↻ 7+

SYSPROCESSID()   **N**   Returns the process ID of the current SAS process.

SYSPROCESSNAME ↻ 7+

SYSPROCESSNAME()   SYSPROCESSNAME(*process ID*)   **N**   Returns the process name of the SAS process.

SYSPROD

SYSPROD(*name*)   **N**   *name:* AF, ASSIST, ETS, FSP, GRAPH, etc. Returns SAS product licensing information: 1 if the name is a licensed SAS product, 0 if the name is an unlicensed SAS product, –1 if the name is not a SAS product. If 1 is returned, it is possible that the product is installed and available for use. Otherwise, the product is not accessible to the program.

Example SYSPROD('BASE') is 1.

SYSRC

SYSRC()   **N**   *I/O.* Returns a file system error code from a recent action.

SYSTEM

SYSTEM(*operating system command*)   **N**   Executes the operating system command and returns the operating system return code.

TAN

TAN(θ)   **N**   *Trig.* Returns the tangent of the angle.

TANH

TANH(θ)   **N**   *Trig.* Returns the hyperbolic tangent of the angle.

TIME

TIME()   **N**   Returns the current time of day.

TIMEPART

TIMEPART(*SAS datetime*)   **N**   Returns the SAS time.

TINV

TINV(*P, d.f.*)   TINV(*P, d.f., nc*)   **N**   *Probability.* The inverse distribution function of the *t* distribution with the indicated parameters.

TNONCT

TNONCT(*x, d.f., P*)   **N**   *Probability.* Returns the nonnegative noncentrality parameter for a noncentral *t* distribution with the parameters indicated.

TODAY

TODAY()   **N**   Returns the current date.

TRANSLATE

TRANSLATE(*string, replacement chars, chars, . . .*)   **$** same   Returns the string with all occurrences of the characters replaced by the corresponding replacement characters.

TRANWRD

TRANWRD(*string, substring, replacement substring*)   **$**   Returns the string with all occurrences of the substring replaced by the replacement substring.

TRIGAMMA

TRIGAMMA(*x*)   **N**   *Math.* The second derivative of the log gamma function.

TRIM

TRIM(*string*)   **$** 1–same   Returns the string with trailing spaces removed. For a blank argument, it returns a single space.

TRIMN

TRIMN(*string*)   **$** ≤same   Returns the string with trailing spaces removed. For a blank argument, it returns a null string.

TRUNC

TRUNC(*x, length*)   **N**   *Rounding.* Shortens the number to the indicated length in bytes, which reduces its precision.

Example TRUNC(844.5001, 3) is 844.5.

UNIFORM

UNIFORM(*seed*)   **N**   *Random number.* Returns a random number from the uniform distribution on the interval [0, 1].

UPCASE

UPCASE(*string*)   **$** same   Converts lowercase letters to uppercase.

URLDECODE ↻ 8+

URLDECODE(*string*)   **$**   Decodes URL text.

URLENCODE ↻ 8+

URLENCODE(*string*)   **$**   Encodes a string as URL text (using numeric codes for characters not in the URL character set).

USS

USS(*sample*)   **N**   *Statistic.* The uncorrected sum of squares.

UUIDGEN ↻ 9.1+

UUIDGEN(*optional n, optional binary indicator*)   **$**   Generates a UUID (a unique identifying value) and returns the 36-character text form. Returns the 16-byte binary form if the binary indicator is a nonzero value. Writes no more than *n* warning messages in the log.

VAR

VAR(*sample*)   **N**   *Statistic.* The variance.

VAR...

VAR...(*dataset ID, n*)   I/O. These functions return attributes of the *n*th variable in the SAS dataset.

VARFMT(*dataset ID, n*)   **$**   Format.

VARINFMT(*dataset ID, n*)   **$**   Informat.

VARLABEL(*dataset ID, n*)   **$**   Label.

VARLEN(*dataset ID, n*)   **N**   Length.

VARNAME(*dataset ID, n*)   **$** 1–32   Name.

VARTRANSCODE(*dataset ID, n*)   **N**   Whether transcoding is permitted for the character variable. ↻ 9.1+

VARTYPE(*dataset ID, n*)   **$** 1   Type: C for character, N for numeric.

VARNUM

VARNUM(*dataset ID, variable name*)   **N**   I/O. Returns the number of the named variable in the SAS dataset.

VERIFY

VERIFY(*string, chars*, . . .)   **N**   Returns the location of the first character in the string that is not one of the characters listed. Otherwise, it returns 0.

Example VERIFY('AAAAA', 'AB') is 0.

V...∕V...X ⑤ 7+

V...(*name*)   V...X(*string*)   ¬%   *Variable information.* These functions return information items about variables in the program. The name argument must be a name or an array reference, not a character constant or expression. The string argument is a character expression whose value is a name. The value of the string argument cannot be an array reference.

VARRAY(*name*)   VARRAYX(*string*)   **N**   Whether the name is the name of an array.

VFORMAT(*name*)   VFORMATX(*string*)   **$**   The variable's format attribute.

VFORMATD(*name*)   VFORMATDX(*string*)   **N**   The decimal argument of the variable's format attribute.

VFORMATN(*name*)   VFORMATNX(*string*)   **$**   The format name of the variable's format attribute (including the $ prefix of a character format name).

VFORMATW(*name*)   VFORMATWX(*string*)   **N**   The width argument of the variable's format attribute.

VINARRAY(*name*)   VINARRAYX(*string*)   **N**   Whether the variable is an element of an array.

VINFORMAT(*name*)   VINFORMATX(*string*)   **$**   The variable's informat attribute.

VINFORMATD(*name*)   VINFORMATDX(*string*)   **N**   The decimal argument of the variable's informat attribute.

VINFORMATN(*name*)   VINFORMATNX(*string*)   **$**   The informat name of the variable's informat attribute (including the $ prefix of a character informat name).

VINFORMATW(*name*)   VINFORMATWX(*string*)   **N**   The width argument of the variable's informat attribute.

VLABEL(*name*)   VLABELX(*string*)   **$** ≤256   The variable's label attribute, or its name if it does not have a label.

VLENGTH(*name*)   VLENGTHX(*string*)   **N**   The variable's length attribute.

VNAME(*name*)   VNAMEX(*string*)   **$** 1–32/200   The variable's name.

VTRANSCODE(*name*)   VTRANSCODEX(*string*)   **N**   Whether transcoding is permitted for the character variable.   ⑤ 9.1+

VTYPE(*name*)   VTYPEX(*string*)   **$** 1   The variable's type: C for character, N for numeric.

VVALUE(*name*)   VVALUEX(*string*)   **$**   The variable's formatted value.   ⑤ 9+

WAKEUP ⟳ W X

WAKEUP(*SAS time or SAS datetime*)   **N**   Suspends execution and displays a dialog box until the SAS time or SAS datetime, unless the SAS datetime is already passed. Returns the number of seconds execution was suspended. If the argument is negative, the function adds 86400 to it make it a SAS time value.

WEEKDAY

WEEKDAY(*SAS date*)   **N**   Returns the weekday number, with Sunday=1, . . . , Saturday=7.

YEAR

YEAR(*SAS date*)   **N**   Returns the year.

YIELDP ⟳ 8+

YIELDP(*par value, nominal paid interest rate, interest payment frequency, number of payments remaining, time till next payment, present value*)   **N**   *Financial.* Returns the yield to maturity.

YRDIF ⟳ 7+

YRDIF(*date, date, calendar code*)   **N**   Returns the number of years from the first date to the second date. **Calendar code** 'Actual' 'Act/Act'   Calculates the actual number of days.   '360'   '30/360' Calculates based on 30-day months.

YYQ

YYQ(*year, quarter*)   **N**   Returns the SAS date.

ZIPCITY ⟳ 9.1+

ZIPCITY(*ZIP code*)   **$**   Returns a string containing the city name in uppercase letters, a comma, and the two-letter postal code for the state.

Example ZIPCITY('27949') is KITTY HAWK, NC.

Note The ZIP code argument can be character or numeric, with or without leading zeros.

ZIPNAME

ZIPNAME(*ZIP code*)   **$** 20   Returns the state name in uppercase letters.

ZIPNAMEL

ZIPNAMEL(*ZIP code*)   **$** 20   Returns the state name.

Example ZIPNAMEL('33333') is Florida.

ZIPSTATE

ZIPSTATE(*ZIP code*)   **$** 2/20   Returns the two-letter postal code for the state.

Example ZIPSTATE('90210') is CA.

17

CALL Routines

CALL routines are almost the same as functions. Like functions, they take actions based on a list of arguments. Unlike a function, a CALL routine does not return a value that can be used in an expression. Instead, it is executed in a separate statement in the data step. However, many CALL routines do return values by assigning values to variables used as arguments. You can also think of a CALL routine as a special kind of data step statement with a simpler syntax; the only terms in the statement are the arguments.

Most CALL routines can also be used in macro programming. See the %SYSCALL macro statement for details. CALL routines that cannot be used in the macro environment are marked with the symbol ¬%.

ALLPERM ↺ 9+
CALL ALLPERM(*index, x, x, . . .*);   *Math.* Generates a permutation of the variables. The *x* variables must be the same type and, if character, the same length. There can be no more than 18 variables. Loop from 1 to FACT(N), if N is the number of variables, to generate all permutations.

CAT... ↺ 9+
CALL CATS(*result, string, . . .*);   CALL CATT(*result, string, . . .*); CALL CATX(*delimiter, result, string, . . .*);   Concatenates strings. See the functions of the same names for details.

COMPCOST ↺ 9+
CALL COMPCOST(*operation, cost, . . .*);   *Text analysis.* Sets the costs of operations used in computing generalized edit distance in the COMPGED function. **Operations and default costs** APPEND 50 BLANK 10 DELETE 100 DOUBLE 20 FDELETE 200 FINSERT 200 FREPLACE 200 INSERT 100 MATCH 0 PUNCTUATION 30 REPLACE 100 SINGLE 20 SWAP 20 TRUNCATE 10

EXECUTE

CALL EXECUTE(*text*);   ¬%   Resolves the macro expression that is contained in the character argument. Resulting SAS statements or tokens are executed immediately after the data step.

LABEL

CALL LABEL(*variable, character variable*);   ¬%   Assigns the variable's label (or if the variable does not have a label, the variable's name) to the character variable.

LOGISTIC ↺ 9.1+

CALL LOGISTIC(*numeric variable, . . .*);   *Math.* Replaces each value with its logistic value.

MISSING ↺ 9.1+

CALL MISSING(*variable, . . .*);   ¬%   Assigns missing values to the variables.

POKE ↺ 7+

CALL POKE(*value, address, optional length*);   The same as POKELONG, but valid only in 32-bit environments.

POKELONG ↺ 8.2+

CALL POKELONG(*value, address, optional length*);   Writes a value in memory. See the POKELONG function for details.

PRXCHANGE ↺ 9+

CALL PRXCHANGE(*pattern ID, n, string variable*);   *PRX.* Replaces a pattern match *n* times.

CALL PRXCHANGE(*pattern ID, n, source string, target string variable, optional result variables*);   Replaces a pattern match *n* times, places the result in the target string variable, and returns these optional result variables: the length of the result; a Boolean indicator, 0 if the result string is truncated because the target string variable is shorter, 1 if the result string is intact; the number of replacements made.

Use *n* = –1 to replace all matches.

PRXDEBUG ↺ 9+

CALL PRXDEBUG(1);   *PRX.* Turns PRX debugging on. The argument can be any positive value.

CALL PRXDEBUG(0);   Turns PRX debugging off.

PRXFREE ↺ 9+

CALL PRXFREE(*pattern ID*);   *PRX.* Frees the memory used by a pattern ID and the associated regular expression. Sets the value of the argument variable to missing.

PRXNEXT ⟳ 9+

CALL PRXNEXT(*pattern ID, start position variable, end position, source string, position variable, optional length variable*);   PRX. Searches the source string between the start position and the end position for a pattern. Returns the position and length, or 0 if a match is not found. Updates the start position variable with the next character position after the match.

PRXPOSN ⟳ 9+

CALL PRXPOSN(*pattern ID, n, position variable, optional length variable*);   PRX. Locates submatch *n*. Returns 0 if fewer than *n* submatches are present.

PRXSUBSTR ⟳ 9+

CALL PRXSUBSTR(*pattern ID, source string, position variable, optional length variable*);   PRX. Searches the source string for a pattern and returns the position and length, or 0 if no match is found

RANBIN

CALL RANBIN(*seed variable, n, P, random number variable*); *Random number.* Generates a random number from a binomial distribution.

RANCAU

CALL RANCAU(*seed variable, random number variable*);   *Random number.* Generates a random number from a Cauchy distribution with $\alpha = 0$ and $\beta = 1$.

RANEXP

CALL RANEXP(*seed variable, random number variable*);   *Random number.* Generates a random number from an exponential distribution with $\lambda = 1$.

RANGAM

CALL RANGAM(*seed variable, a, random number variable*); *Random number.* Generates a random number from a gamma distribution with $b = 1$.

RANNOR

CALL RANNOR(*seed variable, random number variable*);   *Random number.* Generates a random number from a normal distribution with $\mu = 0$ and $\sigma = 1$.

RANPERK ⟳ 9+

CALL RANPERK(*seed variable, k, x, x, . . .*);   *Math.* Generates a random permutation selecting k values from a set of values. The *x* variables must be the same type and, if character, the same length.

RANPERM ↻ 9+

CALL RANPERM(*seed variable, x, x, . . .*);   *Math.* Generates a random permutation of the set of values. The *x* variables must be the same type and, if character, the same length.

RANPOI

CALL RANPOI(*seed variable, λ, random number variable*);
Random number. Generates a random number from a Poisson distribution.

RANTBL

CALL RANTBL(*seed variable, f(1), f(2), . . . , random number variable*);   *Random number.* Generates a random counting number from the indicated distribution table.

RANTRI

CALL RANTRI(*seed variable, hypotenuse, random number variable*);   *Random number.* Generates a random number from a triangular distribution on the interval [0, 1].

RANUNI

CALL RANUNI(*seed variable, random number variable*);   *Random number.* Generates a random number from the uniform distribution on the interval [0, 1].

RXCHANGE ↻ 7+

CALL RXCHANGE(*RX ID, times, character variable*);
CALL RXCHANGE(*RX ID, times, source string, target variable*);
times < 2^{31} *Regular expression.* Makes a substring substitution for a pattern in a character string up to the indicated number of times. Use the RXPARSE function to generate the RX ID that indicates the pattern and substitution. The routine can change a character variable in place, or if you supply a target variable as the fourth argument, the changed character string is placed in that variable.

RXFREE ↻ 7+

CALL RXFREE(*RX ID*);   *Regular expression.* Frees the memory used by an RX ID.

RXSUBSTR ↻ 7+

CALL RXSUBSTR(*RX ID, source string, position variable, optional length variable, optional score variable*);   *Regular expression.* Searches the source string for a pattern. Use the RXPARSE function to generate the RX ID that indicates the pattern. The routine returns the position, length, and score of the substring it finds to match the pattern, or 0 if no match is found.

SCAN ↻ 9+

CALL SCAN(*string, n, position, length, optional delimiters*);   Finds the *n*th token in the string. If *n* < 0, it scans backward from the end of the string.

SCANQ ⑤ 9+
CALL SCANQ(*string, n, position, length, optional delimiters*);
Finds the *n*th token in the string, not counting delimiters inside
quoted strings. If *n* < 0, it scans backward from the end of the string.

SET
CALL SET(*dataset ID*);   *I/O.* Establishes an association between
variables of the SAS dataset and variables of the same name in the
program, so that subsequent calls to the FETCH or FETCHOBS functions retrieve values directly into the program variables.

SLEEP
CALL SLEEP(*n*);   Pauses for *n* seconds.

SOFTMAX ⑤ 9.1
CALL SOFTMAX(*numeric variable, . . .*);   *Math.* Replaces each
value with its softmax value (relative magnitude).

STDIZE ⑤ 9+
CALL STDIZE(*options, . . . , x, x, . . .*);   *Statistics.* Standardizes a
set of values. Standardization subtracts an estimate of the mean and
divides by an estimate of the standard deviation to generate values
with a mean of 0 and a standard deviation of 1.

STREAMINIT ⑤ 8.1+
CALL STREAMINIT(*seed*);   **N** *Random number.* Provides the seed
value to initialize the random number stream for the RAND function.

SYMDEL ⑤ 8.2+
CALL SYMDEL('*name*');   Deletes the global macro variable.

SYMPUT
CALL SYMPUT(*macro variable name, character value*);   ¬%
Assigns the value to the macro variable.

SYMPUTX ⑤ 9+
CALL SYMPUTX(*macro variable name, value, optional symbol table*);   ¬% Converts the value and assigns it to the macro variable.
It applies the BEST12. format and removes leading and trailing spaces
to convert a numeric value to a character value.   **Symbol table codes**
G Global. L The most local. F The most local in which the macro
variable exists.

SYSTEM
CALL SYSTEM(*command*);   Executes the operating system command.

TANH ⑤ 9.1+
CALL TANH(*numeric variable, . . .*);   *Math.* Replaces each value
with its hyperbolic tangent.

VNAME

CALL VNAME(*variable name, character variable*);   ¬%   Assigns the variable's name to the character variable.

VNEXT ♂ 9+

CALL VNEXT(*name, optional type, optional length*);   ¬%   Returns the name and, optionally, the type and length of a data step variable. Call the routine repeatedly to get all variables of the data step. It returns a blank value if there are no more variables.

Type values N   Numeric.   C   Character.

18

Procedures

A procedure is run by a proc step, which is a separate step in a SAS program. This chapter describes the syntax for base SAS procedures. Procedures also use the proc step statements described in chapter 6. In particular, refer to the descriptions there for the BY, RUN, and QUIT statements and the DATA= option. See chapter 12 for additional statements and options for descriptive statistics.

APPEND
PROC APPEND DATA=*SAS dataset* OUT=*SAS dataset options*;
Copies a SAS dataset or appends the observations of one SAS dataset to another.

If the output SAS dataset does not already exist, the procedure copies the input SAS dataset to the output SAS dataset. If the output SAS dataset exists and the input SAS dataset matches it closely enough, the procedure copies the observations of the input SAS dataset to the end of the output SAS dataset.

Terms/Options
DATA= NEW= The input SAS dataset.

OUT= BASE= The output SAS dataset, to which observations are appended.

FORCE Drops or truncates input variables, if necessary.

APPENDVER=V6 Updates indexes after every output observation.
↻ 7+

CALENDAR
PROC CALENDAR DATA=*SAS dataset* *options*;
START *variable*;
optional statements
Prints a SAS dataset in the form of a monthly calendar.

Terms/Options
CALEDATA=*SAS dataset* Input calendar dataset that contains work

schedules.

DATETIME Uses SAS datetime values instead of SAS date values.

DAYLENGTH=*hours*:*minutes* For a schedule calendar, the length of the standard work day.

FILL Prints months with no input observations.

FORMCHAR='*characters*' FORMCHAR(*index . . .*)='*characters*' Overrides all or selected characters of the FORMCHAR= system option.

HOLIDATA=*SAS dataset* Holiday dataset: the input SAS dataset that defines holidays.

HEADER=SMALL *or* MEDIUM *or* LARGE 1-, 4-, or 7-line header.

INTERVAL=DAY *or* WORKDAY How durations are measured.

LEGEND Prints a box identifying variables that are printed.

MEANTYPE=NOBS *or* NDAYS Weight for calculating means.

MISSING Prints missing values, instead of ignoring them.

WEEKDAYS Does not print Saturdays and Sundays.

WORKDATA=*SAS dataset* An input workdays dataset that defines standard shifts.

Statements

START *variable*; The variable that contains the starting date of the activity. **Alias** STA, DATE, ID

DUR *variable*; The variable that contains the duration of the activity. **Alias** DURATION FIN *variable*; The variable that contains the concluding date of the activity. **Alias** FINISH

VAR *variables*; Variables to be displayed in the calendar. **Alias** VARIABLE

HOLISTART *variable*; The variable in the holiday dataset that contains the starting date of the holiday. **Alias** HOLISTA, HOLIDAY

HOLIDUR *variable*; The variable in the holiday dataset that contains the duration of the holiday. **Alias** HOLIDURATION

HOLIFIN *variable*; The variable in the holiday dataset that contains the concluding date of the holiday. **Alias** HOLIFINISH

HOLIVAR *variable*; The variable in the holiday dataset that contains the name of the holiday. **Alias** HOLIVARIABLE, HOLINAME

OUTSTART *day of week*; The starting day of the week.
Alias OUTSTA

OUTDUR *n*; $1 \le n \le 7$ The number of days that are displayed in the week. **Alias** OUTDURATION

OUTFIN *day of week*; The last day displayed in the week.
Alias OUTFINISH

CALID *variable* / *option*; A group variable that identifies multiple output calendars. **Option** OUTPUT=SEPARATE *or* COMBINED *or* MIX **Default** CALID _CAL_ / OUTPUT=COMBINED;

statistic variables / *format option*; Displays the statistic of these variables for each month. **Statistics** MEAN SUM **Format option** F *or* FORMAT=*format*

CATALOG

PROC CATALOG CATALOG=*catalog entry type option options*;
optional statements

Allows actions on entries in a catalog. (Run-group)

Terms/Options

CATALOG=catalog   Identifies the catalog. **Alias** CAT, C

KILL   Deletes all entries in the catalog.

FORCE   Executes statements even if exclusive access to the catalog is
not available. ○ 7+

Entry type option

ENTRYTYPE *or* ET=*entry type*   Restricts processing to one entry type.

Statements

CHANGE *entry=new name . . . / entry type option*;   Changes the
names of entries.

CONTENTS *option*;   Lists the catalog's entries. **Options** FILE=*fileref*
OUT=*SAS dataset*

COPY OUT=*catalog copy options /entry type option*; SELECT *or*
EXCLUDE *entries / entry type option*;   Copies some or all entries.
Copy options IN=*catalog*   MOVE Deletes after copying.   NEW
Replaces the destination catalog if it already exists. ○ 7+   NOEDIT
Locks copies of AF entries. NOSOURCE NOSRC Omits program
source code from copies of AF entries.

DELETE *entry list / entry type option*;   SAVE *entry list / entry type
option*;   Deletes entries.

EXCHANGE *entry=entry . . . / entry type option*;   Swaps the names
of a pair of entries.

MODIFY *entry* (DESCRIPTION='*label*') / *entry type option*;
Changes the description of an entry.

Examples

This step changes the name of WORK.MEDICAL.CLINIC.SCREEN to
WORK.MEDICAL.HOSPITAL.SCREEN and changes its description:

```
PROC CATALOG CATALOG=WORK.MEDICAL;
  CHANGE CLINIC.SCREEN=HOSPITAL.SCREEN;
  MODIFY HOSPITAL.SCREEN
    (DESCRIPTION='Clinical Data Entry Form');
QUIT;
```

This step copies only the PROGRAM and KEYS entries from the
catalog WORK.NHTRUST to the catalog DEV.NHTRUST:

```
PROC CATALOG CATALOG=WORK.NHTRUST;
  COPY OUT=DEV.NHTRUST ET=PROGRAM;
  COPY OUT=DEV.NHTRUST ET=KEYS;
```

CHART

PROC CHART DATA=*SAS dataset   options*;
optional statements

Produces charts using text characters.

Options

FORMCHAR(*index . . .*) = '*characters*' Overrides selected characters of the FORMCHAR= system option.

LPI=*ratio* Determines proportions. Use a value that is 10 times the ratio of character width to line height in your printer's output. **Default** 6.0

Statements

BLOCK *variables / chart options group options*; Creates a block chart.

HBAR *variables / chart options group options statistic options bar chart options*; Creates a horizontal bar chart.

PIE *variables / chart options*; Creates a pie chart.

STAR *variables / chart options*; Creates a star chart.

VBAR *variables / chart options group options bar chart options*; Creates a vertical bar chart.

Chart options

AXIS=*min max* AXIS=*max* AXIS=*list* Defines the axis range.

FREQ=*variable* Identifies the frequency variable.

LEVELS=*n* Number of midpoints for continuous variables.

MIDPOINTS=*list* Values of midpoints.

MISSING Includes missing values.

NOHEADER NOHEADING Suppresses header line (except in bar charts).

SYMBOL='*character(s)*' Symbol to form bars and blocks (if subgroups are not used).

SUMVAR=*variable* Identifies variable to be analyzed.

TYPE= Identifies type of data to be charted: CFREQ Cumulative frequency. CPERCENT CPCT Cumulative percent. FREQ Frequency. MEAN Mean. PERCENT PCT Percent. SUM Sum.

Group options

DISCRETE Indicates the discrete chart variable.

GROUP=*variable* Produces side-by-side charts that are grouped by this variable.

G100 Each group is 100%.

NOSYMBOL NOLEGEND Suppresses the subgroup symbol table.

SUBGROUP=*variable* Subdivides bars to show groups defined by this variable.

Statistic options

CFREQ Prints the cumulative frequency.

CPERCENT Prints the cumulative percent.

FREQ Prints the frequency.

NOSTATS NOSTAT Suppresses statistics.

PERCENT Prints the percent.

SUM Prints total frequency.

Bar chart options

DESCENDING   Prints bars in descending order of size.

GSPACE=*n*   The space between groups.

NOSPACE   Allows vertical bars with no space between them.

NOZEROS   Suppresses bars with zero frequencies.

REF=*number . . .*   Draws reference lines.

SPACE=*n*   The space between bars.

WIDTH=*n*   The width of bars.

CIMPORT

PROC CIMPORT INFILE=*file type=output file options*;
optional statements

Converts a transport file to a SAS file (or SAS files).

Terms/Options

INFILE=*file*   Identifies the input transport file.

LIBRARY *or* LIB=*libref*   CATALOG *or* CAT *or* C=*catalog*   DS *or*
DATA=*SAS dataset*   Identifies the output library or SAS file.

EXTENDSN=YES *or* NO   Whether to add 1 byte to the length of
numeric variables 2 to 7 bytes in length to avoid possible truncation.

NEW   Replaces the output catalog if it already exists. ○ 7+

MEMTYPE=*member types*   Imports the selected member type(s).
Member types DATA *or* DS   CATALOG *or* CAT   ALL ○ 7+

ET=(*entry types*)   Imports selected entry types.   EET=(*entry types*)
Excludes entry types.

NOEDIT   Locks imported AF entries.   NOSOURCE   NOSRC   Omits
program source code from imported AF entries.

NOCOMPRESS   Does not compress SAS data files and catalogs.

TAPE   Indicates a sequential input file.

DATECOPY   Copies file creation and modification dates. ○ 8.1 +

Statements

SELECT *or* EXCLUDE *members or entries / option*;   Copies only
selected members of a library or entries of a catalog. **Options**
MEMTYPE *or* MTYPE *or* MT=*member type(s)*   ENTRYTYPE *or* ETYPE
or ET=*entry type* ○ 7+

COMPARE

PROC COMPARE DATA=*SAS dataset   options*;
optional statements

Compares two SAS datasets or compares variables.

Options

DATA *or* BASE=*SAS dataset*   The SAS dataset to compare to.

COMPARE *or* COMP *or* C=*SAS dataset*   The SAS dataset to compare,
if it is different from the DATA= SAS dataset.

OUT=*SAS dataset*   The output SAS dataset.

Contents of output SAS dataset: OUTALL   OUTBASE   OUTCOMP
OUTDIF   OUTNOEQUAL   OUTPERCENT

METHOD= The comparison method: ABSOLUTE EXACT RELATIVE RELATIVE(ε)

Computation: CRITERION=ε FUZZ=ε NOMISSBASE NOMISSCOMP NOMISSING *or* NOMISS

OUTSTATS=*SAS dataset* Creates an output SAS dataset of summary statistics.

Log notes: NOTE Results. WARNING ERROR Message when differences are found.

Print output: ALLOBS ALLSTATS ALLVARS BRIEF LISTALL *or* LIST LISTBASE LISTBASEOBS LISTBASEVAR LISTCOMP LISTCOMPOBS LISTCOMPVAR LISTEQUALVAR LISTOBS LISTVAR MAXPRINT=*n or* (*n, n*) NODATE NOPRINT NOSUMMARY NOVALUES PRINTALL STATS TRANSPOSE

Statements

ID *optional* DESCENDING *variable . . . optional* NOTSORTED; Variables that match observations.

VAR *variables*; Variables in the base dataset to compare to.

WITH *variables*; Variables in the comparison dataset to compare, if they have different names.

Example

The step below compares the values of the variables TIME and ACCUR in the SAS dataset AFTER with the same variables in the SAS dataset BEFORE. Both SAS datasets are in sorted order by the variables DATE and NAME.

```
PROC COMPARE DATA=BEFORE COMPARE=AFTER METHOD=EXACT;
ID DATE NAME;
VAR TIME ACCUR;
RUN;
```

CONTENTS

PROC CONTENTS DATA=*SAS dataset or libref.*_ALL_ *options*; Describes the contents of a SAS dataset.

Options

DIRECTORY Lists the members of the library that contains the SAS dataset.

DETAILS Also includes observation count, entry count, index, and label columns in the directory listing. NODETAILS Omits those columns.

MEMTYPE *or* MTYPE *or* MT=*member type or* (*member type, . . .*) *or* ALL Selects one or more member types.

NODS Suppresses print output except for the directory page. NOPRINT Suppresses all print output.

ORDER= Order of variable names: IGNORECASE Alphabetical order. VARNUM Logical position. ↻ 9+

SHORT Lists names of variables only.

FMTLEN Lists the default length of an informat or format, if applicable.

CENTILES   Shows centiles of indexes. ○ 7+

OUT=*SAS dataset*   Output SAS dataset, with one observation for each variable.

OUT2=*SAS dataset*   Output SAS dataset, with one observation for each index or integrity constraint. ○ 8+

CONVERT
PROC CONVERT *input type=fileref* OUT=*SAS dataset options*;
Imports BMDP, OSIRIS, and SPSS files. **Options** BMDP=*fileref*
OSIRIS=*fileref* DICT=*fileref* SPSS=*fileref* FIRSTOBS=*n* OBS=*n*

COPY
PROC COPY IN=*libref* OUT=*libref options*;
optional statement
Copies SAS files.

Options

MEMTYPE *or* MTYPE *or* MT=(*member types*)   Copies selected member types.

MOVE   Deletes after copying.   ALTER=*password*   The alter password if you use the MOVE option for alter-protected members.

FORCE   Allows the MOVE option for a SAS dataset that has an audit trail. The audit file is discarded. ○ 9+

DATECOPY   Copies file creation and modification dates. ○ 8.1+

When copying SAS data files: INDEX=YES *or* NO   Whether to copy indexes   CONSTRAINT=YES *or* NO   Whether to copy integrity constraints when copying indexes.   CLONE   NOCLONE   Whether to reproduce attributes of compression, buffer size, encoding, etc.

Statements
SELECT *or* EXCLUDE *members / option*;   Copies selected members
Option MEMTYPE *or* MTYPE *or* MT=(*member types*)

Example
This step copies all members of the SAS data library HERE to the SAS data library THERE:
PROC COPY IN=HERE OUT=THERE INDEX=YES;
RUN;

CORR
PROC CORR DATA=*SAS dataset   options*;
optional statements
Measures correlations.

Options

Print output: BEST=*n* NOCORR NOPRINT NOPROB NOSIMPLE
RANK

Hoeffding's D statistics: HOEFFDING OUTH=*SAS dataset*

Kendall tau-b coefficients: KENDALL   OUTK=*SAS dataset*

Spearman rank-order correlations: SPEARMAN   FISHER
OUTS=*SAS dataset*

Pearson product-moment correlations: PEARSON ALPHA COV
CSSCP NOMISS SINGULAR=*x* SSCP FISHER OUTP=*SAS dataset*

VARDEF=N *or* DF *or* WEIGHT *or* WGT *or* WDF
EXCLNPWGT ↻ 7+

Statements

VAR *variables*;   Measures correlations of these variables.

WITH *variables*;   Measures correlations between these variables and the variables listed in the VAR statement.

PARTIAL *variables*;   Variables for partial correlation.

FREQ *variables*;   The frequency variable.

WEIGHT *variables*;   The weight variable.

CPORT

PROC CPORT *type=input file* FILE=*file options*;
optional statements
Creates a transport file.

Terms/Options

LIBRARY *or* LIB=libref CATALOG *or* CAT *or* C=*catalog* DATA *or* DS=*SAS dataset* The input library or SAS file.

FILE=*file* Copies to this transport file.

OUTLIB *or* OUT=*libref* Copies to this SAS data library.

AFTER=*SAS date* Omits catalog entries that are not modified on or after this date.

ET=(*entry types*) Copies selected entry types. EET=(*entry types*) Excludes entry types.

INDEX=YES *or* NO Whether to copy indexes of SAS data files.

CONSTRAINT *or* CON=YES *or* NO Whether to copy integrity constraints when copying indexes. ↻ 7+

INTYPE=*DBCS type* OUTTYPE=*DBCS type or* UPCASE

MEMTYPE *or* MTYPE *or* MT=*member type or* (*member type   member type . . .*) Copies selected member types.

NOEDIT Locks exported AF entries. NOSOURCE NOSRC Omits program source code from exported AF entries.

NOCOMPRESS Does not compress the transport file.

GENERATION *or* GEN= When copying a generation dataset: YES Copies all generations. NO Copies only one generation. ↻ 7+

DATECOPY Copies file creation and modification dates. ↻ 8.1+

TAPE Indicates a sequential output transport file.

TRANSLATE=(*n* TO *n* . . .) Translates characters.

Statements

TRANTAB NAME=*translation table options*; Uses the translation table to translate characters in exported entries. **Options** TYPE=(*list*) Applies the translation table to: *entry types* The listed entry types. CATDESC Entry descriptions. DATASET Values and labels of SAS datasets. OPT=(*list*) Applies the translation table to: DISP Entries with windows. SRC SOURCE entries.

SELECT *or* EXCLUDE *members or entries / option*;   Copies only selected members of a library or entries of a catalog. **Options**

MEMTYPE *or* MTYPE *or* MT=*member type(s)*   ENTRYTYPE *or* ETYPE
or ET=*entry type* ⟳ 7+

DATASETS

PROC DATASETS *options member type option   password options*;
optional statements
Allows actions on members of a SAS data library. (Run-group)

Options

LIBRARY=*libref* The SAS data library.

NOLIST   Does not write a list of members in the log.

NOWARN   Does not generate notes when a member that is named in
a statement does not exist.

KILL   Deletes all members in the library.

DETAILS   Also includes observation count, entry count, variable
count, and label columns in the directory listing   NODETAILS   Omits
those columns.

FORCE   Executes a run group even if it contains errors. Also equivalent to the FORCE option in the APPEND statement.

Member type option

MTYPE=   Selects member types to be processed: *member type*   A
specific member type. (*member type*   ) Multiple member types
(only in the PROC statement).   ALL   All member types. You can also
write this option, in parentheses, after a member name in a statement
in the proc step, to have the option apply to that specific member.
Default ALL **Alias** MEMTYPE, MT

Statements

AGE *member member . . . / member type option password option*;
Renames each member listed with the next name on the list and
deletes the last member in the list. The first member in the list should
already exist.

CHANGE *member=name . . . / member type option password
option generation option*;   Renames the member.

EXCHANGE *member=member . . . / member type option password
option*;   Swaps the names of a pair of members.

APPEND DATA=*SAS dataset* OUT=*SAS dataset option*;   Equivalent
to the APPEND procedure

CONTENTS DATA=*SAS dataset or libref._ALL_ options*;
Equivalent to the CONTENTS procedure.

COPY OUT=*libref options*; *optional secondary statement*
Equivalent to the COPY procedure.

DELETE *member list / member type option password option generation option*;   SAVE *member list / member type option*;   Deletes
members.

REPAIR *member / member type option password option generation option*;   Attempts to repair a SAS data file or catalog. ⟳ 7+

AUDIT *member password option generation option*; *secondary
statements*   Creates or manages an audit trail for the SAS data file.
⟳ 8+

MODIFY *member* (*dataset options*) / *member type option*
generation option   change option; *optional secondary statements*   Modifies a SAS data file. **Dataset options** LABEL=
TYPE= *password option* SORTEDBY= GENMAX= GENNUM=
Change options DTC=*SAS datetime constant* Sets the creation
date. ↻ 8.1+ CORRECTENCODING=*encoding* Use this option to
change a SAS dataset's encoding attribute to match its actual character
data. ↻ 9.1+

Generation option

GENNUM= Selects the generation to process for a generation dataset.
n The generation number. 0 The current generation. -*n* The relative generation number. ALL All generations (in the CHANGE or
DELETE statement). HIST All generations except the current one (in
the DELETE statement). REVERT Removes the current generation
to revert to the previous one (in the DELETE statement). ↻ 7+

Secondary statements for MODIFY

RENAME *variable*=*name* . . . ;   Changes the name of a variable.

INFORMAT *variables informat* . . . ;   Changes the informat
attribute of variables.

INFORMAT *variables*;   Clears the informat attribute of variables.

FORMAT *variables informat* . . . ;   Changes the format attribute of
variables.

FORMAT *variables*;   Clears the format attribute of variables.

LABEL *variable*='*label*' . . . ;   Changes the label attribute of a variable.

LABEL *variable*= . . . ;   Clears the label attribute of a variable.

INDEX CREATE *index or index*=(*variable variable* . . .) . . . / *index
options*;   Creates an index. **Index options** NOMISS Excludes
from the index any observation that has missing values for all key
variables. UNIQUE Prevents observations that duplicate existing
key values from being added to the SAS dataset. UPDATECENTILES
or UPDCEN=*n or* ALWAYS *or* NEVER Updates centiles for the index
when the SAS dataset is closed after changes to key values of *n* percent
of observations. *ALWAYS:* 0 *NEVER:* 101. Default: 5. ↻ 7+

INDEX DELETE *index* . . . ;   Deletes an index. If the index is required
for an integrity constraint, the index is not deleted until the integrity
constraint is deleted.

INDEX DELETE _ALL_;   Deletes all indexes, except those required for
integrity constraints. ↻ 8+

INDEX CENTILES *index* . . . / *options*;   **Options** REFRESH Updates
centiles immediately. UPDATECENTILES=*n or* ALWAYS *or* NEVER
Changes the centiles setting. ↻ 7+

IC CREATE *integrity constraint*=*rule options*;   Creates an integrity
constraint. An integrity constraint creates an error condition when
you try to add an observation to the SAS dataset that violates a data
integrity rule. ↻ 7+ **Options** MESSAGE='*message text*' The error
message when the integrity constraint creates an error condition.
MSGTYPE=USER Replaces the standard error message. ↻ 8.1+
Integrity rules CHECK(WHERE=(*condition*)) Requires a condition
to be met. NOT NULL(*variable*) Requires nonmissing values for a
variable. UNIQUE *or* DISTINCT(*variable(s)*) Requires a variable to

have a different value in each observation. Requires a set of variables to have a different set of values in each observation. PRIMARY KEY(*variable(s)*) Defines a primary key. Requires a different nonmissing value (or set of values) in each observation. A SAS data file can have only one primary key. FOREIGN KEY(*variable(s)* REFERENCES *SAS dataset optional variable action options*) Defines a foreign key. This creates a link to a primary key of another SAS dataset. It requires the key value to match that primary key. Action options define a response when the primary key is changed. **Foreign key action options** ON DELETE RESTRICT ON UPDATE RESTRICT Allows a deletion of or change in the primary key only if no foreign key matches that observation. ON DELETE SET NULL ON UPDATE SET NULL Sets values to missing in the foreign key when a corresponding primary key value is deleted or changed. ON UPDATE CASCADE Updates values in the foreign key when a primary key value is updated. ⟳ 8.1+

IC DELETE *integrity constraint* . . . ; Deletes integrity constraints. Deleting an integrity constraint also deletes any indexes created by (or owned exclusively by) the integrity constraint. ⟳ 7+

IC DELETE _ALL_; Deletes all integrity constraints. ⟳ 8+

IC REACTIVATE *integrity constraint* REFERENCES *libref*; Reactivates an integrity constraint. (Use this statement after an error deactivates a foreign key integrity constraint.) ⟳ 7+

Secondary statements for AUDIT

The AUDIT statement names the SAS dataset with the audit trail. These statements follow to indicate specific actions for the audit trail.

INITIATE *option*; Creates the audit file and initiates the audit trail. **Option** AUDIT_ALL=YES All operations are logged and logging cannot be suspended. ⟳ 9.1+

LOG *image options*; Determines whether a new audit trail stores audit observations for specific operations on observations. **Image options** BEFORE_IMAGE=YES *or* NO Before an update. DATA_IMAGE=YES *or* NO After a successful update. ERROR_IMAGE=YES *or* NO After an unsuccessful update. ADMIN_IMAGE=YES *or* NO On suspending and resuming. ⟳ 9.1+

USER_VAR=*variable attribute options* . . . ; Creates user variables for a new audit trail. These variables are stored in the audit file, but accessed in the SAS data file. **Attribute options** $ *length* LABEL='*label*'

SUSPEND; Suspends the audit trail. The audit file is kept, but logging stops.

RESUME; Reactivates an audit trail that was previously suspended.

TERMINATE; Terminates the audit trail and deletes the audit file. ⟳ 8+

Examples

This step deletes all members of the WORK library:

```
PROC DATASETS LIBRARY=WORK NOLIST KILL;
QUIT;
```

This step deletes LIVE.PRIOR, renames LIVE.CURRENT as LIVE.PRIOR, and renames LIVE.NEXT as LIVE.CURRENT:

```
PROC DATASETS LIBRARY=LIVE NOLIST NOWARN;
AGE NEXT CURRENT PRIOR / MT=DATA;
QUIT;
```

This step creates a simple index on the variable KEY in the SAS dataset BIG.BIGFILE and deletes the index on the variable OLDKEY:

```
PROC DATASETS LIBRARY=BIG NOLIST;
MODIFY BIGFILE;
INDEX CREATE KEY;
INDEX DELETE OLDKEY;
QUIT;
```

This step changes the names of the variables STATE and L_NAME to TERR and LASTNAME in the SAS dataset PEOPLE.WEST:

```
PROC DATASETS LIBRARY=PEOPLE NOLIST;
MODIFY WEST;
RENAME STATE=TERR L_NAME=LASTNAME;
QUIT;
```

DBCSTAB ○ 8+
PROC DBCSTAB TABLE=*name options*;
Creates DBCS (double-byte character set) conversion tables. The tables are stored as DBCSTAB entries.

Terms/Options
TABLE=*name* The entry name of the DBCS conversion table.
Alias N, NAME

CATALOG=*name* The entry is stored in this catalog.
Default SASUSER.DBCS

DESC='*description*' The description for the entry.

DBCSLANG=*name* The language.

DATA=*SAS dataset* The input SAS dataset containing the code values for the tables. Variable names should be valid values for the DBCSTYPE= system option. Values are DBCS characters coded for those types. Each observation represents a different character.

BASETYPE=*DBCS type* A base type for the code conversion process. Instead of converting from every type to every other type, every type is converted to and from the base type.

VERIFY Checks for invalid double-byte code values.

FORCE Produces output even if data errors are present.

DISPLAY
PROC DISPLAY CATALOG=*entry option*;
Executes an AF entry. **Option** BATCH

DOCUMENT ○ 9+
PROC DOCUMENT NAME=*ODS document access option*;

action statements
Accesses an ODS document.

Access options

READ   Read-only.   WRITE   Read-write.   UPDATE   Update (append).

Action statements

DIR;   Displays the current path.

DIR *path*;   Sets the path.

LIST *path*, . . . / *options*;   Lists the contents of an entry or entries.
Options LEVELS=*n or* ALL   How many levels to show.   FOLLOW
Resolve links.   ORDER=ALPHA *or* INSERT *or* DATE   The order of the
listing.   DETAILS   Shows properties of entries.

DOC;   DOC LIBRARY=*libref*;   Lists ODS documents.

DOC NAME=*ODS document options*;   Opens an ODS document.
Options *access options*   LABEL='*label*'

DOC CLOSE;   Closes the current document.

HIDE *path*, . . . ;   Hides items (they are not displayed when the
document is displayed).

UNHIDE *path*, . . . ;   Unhides items.

DELETE *path*, . . . ;   Deletes items.

COPY *or* MOVE *path*, . . . TO *path* / *options*;   Copies or moves
items. **Options** LEVELS=*n or* ALL   How many levels to use.   FIRST
BEFORE=*path*   AFTER=*path*   LAST   Destination location.

MAKE *path*, . . . / *options*;   Creates a new location or locations.
Options FIRST   BEFORE=*path*   AFTER=*path*   LAST   New location.

RENAME *path* TO *path*;   Renames a location or object.

LINK *path* TO *path* / *options*;   Creates a link. **Options** LABEL
Uses the target label as the link label.   FIRST   BEFORE=*path*
AFTER=*path*   LAST   Link location.   HARD   The link is an indepen-
dent reference to an output object within the same document

SETLABEL *path* '*label*';   Assigns a label.

NOTE *path optional* '*text*' / *options*;   Creates a note (a text object).
Options FIRST   BEFORE=*path*   AFTER=*path*   LAST   Note location.
JUST=LEFT *or* CENTER *or* RIGHT   Text justification.

REPLAY *optional path*, . . . / *options*;   Sends items to open ODS
destinations (print0). **Options** LEVELS=*n or* ALL   How many levels
to use.   ACTIVETITLE ACTIVEFOOTN ACTITLE ACFOOTN Uses
the current title and footnote lines instead of the stored title and
footnote lines.   DEST=(*destination* . . .)   Sends output to the selected
ODS destination(s).

IMPORT *source* TO *path* / *option*;   Imports an object. **Source**
DATA=*SAS dataset*   GRSEG=*graph segment entry* **Options** FIRST
BEFORE=*path*   AFTER=*path*   LAST   Target location.

OBPAGE *output object* / *options*;   Inserts (or deletes) a page break
before (or after) the output object. **Options** DELETE   AFTER

OBBNOTE*n output object optional* '*text*' / *option*; $1 \leq n \leq 10$ Defines an object header text line. **Option** JUST=LEFT   CENTER   RIGHT

OBANOTE*n output object optional* '*text*' / *option*; $1 \leq n \leq 10$ Defines an object footer text line. **Option** JUST=LEFT   CENTER   RIGHT

OBTITLE*n output object optional 'text' / option*; $1 \leq n \leq 10$
Defines a title line for the output object. **Option** JUST=

OBSTITLE*n output object optional 'text' / option*; $1 \leq n \leq 10$
Defines a subtitle line for the output object. **Option** JUST=

OBFOOTN*n output object optional 'text' / option*; $1 \leq n \leq 10$
Defines a footnote line for the output object. **Option** JUST=

DOWNLOAD ○ SAS/CONNECT

PROC DOWNLOAD *options*;
optional statements
Copies a file from the remote session to the local session.

Options

DATA=*SAS dataset* OUT=*SAS dataset* Transfers the SAS dataset.
INCAT=*catalog* OUTCAT=*catalog* Transfers the catalog. IN=*libref*
OUT=*libref* Transfers the library. INDEX=YES *or* NO Whether to
copy indexes. CONSTRAINT=YES *or* NO Whether to copy integrity
constraints. DATECOPY Copies SAS dataset creation and modification dates. EXTENDSN=YES Increases the length of short numeric
variables by 1. MTYPE=(*member type, . . .*) Copies only these
member types in the library. ENTRYTYPE=*entry type* Copies only
this entry type in the catalog. GEN=NO Omits historical generations
of generation datasets from the library. V6TRANSPORT Creates a
transport file for transfer.

INFILE=*file* OUTFILE=*file* Transfers the text file. BINARY Uses a
binary transfer instead of a text transfer.

AFTER=*date* Transfers only files that have been modified since the
date given.

STATUS=YES *or* NO Whether to display the Transfer Status dialog.

Statements

SELECT *or* EXCLUDE *members or entries / option*;   Copies only
selected members of a library or entries of a catalog. **Options**
MEMTYPE=*member type(s)* ENTRYTYPE=*entry type*

TRANTAB *translation table options*;   Selects a translation table
for text translation. **Options** TYPE=(*entry type, . . .*) Applies the
selected translation table to these entry types. OPT= Translates
only: DISP Display text. SRC Programs. (DISP SRC) Both.

EXPLODE

PROC EXPLODE;
PARMCARDS *or* PARMCARDS4;
parameter lines
; *or* ;;;;
Prints oversized text formed out of regular text characters.

Parameter lines

L   Forms characters out of asterisks. This is the default.

D   Forms darker characters by overprinting H, Q, and T. This
works only with the system option OVP.

S*n*   Skips *n* lines.

P   Starts a new page.

n message $0 \le n \le 9$ Skips *n* lines and prints the message. The message can contain capital letters, digits, and commonly used symbols. Use the PARMCARDS4 statement if the message contains a semicolon.

U *characters*   Forms an underline out of asterisks. Any non-blank character prints as an underline.

Example
```
PROC EXPLODE;
PARMCARDS;
L
5 PEACE
5 NOW
U NOW
;
```

EXPORT
PROC EXPORT DATA=*SAS dataset options*;
optional statements

Copies data from a SAS dataset to another data file format. ◌ W X 7+

Options
OUTFILE=*file*   The output file.
OUTTABLE=*table*   The output database table. ◌ SAS/ACCESS
DBMS=*data format*   The output data file format or DBMS.
Data formats DLM   Delimited.   TAB   Tab-delimited.   CSV   Comma separated values.   *SAS/ACCESS DBMS name*   The interface to a database or file format. ◌ SAS/ACCESS
REPLACE   Replaces the output file.

Optional statements
An optional equals sign can follow the initial keyword in each of these statements.
DELIMITER '*char*';   The delimiter character.
DATABASE '*database*';   The database name. ◌ SAS/ACCESS
UID '*user ID*';   PWD '*password*';   The DBMS user ID and password.
WCDB '*database*';   The workgroup database that contains the DBMS user ID and password. ◌ SAS/ACCESS

FONTREG ◌ 9.1+
PROC FONTREG *options*;
additional statements

Registers system font files in the SAS Registry.

Options
MODE=   Selects fonts: ALL   All fonts found.   ADD   Only fonts that are not already registered.   REPLACE   Updates previously registered fonts, but does not add new fonts.
USESASHELP   Registers fonts in the SASHELP part of the SAS Registry. The default is to use the SASUSER part of the SAS Registry.
NOUPDATE   Checks font files, but does not update the SAS Registry.
MSGLEVEL=   Detail of log notes about fonts: NONE   None.   TERSE A summary of fonts found.   NORMAL   Also, a list of fonts added. VERBOSE   Also, lists of fonts not added and not understood.

Statements

FONTFILE '*physical file name*' . . . ;   Searches files for fonts.

FONTPATH '*directory*' . . . ;   Searches directories for fonts.

TRUETYPE '*directory*' . . . ;   Searches directories for TrueType fonts.

TYPE1 '*directory*' . . . ;   Searches directories for Type 1 fonts.

FORMAT

PROC FORMAT *options*;
optional statements
Defines and prints formats and informats. (Run-group)

Options

LIBRARY=*libref*   The library in which the formats and informats are stored in a catalog called FORMATS.   LIBRARY=*catalog*   A catalog in which the formats and informats are stored.

FMTLIB   Prints the contents of the FORMATS catalog.   PAGE   Prints each entry on a separate page.

CNTLIN=*SAS dataset*   The input control dataset. Informats and formats that are defined by the dataset are added to the FORMATS catalog.

CNTLOUT=*SAS dataset*   The output control dataset. Entries in the FORMATS catalog are converted to a SAS dataset format.

MAXLABELEN=*n*   The maximum label length that is printed or written to a SAS dataset.

MAXSELEN=*n*   The maximum range value length that is printed or written to a SAS dataset.

NOTSORTED   Stores ranges in the order you specify, rather than in sorted order.

NOREPLACE   Does not replace existing catalog entries.

Statements

SELECT *entries*; *or* EXCLUDE *entries*;   Defines a subset of entries to read from the FORMATS catalog or write to the output control dataset. Write an informat entry name as the informat name preceded by @.

INVALUE *informat* (*informat options*) *range* = *value* . . . ;   Defines a value informat.

VALUE *format* (*format options*) *range* = *value* . . . ;   Defines a value format.

PICTURE *format* (*format options*) *range* = *picture* (*picture options*) . . . ;   Defines a picture format.

Format and informat options

DEFAULT=*n*   The default width.   MAX=*n*   The maximum width. MIN=*n*   The minimum width.

FUZZ=*number*   Extends ranges by the amount specified.
Default 1E-12

NOTSORTED   Stores ranges in the order indicated in the program, rather than in sorted order. ◌ 7+

For formats: MULTILABEL   Allows a range to appear more than once (or ranges that overlap) to indicate different formatted values. Second and subsequent formatted values are used as secondary labels in some contexts. ⊙ 7+

For picture formats: ROUND   Rounds the numeral instead of truncating it.

For informats: UPCASE   Converts the input value to uppercase before comparing it to the ranges.   JUST   Removes leading spaces from the input value before comparing it to the ranges.

Ranges

For character formats and character informats, ranges consist of character values. For numeric formats, ranges consist of numeric values. For numeric informats, ranges can include numeric and character values.

constant   LOW   HIGH   *value - value*   *value -< value*
value <- value   *value <-< value*   OTHER   *range, range, . . .*

Values

The "label" value that results from a range is a character constant, except for numeric informats, where values should usually be numeric constants. A value can also be a reference to another informat or format.

constant

[*informat*]   [*format*]   (|*informat*|)   (|*format*|)

SAME   Unchanged (for character informats) or treated as ordinary numeric data (for numeric informats).

ERROR   Treated as invalid data (for informats).

Pictures

A picture is a character constant that contains digit selectors and literal characters. Any character other than a digit is a literal character that appears in the formatted value. A picture is simply a literal value if it does not contain any digits or if the NOEDIT option is used.

A different kind of picture is used for SAS date, SAS time, or SAS datetime values. These pictures contain picture directives, which are escape sequences that begin with a percent sign.

Digit selectors

Digits in a picture are used as digit selectors. If the picture contains any digit selectors, then the first character of the picture must be a digit selector. Each digit selector represents a position for a digit or fill character in the formatted value. Fill characters are used only for zero digit selectors at the beginning of the picture. Use nonzero digit selectors to generate leading zeroes. Also use nonzero digit selectors at the end of the picture and after a decimal point.

Picture directives ⊙ 7+

Picture directives are case-sensitive, produce numbers without leading zeros, and are localized when executed according to the DFLANG= system option. Use the DATATYPE= picture option to indicate how data values are interpreted. Write a 0 before the letter of the picture directive to obtain leading zeros for two-digit elements. Use single quotes to avoid macro reference errors. Add trailing spaces to make the picture an appropriate width.

%%   Percent sign (%).

%Y Year. %y Year without century. %m Month number. %B Month name. %b Month name, abbreviated. %d Day. %A Weekday name. %a Weekday name, abbreviated. %w Weekday number (Sunday=1, . . ., Saturday=7). %j Day of year. %U Week of year (week 1 beginning on first Sunday).

%H Hour. %I Hour of 12-hour clock. %p AM or PM. %M Minute. %S Second.

Picture options

FILL='*char*' The fill character: replaces digit selector zeroes at the beginning of the picture if the numeral has fewer digits than the number of digit selectors. **Default** ' '

MULTIPLIER *or* MULT=*factor* The value is multiplied by this factor before being converted to a numeral.

DATATYPE=*type* Interpretation of the input value: DATE SAS date value. TIME SAS time value. DATETIME SAS datetime value. ⚲ 7+

DECSEP=*char* Decimal point character. DIG3SEP=*char* Separator character for each 3 digits. ⚲ 7+

NOEDIT The picture is treated as a literal value.

Control dataset variables

Required variables: FMTNAME START LABEL

TYPE The type of routine: C Character format N Numeric format J Character informat I Numeric informat P Picture format

FMTNAME Name.

DEFAULT MIN MAX Width.

START END Range interval (input) values.

SEXCL EEXCL Exclude endpoints from interval: Y N

LABEL Label or picture (output value).

LENGTH FUZZ MULT NOEDIT PREFIX FILL DECSEP DIG3SEP DATATYPE LANGUAGE Options.

HLO Special range codes: H High. L Low. O Other. N No ranges. Other codes: I Numeric interval for informat. F Label is format/informat. U Upcase. J Just. R Round. S Notsorted.

Examples
```
PROC FORMAT;
VALUE BOOLEAN 0 = 'False'  1 = 'True';
INVALUE TIX   0-5=0   6-17, 75-HIGH=2.00   OTHER=4.00;
VALUE SIGN (MIN=1)   LOW-<0 = 'NEGATIVE'   0 = 'ZERO'
   0<-HIGH = 'POSITIVE'   ._-.Z = 'UNKNOWN';
PICTURE HM
   0-86399 = '%H hours %M minutes' (DATATYPE=TIME);
RUN;
```

FORMS
PROC FORMS DATA=*SAS dataset options*;
optional statement
LINE *n variables / options*; . . .

Prints data in rectangular blocks (form units). Each input observation is printed as a block.

Options

FILE *or* DDNAME *or* DD=*fileref* The output file.

Page: DOWN *or* D=*n* Skips *n* lines at the top of the page. CC Uses a carriage-control character to start a new page. INDENT *or* I=*n* The left margin. PAGESIZE *or* PS=*n* The number of lines on the page.

Size of a block: WIDTH *or* W=*n* Width. LINES *or* L=*n* Lines.

The number of blocks: ACROSS *or* A=*n* Across the page. NDOWN *or* ND=*n* Down the page.

Space between blocks: BETWEEN *or* B=*n* Horizontal spacing. SKIP *or* S=*n* Vertical spacing.

ALIGN=*n* Starts with *n* blocks filled with Xs. COPIES *or* C=*n* Prints each observation *n* times. SETS=*n* Prints the entire output *n* times.

Statements

FREQ *variable*; Identifies a frequency variable, which indicates the number of times to print each observation.

LINE *n variables / options*; Prints the variables on the indicated line of the block. **Options** INDENT *or* I=*n* Indents the line. LASTNAME *or* L Reorders the character value to print first the words that come after the comma in the value, then the words that come before the comma. PACK *or* P Removes trailing spaces from variable values. REMOVE *or* R Omits the line if the variables are missing or blank.

FREQ

PROC FREQ DATA=*SAS dataset options*;
optional statements

Prints tables of frequencies. The tables show the number of observations in the input SAS dataset that have each value of a variable or combination of variables.

Options

FORMCHAR(1, 2, 7)='*chars*' FORMCHAR='*chars*' Overrides characters of the FORMCHAR= system option.

ORDER= The order of output values: DATA Their order of appearance in the input data. INTERNAL Sorted. FORMATTED Sorted order of the formatted values. FREQ Descending order of frequency.

NLEVELS Prints the "Number of Variable Levels" table that indicates the number of distinct formatted values for each variable. ◯ 9.1+

PAGE Prints only one table on a page.

NOPRINT Suppresses print output.

Statements

WEIGHT *variable / option*; Identifies a weight variable. **Option** ZEROS Includes observations and levels with zero weights. ◯ 9+

TABLES *requests / options*; Prints tables.

OUTPUT OUT=*SAS dataset statistics*; Creates an output SAS dataset from the last table request. **Statistics** AJCHI BDCHI BINOMIAL (LEVEL=*n*) CMHCOR CMHGA CMHRMS COCHQ CONTGY CRAMV EQKAP EQWKP FISHER EXACT GAMMA JT KAPPA KENTB LAMCR LAMDAS LAMRC LGOR LGRRC1 LGRRC2 LRCHI MCNEM MHCHI MHOR MHRRC1 MHRRC2 N NMISS

OR PCHI PCORR PHI PLCORR RDIF1 RDIF2 RELRISK RISKDIFF RISKDIFF1 RISKDIFF2 RRC1 RRC2 RSK1 RSK11 RSK12 RSK2 RSK21 RSK22 SCORR SMDCR SMDRC STUTC TREND TYSMM U UCR URC WTKAP **Statistic groups** ALL AGREE CHISQ CMH CMH1 CMH2 MEASURES

TEST *statistics*;   Computes asymptotic tests. **Statistics** AGREE GAMMA KAPPA KENTB MEASURES PCORR SCORR SMDCR SMDRC STUTC WTKAP ○ 7+

EXACT *statistics / option*;   Computes exact statistics. **Statistics** AGREE BINOMIAL (LEVEL=*n*) CHISQ FISHER EXACT JT KAPPA LRCHI MCNEM MEASURES MHCHI OR PCHI PCORR POINT SCORR TREND WTKAP **Option** MAXTIME=*time* A time limit in seconds. MC N= SEED= ALPHA= Options for Monte Carlo estimation. ○ 7+

Requests
A table request consists of one variable or a list of variables connected by asterisks. For a two-way table, the first variable forms rows. The last variable forms columns. You can also use variable lists in parentheses to define multiple tables.

TABLES statement options
FORMAT=*format* Format for frequency values. ○ 8.1+

LIST Prints in list format.

MISSING Uses missing values.

MISSPRINT Prints missing value frequencies in tables.

OUT=*SAS dataset* Creates a SAS dataset from the last table that is requested.

Include in the output SAS dataset: OUTPCT Percent variables. OUTEXPECT Expected frequencies. OUTCUM Cumulative frequencies and percents of a one-way table. ○ 7+

NOPRINT Does not print tables.

SPARSE Uses all possible combinations, even ones that do not appear in the data.

TOTPCT Prints percent of total in tables with more than two dimensions.

CONTENTS='*text*' Link text for ODS table of contents. ○ 7+

Statistics: AGREE ALL ALPHA=*number* BINOMIAL (P=*P* LEVEL=*n*) BINOMIALC CELLCHI2 CHISQ TESTF=(*n . . .*) TESTP=(*P . . .*) NOWARN CL CMH BDT CMH1 CMH2 CUMCOL DEVIATION EXPECTED FISHER EXACT JT MEASURES NOCOL NOCUM NOFREQ NOPERCENT NOROW PLCORR CONVERGE= MAXITER=*n* PRINTKWT RELRISK RISKDIFF RISKDIFFC SCORES=MODRIDIT *or* RANK *or* RIDIT *or* TABLE SCOROUT TREND

Examples
This step prints a separate frequency table for each variable in the SAS dataset SUBJECTS:

```
PROC FREQ DATA=SUBJECTS;
RUN;
```

The step below prints three two-way frequency tables, which combine the variable CLASS (which forms rows) with each of the variables SCORE1, SCORE2, and SCORE3 (which form columns).

```
PROC FREQ DATA=SUBJECTS;
TABLES CLASS*(SCORE1-SCORE3);
RUN;
```

FSLIST ○ 7+

PROC FSLIST FILE=*fileref options*;

Displays a text file. **Options** Display: NUM   NONUM   CAPS NOCAPS   NOBORDER   HSCROLL=*n or* PAGE *or* HALF   Carriage-control characters: CC   FORTCC   NOCC   OVP   NOOVP

IMPORT

PROC IMPORT OUT=*SAS dataset options*;
optional statements

Interprets a data file and copies data to a SAS data file. ○ W X 7+

Options

DATAFILE=*file*   The input file.
TABLE=*table*   The input database table. ○ SAS/ACCESS

DBMS=*data format*   The input data file format or DBMS.
Data formats DLM   Delimited.   TAB   Tab-delimited.   CSV   Comma separated values.   *SAS/ACCESS DBMS name*   The interface to a database or file format. ○ SAS/ACCESS

REPLACE   The output SAS data file replaces an existing file of the same name.

Optional statements

An optional equals sign can follow the initial keyword in each of these statements.

DELIMITER '*char*';   The delimiter character.

GETNAMES YES *or* NO;   Whether to get variable names from the column names of a table or the first record of a file. If not, the procedure creates variable names VAR0, VAR1, . . .

DATABASE '*database*';   The database name.   UID '*user ID*'; PWD '*password*';   The DBMS user ID and password.   WGDB '*database*'; The workgroup database that contains the DBMS user ID and password.   DBPWD '*password*';   The database (or file) password.   For DBF: GETDELETED YES *or* NO;   Whether to read deleted records. For spreadsheets: SHEET *name*;   The spreadsheet to read. The default is the first spreadsheet in the file.   RANGE=*name or range* The range (rectangular area) to read. ○ SAS/ACCESS

ITEMS ○ z

PROC ITEMS NAME=*item store*;
optional statements

Creates or manages an item store.

Statements

LIST *selection   option*;   Lists items in the log. **Option** DUMP=*fileref*   Writes to this file instead of the log.

DELETE *selection*;   Deletes the selected item or directory, or the entire contents of the item store.

MERGE SOURCE=*item store*;   Merges the contents of another item store into the item store.

IMPORT FILEREF=*fileref selection*;   Imports an HTC file into the item store or the selected directory, or imports a file into the selected item.

EXPORT FILEREF=*fileref selection*;   Exports an HTC file.

Selection

The default selection is the entire item store.

DIR='*name*' Selects this item store directory.

ITEM='*name*' Selects this item.

MEANS

The SUMMARY procedure with the PRINT option as the default. The default analysis variables are all numeric variables. **Example** This step prints several descriptive statistics for all numeric variables in a SAS dataset: PROC MEANS DATA=WORK.SUBJECTS; RUN;

MIGRATE ⟳ 9+

PROC MIGRATE IN=*libref* OUT=*libref options*;
Converts SAS files from an older version.

Options

KEEPNODUPKEY Keeps the NODUPKEY sort attribute of a SAS data file, even though it is not necessarily accurate.

BUFSIZE= Changes the buffer size: *n* *n*K *n*M *n*G *n*X MAX

MOVE Deletes after copying. This prevents most validation.

SLIBREF=*remote libref* Remote library services libref for the library, required when converting 32-bit catalogs to a 64-bit platform.

OPTIONS

PROC OPTIONS *options*;
Lists values of system options.

Options

SHORT LONG DEFINE VALUE

HOST PORTABLE *or* NOHOST OPTION=*option name*

GROUP=*option group name* ⟳ 7+

OPTLOAD ⟳ 8.2+

PROC OPTLOAD *options*;
Loads a stored set of system option settings.

Options

Loads option settings from: KEY="*registry key*" The SAS registry. DATA=*SAS dataset* The variables OPTNAME and OPTVALUE in a SAS dataset. The default location for option settings is the SAS dataset SASUSER.MYOPTS.

OPTSAVE ⟳ 8.2+

PROC OPTSAVE *options*;
Stores system option settings. Startup options, passwords, and a few other system options are not included.

Options

Stores option settings in: KEY="*registry key*" The SAS registry.
DATA=*SAS dataset* The variables OPTNAME and OPTVALUE in a
SAS dataset. The default location for option settings is the SAS dataset
SASUSER.MYOPTS.

PDS ⊘ z

PROC PDS DDNAME=*file options*; *optional statements* Allows
actions on members of a PDS. **Options** NOLIST Suppresses the
list of PDS members. KILL Deletes all members of the PDS.
Statements DELETE *member . . .* ; Deletes PDS members.
CHANGE *member=name . . .* ; Changes the names of PDS members.
EXCHANGE *member=member . . .* ; Swaps names of PDS members.

PDSCOPY ⊘ z

PROC PDSCOPY INDD=*file* OUTDD=*file options*; *optional statement*
Copies a PDS. **Options** ALIASMATCH=BOTH *or* EITHER *or* NAME
or TTR BLKSIZE=*n* DC DCBS *or* NODCBS INTAPE MAXBLK=*n*
NE NEW MOD NOALIAS *or* NOA NOREPLACE *or* NOR NOTEST
OUTTAPE SHAREINPUT *or* SHAREIN **Statements** SELECT *or*
EXCLUDE *PDS members*; Copies selected PDS members.

PLOT

PROC PLOT DATA=*SAS dataset page options*;
PLOT *request . . . / plot options*;
Produces scatter graphs using text characters. (Run-group)

Page options

FORMCHAR(*index . . .*)='*chars*' Overrides one or more characters of
the FORMCHAR= system option.

HPERCENT=*percent* VPERCENT=*percent* The width and height of
each plot as a percent of the page width and height. Allows more than
one plot per page.

MISSING Uses blank values in determining axes.

NOLEGEND Suppresses the legend.

NOMISS Ignores missing values in determining axes.

UNIFORM Scales axes the same way for all BY groups.

VTOH=*ratio* The aspect ratio. Use the ratio of the line height to the
width of a character printed by your printer.

Requests

vertical variable**horizontal variable*

vertical variable or (*variables*)
        optional : or * *horizontal variable or* (*variables*)
        optional $ label variable
        optional ='*plot character*' *or plot variable*

List operators

(*list*) * (*list*) Creates all possible combinations of items in the lists.

(*list*) : (*list*) Combines items one by one.

Plot options

Axes and reference lines: HAXIS=*marks* HPOS=*length* HZERO
HEXPAND HREVERSE HSPACE=*n* VAXIS=*marks* VPOS=*length*
VZERO VEXPAND VREVERSE VSPACE=*n* HREF=*marks*
HREFCHAR='*char*' VREF=*marks* VREFCHAR='*char*' **Marks** *n . . .*
start TO *stop* BY *interval* BY *interval*

Layout: BOX OVERLAY

Contour levels: CONTOUR=*levels* S*level*='*char*' SLIST='*char*' . . .

Label: PLACEMENT *or* PLACE=(*label placement*) SPLIT='*char*'
OUTWARD='*char*' PENALTY(*index . . .*)=*penalty . . .* STATES
LIST=*penalty threshold*

Example

This step plots X against Y and X against Z on the same axes:

```
PROC PLOT DATA=SPACE;
PLOT Y*X='Y' Z*X='Z' / OVERLAY;
RUN;
```

PMENU

```
PROC PMENU options;
MENU entry name;
ITEM statements
other statements
```

Defines a PMENU entry. (Each run group defines a separate entry.)

Options

CATALOG=*catalog* The PMENU entry is stored in this catalog.

DESC '*description*' A description stored with the PMENU entry.

MENU statement

MENU *name*; Begins the definition of a menu. The first statement in
a run group is a MENU statement that names the PMENU entry and
defines a menu bar. Subsequent MENU statements define pull-down
menus.

ITEM and SEPARATOR statements

Each MENU statement is immediately followed by ITEM statements,
which define menu items. The order of the ITEM and SEPARATOR
statements determines the order of menu items.

ITEM '*name*' *or name options*; Defines a menu item.

SEPARATOR; Defines a separator line (displayed in most operating
systems).

Options

SELECTION=*selection* MENU=*menu* SUBMENU=*submenu*
DIALOG=*dialog box* Associates the menu item with a subsequent
statement to define the action taken when the item is selected.
GRAY Indicates that the menu item is inactive.

ACCELERATE='*char*' A character that can be typed in the menu to
select the menu item (in some operating systems).

MNEMONIC='*char*' A character that can be typed as the equivalent of
selecting the menu item (in some operating systems).

SELECTION statement

SELECTION *selection* '*string*' *or command*;   Defines a command string that results from selecting a menu item.

SUBMENU statement

SUBMENU *submenu entry*;   Indicates the entry in which the submenu is stored. ⟲ 7+

DIALOG statement

The DIALOG statement and subsequent TEXT, CHECKBOX, RADIOBOX, and RBUTTON statements define a dialog box.

DIALOG *dialog box* '*command string*';   Defines a dialog box. The command string results when the user selects the OK button in the dialog box; no action results when the user selects the Cancel button. The command string can contain symbols that represent values from text boxes, check boxes, and radio boxes in the dialog box:

@*n*   The value from text box *n*.

%*n*   The value from radio box *n*.

&*n*   The value from check box *n*.

TEXT statement

TEXT #*line* @*column* '*text*' *options*;   Displays a message in the dialog box.

TEXT #*line* @*column* LEN=*length* *options*;   Defines a text box, where the user can enter a text value.

Options

COLOR=*color*   The color of the text.

ATTR=HIGHLIGH *or* BLINK *or* REV_VIDE *or* UNDERLIN   The video attribute of the text.

CHECKBOX statement

A check box represents an on/off choice.

CHECKBOX *optional* ON #*line* @*column* '*text*' *options*;   Defines a check box. The text is displayed next to the check box. If the check box is checked, the text is substituted in the dialog box's command string.

Options

ON   The check box is checked by default.

COLOR=*color*   The color of the text.

SUBSTITUTE='*text*'   This text is substituted in the dialog box command string, in place of the displayed text, if the check box is checked.

RADIOBOX and RBUTTON statements

A radio box consists of radio buttons. The user selects one radio button in the radio box.

RADIOBOX DEFAULT=*n*; RBUTTON *optional* NONE #*line* @*column* '*text*' *options*; . . .   Defines a radio box. The radio button that is defined by the *n*th RBUTTON statement is selected by default.

Options

NONE   This radio button indicates no selection from the radio box.

COLOR=*color*   The color of the text.

SUBSTITUTE='*text*' This text is substituted in the dialog box command string, in place of the displayed text, if the radio button is selected.

Example

This step defines a menu bar with the items Large, Small, and End — each associated with a display manager command:

```
PROC PMENU CATALOG=WORK.DEV DESC 'Alice in Wonderland';
   MENU RESIZE;
   ITEM 'Large' SELECTION=LARGE;
   ITEM 'Small' SELECTION=SMALL;
   ITEM 'End';
   SELECTION LARGE 'WDEF 2 2 20 78';
   SELECTION SMALL 'WDEF 8 20 9 40';
QUIT;
```

PRINT

PROC PRINT DATA=*SAS dataset   options*;
optional statements

Prints a SAS dataset in table form, with observations as rows and variables as columns.

Options

DOUBLE   D   Double-spaces (between observations).

LABEL   L   Uses variable labels.   SPLIT *or* S='*char*'   Uses labels and splits column headings wherever this character appears in the label.

N   Prints the number of observations.

N='*text*'   N='*BY group text*' '*total text*'   Prints the number of observations with the explanatory text. Use two text labels if you use both a BY statement and a SUM statement.   ↻ 7+

OBS='*text*'   The header for the observation number column.   ↻ 7+

NOOBS   Suppresses the observation number column.

ROUND   Rounds numbers to two decimal places (for summing purposes).

HEADING=   The orientation of column headings: HORIZONTAL   H
VERTICAL   V

ROWS=PAGE   Prints only one row of variables per page, even if more than one row is required.

WIDTH=   Column width: FULL   The variable's formatted width.
MINIMUM   MIN   The longest formatted value on the page.   UNIFORM
U   The formatted width if the variable has a format with an explicit width; otherwise, the longest formatted value.   UNIFORMBY   UBY
The formatted width if the variable has a format with an explicit width; otherwise, the longest formatted value in the BY group.

CONTENTS='*text*'   Link text for ODS table of contents.   ↻ 7+
STYLE=*style*   ODS style definition.   ↻ 8.2+

Statements

ID *variables / option*;   Prints these variables at the left side of the line.   **Option** STYLE=*style* ↻ 8.2+

VAR *variables / option*;   Prints these variables. If there is no VAR statement, all variables are printed.   **Option** STYLE=*style* ↻ 8.2+

SUM *variables / option*;   Prints these variables and the totals for
them. **Option** STYLE=*style* ↻ 8.2+

SUMBY *variable*;   Prints the subtotals at the end of a BY group for
this BY variable and for any preceding BY variable.

PAGEBY *variable*;   Starts a new page at the end of a BY group for
this BY variable.

Examples

This step prints all the variables of the most recently created SAS
dataset in the PRINT procedure's default format, including a column
of observation numbers at the left side:

```
PROC PRINT HEADING=H;
RUN;
```

The step below prints selected variables, with MILE_OUT in the left
column, formed into groups by the variables SIZE and CAR; each new
value of SIZE starts on a separate page. It prints totals of the variables
MILEAGE and PRICE for each value of CAR and SIZE, and for the
SAS dataset as a whole. The report begins on page 1, with a title line at
the top of each page.

```
OPTIONS PAGENO=1 NODATE CENTER;
TITLE1 'Autos 2 Go';
PROC PRINT DATA=RENTAL LABEL;
   BY SIZE CAR;
   ID MILE_OUT;
   VAR MILEAGE PRICE DATE_OUT PT_OUT DATE_IN PT_IN;
   PAGEBY SIZE;
   SUM MILEAGE PRICE;
   SUMBY CAR;
   FORMAT MILE_OUT Z5. MILEAGE 6.2 PRICE DOLLAR7.2
      DATE_OUT DATE_IN MMDDYY8.;
   LABEL SIZE='Size Class' CAR='Car' MILE_OUT='Mileage At Pickup'
      MILEAGE='Distance' PRICE='Price'
      DATE_OUT='Pickup Date' DATE_IN='Dropoff Date'
      PT_OUT='Pickup Location' PT_IN='Dropoff Location';
RUN;
```

PRINTTO

PROC PRINTTO *options*;
Redirects the log or standard print file.

Options

LOG=*file*   Redirects the log.

PRINT *or* FILE *or* NAME=*file*   Redirects the standard print file.

UNIT=*nn*   Redirects the standard print file to fileref FT*nn*F001.

NEW   Replaces the file.

LOG=*entry* PRINT=*entry*   Redirects the log/standard print file to a
catalog entry of type LOG or OUTPUT. LABEL='*label*' Provides a
descriptive label for the catalog entry or entries.

LOG=LOG   PRINT=PRINT   Restores the defaults.

Example
These statements identify a print file and redirect standard print output to it:

```
FILENAME LISTING2 'MEANS.LST';
PROC PRINTTO PRINT=LISTING2;
RUN;
```

PRTDEF ⟲ 8.2+
PROC PRTDEF DATA=*SAS dataset options*;
Adds a printer definition to the SAS Registry with settings from a printer attribute dataset.

Options
USESASHELP   Applies changes to the SASHELP part of the SAS Registry. The default action is to change the SASUSER part.

DELETE   Deletes the printer definition from the SAS Registry.
REPLACE   Replaces a printer definition if one of the same name already exists.

FOREIGN   Does not check host-specific items. Use this option if the printer definition is being created for use on another host.

LIST   Lists changes in the log.

Printer attribute dataset variables
Identity (required): MODEL   NAME   DEVICE   DEST
Margins: TOP   BOTTOM   LEFT   RIGHT   UNITS
Default font: TYPEFACE   FONTSIZE   STYLE   WEIGHT   CHARSET
Other: DESC RES   VIEWER   PREVIEW LRECL HOSTOPT OPCODE
PROTOCOL TRANTAB PAPERIN PAPEROUT PAPERSIZ   PAPERTYP

PRTEXP ⟲ 9+
PROC PRTEXP *options*;
optional statement
Extracts printer definition data from the SAS Registry.

Options
USESASHELP   Searches only the SASHELP part of the SAS Registry.

OUT=*SAS dataset*   Creates a printer attribute dataset. Otherwise, the procedure writes printer definitions in the log.

Statements
SELECT *or* EXCLUDE *printers*;   Uses only selected printers.

PWENCODE ⟲ 9.1+
PROC PWENCODE IN='*password*' *options*;
Encodes (encrypts) a password.

Options
OUT=*fileref*   Writes the encoded password in this file. **Default** LOG
METHOD=SAS001   Uses the default SAS001 encoding method.

RANK

PROC RANK DATA=*SAS dataset* OUT=*SAS dataset options*;
VAR *variables*;
optional RANKS *variables*;

Ranks values of numeric variables.

Options

DESCENDING   Ranks from largest to smallest. The default is from smallest to largest.

FRACTION   F   Fractional ranks, with 1 as the highest rank.   FN1   N1   NPLUS1   Fractional ranks, between 0 and 1.   PERCENT   Fractional ranks times 100, with 100 as the highest rank.

GROUPS=*n*   Divides values into *n* groups and assigns quantile ranks from 0 to *n* − 1.

TIES=   Ranks of tied values: HIGH   MEAN   LOW   The default is TIES=MEAN. For fractional ranks, the default is TIES=HIGH.

NORMAL=BLOM *or* TUKEY *or* WV   Computes normal scores.
SAVAGE   Computes Savage scores.

Statements

VAR *variables*;   Analysis variables: ranks these variables.

RANKS *variables*;   Copies the analysis variables to the output SAS dataset and creates these rank variables.

Examples

This step ranks observations by increasing order of TIME to create the variable FINISH (placing finishers in a race):

```
PROC RANK DATA=RACE.TIMES OUT=RACE.ORDER TIES=LOW;
   VAR TIME;
   RANKS FINISH;
RUN;
```

This step converts the variable APTITUDE to percentile ranks:

```
PROC RANK DATA=SCORES OUT=PCTILE GROUPS=100;
   VAR APTITUDE;
RUN;
```

REGISTRY

PROC REGISTRY *options*;
Maintains the SAS Registry. ○ 7+

Options

LIST   Lists the SAS Registry in the log.

LISTUSER   Lists the SASUSER part of the SAS Registry in the log.

LISTHELP   Lists the SASHELP part of the SAS Registry in the log.

LISTREG='*libref.name*'   Lists the registry file in the log. ○ 9+

STARTAT='*key*'   Lists or exports only the key and its subkeys.

COMPAREREG1='*libref.name*'   COMPAREREG2='*libref.name*'
Compares the two registry files and writes the results in the log. ○ 9+

CLEARSASUSER   Erases the SASUSER part of the SAS Registry.

USESASHELP Operates on the SASHELP part of the SAS Registry (for the options listed below). The default is to operate on the SASUSER part of the SAS Registry.

COMPARETO=*file* Compares the file to the SAS Registry part.

EXPORT=*file* Copies the SAS Registry part to the file.

IMPORT=*file* Updates the SAS Registry part with the contents of the file.

UNINSTALL=*file* Updates the SAS Registry part by removing the contents of the file.

FULLSTATUS Generates additional log notes about the IMPORT= and UNINSTALL= options.

RELEASE ♂ z

PROC RELEASE DDNAME=*file options*; Releases unused space at the end of a file. **Options** TOTAL=*n* TRACKS=*n* UNUSED=*n* RELEASE=*n* EXTENT BOUNDARY *or* TYPE=DSCB *or* CYL *or* TRK *or* ALLOC

REPORT

PROC REPORT DATA=*SAS dataset options*;
optional statements

Prints or summarizes a SAS dataset in table format.

Statistics options

EXCLNPWGT Disregards (excludes) observations that have nonpositive weight values. ♂ 7+

VARDEF=N *or* DF *or* WEIGHT *or* WGT *or* WDF

MISSING Treats missing values as valid values of class variables.

THREADS Enables multithreading to increase multiprocessor performance. NOTHREADS Prevents multithreading. ♂ 9.1+

Formatting options

FORMCHAR='*chars*' FORMCHAR(*index . . .*)='*chars*' Overrides all or selected characters of the FORMCHAR= system option. ♂ 7+

BOX Draws table rules around each page and between the rows and columns of the report.

CENTER Centers the report. NOCENTER Left-aligns the report.

COLWIDTH=*n* The default column width. **Default** 9

HEADLINE Draws a horizontal line under the column headers.

HEADSKIP Leaves a blank line under the column headers.

LS=*n* The line size: the number of characters that are used on a line.

NOHEADER Omits column headers. NAMED Omits column headers and writes the column name and an equals sign before each value in the report.

PANELS=*n* The page is divided horizontally into this many panels. **Default** 1

PS=*n* The page size: the number of lines used on a page.

PSPACE=*n* The horizontal spacing between panels. **Default** 4

SHOWALL Displays all columns.

SPACING=*n* The horizontal spacing between columns.

SPLIT='*char*' Splits column headings at this character. Also splits values if you use the FLOW item option. **Default** '/'

WRAP Wraps, if necessary, to display all columns together.

STYLE(*optional part*)=*style element and/or* {*attribute=value . . .* } ODS style of a part of the output. **Parts** CALLDEF COLUMN HEADER LINES REPORT SUMMARY ◯ 7+

CONTENTS='*text*' Link text for ODS table of contents. ◯ 7+

File and user interface options

REPORT=*entry* A REPT entry that is used to format the report.

NOALIAS Allows execution of a report that contains code segments that do not use aliases for variable names. ◯ 7+

LIST Writes the report definition in the log.

OUT=*SAS dataset* Writes an output SAS dataset based on the report, with rows as observations and columns as variables.

OUTREPT=*entry* Stores the report definition in this REPT entry.

NOEXEC Does not produce the report.

WINDOWS WD Opens the REPORT window for interactive report display or modification. PROMPT Opens the REPORT window and displays prompts. NOWINDOWS NOWD Does not open a window.

COMMAND Displays command lines instead of menu bars.

HELP=*catalog* The catalog that contains help entries, which can be CBT and/or HELP entries, for the report.

PROFILE=*catalog* The catalog that contains the REPORT profile in the entry REPORT.PROFILE. **Default** SASUSER.PROFILE

Statements

BY *variable*; Produces a separate report for each BY group. You cannot use this statement with the REPORT window or the OUT= option.

COLUMN *columns . . .* ; Defines the columns of the report.

BREAK BEFORE or AFTER *break variable / break options*; Defines break lines at the beginning or end of each group of observations formed by a value of the break variable. The break variable is a group variable or order variable.

BREAK BEFORE or AFTER / *break options*; Defines break lines at the beginning or end of the report.

DEFINE *item name / item options*; Defines characteristics of an item in the report. The item can be a variable, statistic, or alias.

COMPUTE *computed variable / type option*; *code segment* ENDCOMP; Code to execute to produce values for a computed variable column. **Type option** CHARACTER CHAR The computed variable is a character variable. The default type is numeric. LENGTH=*n* The length of the computed character variable. The default length is 8.

COMPUTE *location / options*; *code segment* ENDCOMP; Code to execute at the specified location in the report. The code segment can be used to compute variables or write break lines. **Locations** BEFORE or AFTER *break variable* At the beginning or end of each group of rows defined by the break variable (an order or group variable). BEFORE or AFTER _PAGE_ At the beginning or end of each page. ⏱ 7+ BEFORE *or* AFTER At the beginning or end of the report. **Options** STYLE=*style element and/or* {*attribute=value* . . . } ODS style of the code segment's output lines. ⏱ 7+ LEFT CENTER RIGHT Alignment of the output lines (for _PAGE_ only). ⏱ 7+

FREQ *variable*; The frequency variable.

WEIGHT *variable*; The weight variable.

Column definitions

variable A column that displays a variable.

statistic A column that displays a statistic (N or PCTN).

variable, statistic or statistic, variable A column that displays a statistic computed for a variable. Available statistics are the standard statistics, except SKEWNESS and KURTOSIS, plus PCT and PCTN.

column definition=alias Defines an alias for use in the DEFINE statement and any code segments.

(list), (list) Multiple columns that combine every item in the first list with every item in the second list.

('header' . . . column definitions) A header that spans multiple columns.

Break options

COLOR=*color* The color of text in the break line.

OL Overline. DOL Double overline.

PAGE Page break.

SKIP A blank line appears after the break lines.

SUMMARIZE A summary line that contains statistics and/or computed variables is written.

SUPPRESS The break variable is omitted from the summary line.

UL Underline. DUL Double underline.

STYLE=*style element and/or* {*attribute=value* . . . } ODS style of the summary line. ⏱ 7+

Item options

'header' . . . The column header. If the first and last characters are one of * + - . : = \ _ or are < and > they are repeated to fill the column width.

Usage: DISPLAY The variable is displayed as a column in the report. ORDER The variable determines the order of rows. GROUP The variable determines the order of rows and forms groups. The entire group is summarized and displayed as one row, if possible. ACROSS The variable forms groups. The entire group is summarized and displayed as a column. ANALYSIS Statistics are computed on the variable. COMPUTED A variable defined in a compute block.

statistic The statistic to be calculated for an analysis variable. The default statistic is SUM.

ORDER= How an order, group, or across variable is sorted: DATA In order of appearance in the input SAS dataset. INTERNAL In sorted order of values. FORMATTED In sorted order of formatted values. FREQ In order of frequency.

DESCENDING Reverses the sort order of an order, group, or across variable.

SPACING=*n*   The horizontal spacing to the left of the column.

WIDTH=*n*   The column width.

FORMAT=*format*

FLOW   Word wraps when values are longer than the width of the column (or splits at the split character, if present in the value).

Alignment of the item and its heading: LEFT   CENTER   RIGHT

COLOR=*color*

STYLE(*optional part*)=*style element and/or* {*attribute=value . . .* } ODS style of the item. **Parts** COLUMN   HEADER   ⟳ 7+

ITEMHELP=*entry name*   The name of the CBT or HELP entry that is used as a help window for the item.

NOPRINT   The column does not appear in the report.   NOZERO   The column appears only if it contains a nonzero, nonmissing value.

ID   The column and all columns to its left appear on every page of the report (useful when there are too many columns to fit on a page).

PAGE   The column starts on a new page.

Code segments

A compute block determines a sequence of actions to take a specific point in building the report. The COMPUTE statement indicates when the actions execute. The subsequent statements form a code segment that defines the actions. An ENDCOMP statement marks the end of the block. Code segments can contain the elements described below.

Variable references in a code segment

A column defined with an alias must use the alias as the variable name in a code segment.

variable   A group, order, display, or computed variable or a variable that is created in a code segment.

variable.statistic   An analysis variable.

_C*n*_   The value in column *n*. Use this form for columns that are headed by across variables.

COL   The column number of the computed variable.

BREAK   An automatic variable that contains: the value of the break variable, if any; RBREAK at the beginning or end of the report; PAGE at the beginning or end of a page; otherwise, blank.

A computed variable code segment can only use values that are associated with columns that appear to its left in the report and variables from previous code segments. You can compute code-segment variables in one or more code segments and then use them in a later code segment. The order of execution of the report and any code segments in it is from top to bottom and left to right.

Code segment statements

Data step statements: Assignment CALL   Comment   Null LENGTH   Sum DO, END   GOTO   IF-THEN, ELSE   LINK, RETURN   SELECT, WHEN, OTHERWISE, END

Global statement: DM

LINE *terms*;   Writes a line in the report. **Terms** @*n* @*variable* Moves the pointer to a column. +*n* +*variable* Advances the pointer by a number of column positions. *variable format* Writes the variable. '*string*' Writes the string. *n**'*string*' Writes the string *n* times.

CALL DEFINE(*location*, '*attribute*', *value*); Sets the value of an attribute. The change applies only to the current row.
Location *column name column number* _COL_
Attribute, value 'FORMAT', '*format*' For REPORT window: 'COLOR', '*color*' 'HIGHLIGHT' *or* 'BLINK' *or* 'RVSVIDEO', 1 *or* 0 'COMMAND', '*command string*' For ODS: 'STYLE', '*style element and/or* {*attribute=value . . .* }' 'URL', '*url*' ⟲ 7+

SORT

PROC SORT DATA=*SAS dataset options*;
BY *optional* DESCENDING *variable* . . . ;
Sorts the observations in a SAS dataset.

Options

OUT=*SAS dataset* The output SAS dataset. By default, the input SAS dataset is sorted in place.

DATECOPY Copies the file creation and modification dates of the input SAS dataset to the output SAS dataset. ⟲ 7+

FORCE Allows the use of options to delete variables and observations while sorting in place. Allows sorting in place of an indexed SAS dataset, and deletes all indexes except those required by integrity constraints.

Order of observations that have the same BY value: EQUALS The same order relative to each other. NOEQUALS No particular order.

NODUPKEY Does not write multiple observations with the same BY variable values to the output SAS dataset.

NODUPRECS NODUP Does not write consecutive identical observations to the output SAS dataset.

DUPOUT=*SAS dataset* An output SAS dataset for duplicate observations. ⟲ 9.1+

REVERSE Reverses the sort order of character variables.

Optional collating sequences: ASCII EBCDIC NORWEGIAN DANISH SWEDISH FINNISH NATIONAL SORTSEQ=*sequence*

SORTSIZE=*n or n*K *or* MAX Limits the use of memory for sorting.

TAGSORT Uses a tag sort algorithm: sorting the BY variables first, then the rest of the variables. This is sometimes more efficient.

OVERWRITE Deletes the input SAS dataset before replacing it with the sorted output. ⟲ 9.1+

THREADS Enables multithreading to increase multiprocessor performance. NOTHREADS Prevents multithreading. ⟲ 9+

Example

This step creates a sorted copy of the SAS dataset US, called USSORT:

```
PROC SORT DATA=US OUT=USSORT;
  BY ASTROLOGICALSIGN;
RUN;
```

SQL

PROC SQL *options*;
SQL statements, RESET statements, and global statements
Executes SQL statements.

Essential SQL terms

Table: SAS data file. Row: observation. Column: variable.

Options

DQUOTE= Values in double quotes are: ANSI Names. SAS Character constants. ◌ 7+

After an SQL error: ERRORSTOP Stops executing SQL statements. NOERRORSTOP Continues execution with the next statement.

EXEC Executes SQL statements. NOEXEC Checks SQL syntax only.

FEEDBACK Displays expanded statements. NOFEEDBACK Does not display expanded statements.

PRINT The results of the SELECT statement are printed. NOPRINT The SELECT statement is executed, but its results are not printed.

NUMBER The SELECT statement generates a column ROW with row numbers. NONUMBER The SELECT statement does not use row numbers.

SORTMSG NOSORTMSG Whether to write log messages about sorting. ◌ 7+

SORTSEQ=*collating sequence* The collating sequence for an ORDER BY clause.

FLOW FLOW=*n* FLOW=*n* *n₂* NOFLOW Controls text flow of character columns that are wider than *n*.

DOUBLE Double-spaces print output. NODOUBLE Single-spaces. This is the default.

INOBS=*n* Limits the number of rows that are used from any one input source in a statement.

LOOPS=*n* Limits the repetitions of the innermost SQL loop.

OUTOBS=*n* Limits the number of output rows in any statement or expression.

PROMPT Prompts the interactive user when the INOBS=, OUTOBS=, or LOOPS= limit is reached. NOPROMPT Stops executing when the limit is reached. This is the default.

Measures and reports elapsed time of: STIMER Each SQL statement separately. NOSTIMER The step as a whole.

THREADS Enables multithreading to increase multiprocessor performance. NOTHREADS Prevents multithreading. ◌ 9+

UNDO_POLICY=NONE *or* OPTIONAL *or* REQUIRED The recovery strategy when errors occur in table updates.

Statements

RESET *options*; Changes options.

query expression optional ORDER BY *column*, . . . ; SELECT statement: prints the results of a query.

VALIDATE *query expression*; Checks the syntax of a query expression.

CREATE TABLE *table* (*column definition*, . . . , *optional integrity rule*, . . .);   CREATE TABLE *table* LIKE *table*;   Creates a new table with no rows.

CREATE TABLE *table* AS *query expression option*;   Creates a new table. **Option** ORDER BY *column*, . . .   Sort order.

CREATE VIEW *view* AS *query expression options*;   Creates a new view. **Options** ORDER BY *column*, . . .   Sort order. USING *LIBNAME statement*, . . .   Defines librefs for the view only. The LIBNAME statements are stored in the view and are used every time you access the view. See the LIBNAME statement in chapter 4. ☉ 7+

CREATE *option* INDEX *index* ON *table* (*column*, . . .);   Creates an index. **Option** UNIQUE

DESCRIBE VIEW *view*, . . . ;   Describes an SQL view.

DESCRIBE TABLE *table*, . . . ;   Describes a table.

DESCRIBE TABLE CONSTRAINTS *table*, . . . ;   Lists the integrity constraints of a table. ☉ 7+

DROP TABLE *table*, . . . ;   Deletes tables.

DROP VIEW *view*, . . . ;   Deletes views.

DROP INDEX *index*, . . . FROM *table*;   Deletes indexes.

ALTER TABLE *table action*;   Modifies a table. **Actions** ADD *column definition*, . . .   Adds columns. MODIFY *column definition*, . . .   Changes column attributes. DROP *column*, . . .   Drops columns. ADD CONSTRAINT *integrity constraint rule message option*   Creates (adds) an integrity constraint. See the DATASETS procedure for integrity rules, but omit WHERE= when writing a CHECK rule. DROP CONSTRAINT *integrity constraint*   Deletes (drops) an integrity constraint.

DELETE FROM *table* WHERE *expression*;   Conditionally deletes rows from a table. DELETE FROM *table*;   Deletes all rows.

INSERT INTO *table or table*(*column*, . . .) SET *column=expression*, ... *or* VALUES (*value*, . . .) . . . *or query expression*;   Adds rows to a table.

UPDATE *table* SET *column=expression*, ... *optional* WHERE *expression*;   Changes the values in a table.

In addition to tables, you can apply the DELETE, INSERT, and UPDATE statements to most SQL views (but not those with an ORDER BY clause) and many SAS/ACCESS views. ☉ 7+

Message options for integrity constraints

MESSAGE="*message*"   Message text displayed when a data change violates the constraint. NEWLINE   Displays the message text on a separate line. USER   Does not display the default message. ☉ 9+

DBMS statements ☉ SAS/ACCESS

CONNECT TO *DBMS optional* AS *alias* (*arguments*);   Opens a connection to a database.

DISCONNECT FROM *DBMS or alias*;   Closes a connection. (Otherwise, the connection is closed at the end of the step.)

EXECUTE (*statement*) BY *DBMS or alias*;   Sends a statement or command to a connected database for execution.

Essential SQL components (simplified)

column definition: name type optional (width) optional attributes
type: NUMERIC, CHARACTER, etc. *attributes:* INFORMAT= . . . ,
FORMAT= . . . , LABEL= . . .

query expression: SELECT *column, . . .* FROM *table or view or*
CONNECTION TO *DBMS or alias (query expression) etc. optional*
WHERE *expression*

Examples

These SQL statements create tables that contain data from the table
ORIGINAL:

```
CREATE TABLE COPY AS SELECT * FROM ORIGINAL;
CREATE TABLE SUBSET AS
    SELECT * FROM ORIGINAL
    WHERE SELECT = 'Y';
```

This SQL statement creates a simple index on the variable NAME in
the table PRODUCT.MASTER:

```
CREATE INDEX NAME ON PRODUCT.MASTER(NAME);
```

This SQL statement prints selected data from the table
PRODUCT.MASTER:

```
SELECT NAME, LIST, ORIGINAL, SALE, CLERNC FROM
PRODUCT.MASTER
WHERE CLERNC IS NOT MISSING AND
CLERNC < .50*ORIGINAL
ORDER BY NAME;
```

STANDARD

PROC STANDARD DATA=*SAS dataset* OUT=*SAS dataset options*;
VAR *variables*;
optional statements

Standardizes numeric variables: converts them to a stated mean or
standard deviation or replaces missing values with the mean value.

Options

MEAN *or* M=*number* Converts the variables to this mean.

STD *or* S=*number* Converts the variables to this standard deviation.

REPLACE Replaces missing values with mean values.

PRINT Prints the mean and standard deviation.

VARDEF=N *or* DF *or* WEIGHT *or* WGT *or* WDF

EXCLNPWGT Disregards (excludes) observations that have nonpositive weight values. ○ 7+

Statements

VAR *variables*; Standardizes these variables.

FREQ *variables*; The frequency variable.

WEIGHT *variables*; The weight variable.

Example

PROC STANDARD DATA=MODEL OUT=MMODEL REPLACE;

RUN;

SUMMARY

PROC SUMMARY DATA=*SAS dataset options statistics*;
optional statements

Computes descriptive statistics and frequencies of variables in a SAS dataset.

Options

PRINT Prints descriptive statistics. This is the default for the MEANS procedure. NOPRINT Does not produce print output. This is the default for the SUMMARY procedure.

MISSING Includes missing class variable values.

NWAY Includes only the highest _TYPE_ value in the output.
DESCENDING DESCEND DESCENDTYPES Orders output by descending _TYPE_ value.

COMPLETETYPES Creates all class combinations, even those not present in the input data. ○ 7+

CLASSDATA=*SAS dataset* Class combination dataset. All class combinations found in this SAS dataset appear in the output. ○ 7+

EXCLUSIVE Uses only the class combinations of the class combination dataset. ○ 7+

IDMIN Uses the minimum ID value, instead of the maximum.

FW=*n* The width of printed statistic values.

NONOBS Does not print the N Obs column of the number of observations in each class group. ○ 7+

PRINTIDVARS PRINTIDS Prints ID variables. ○ 7+

PRINTALLTYPES PRINTALL Prints all class variable combinations. The WAYS or TYPES statement overrides this option. ○ 7+

MAXDEC=*n* The maximum number of decimal places printed.

ORDER= The order of output class values: DATA Their order of appearance in the input data. INTERNAL Sorted. FORMATTED Sorted order of the formatted values. FREQ Descending order of frequency.

VARDEF=N *or* DF *or* WEIGHT *or* WGT *or* WDF

EXCLNPWGT Disregards (excludes) observations that have nonpositive weight values. ○ 7+

CHARTYPE Makes the output _TYPE_ variable a character variable that contains a binary numeral of the type value (or a pseudoarray in which the 1 or 0 in each character position indicates the involvement of the corresponding class variable). ○ 7+

ALPHA=*number* Sets the confidence level used by the confidence level statistics CLM, LCLM, and UCLM.

PCTLDEF *or* QNTLDEF=1 *or* 2 *or* 3 *or* 4 *or* 5 Mathematical definition of percentiles.

QMARKERS=*n* The number of markers to use when using the fixed space method to estimate quantiles. ○ 7+

QMETHOD= Method for calculating quantiles: OS Order statistics. P2 Fixed space estimation. ○ 7+

SUMSIZE=*n* Overrides the system option. ○ 7+

THREADS   Enables multithreading to increase multiprocessor performance.   NOTHREADS   Prevents multithreading.   ○ 9.1+

NOTRAP   Does not attempt to recover from floating point exception errors.   ○ 7+

Additional statistics

CLM   LCLM   UCLM   Confidence limit for the mean.

quantiles   QRANGE   ○ 7+

Statements

CLASS *variables / options*;   Class variables: forms groups according to the values of these variables.   **Options** MISSING   Includes missing class variable values.   GROUPINTERNAL   Forms class combinations of the internal (unformatted) values of class variables.   ORDER=DATA INTERNAL   FORMATTED   FREQ   DESCENDING   The order of output class values.   PRELOADFMT   Refers to the formats of the class variables when determining class combinations.   EXCLUSIVE   Uses only class variable values that are found in their formats.   ○ 7+   MLF Uses both primary and secondary labels to define groups when using a multilabel format.   ○ 8+

WAYS *n or range* . . . ; $0 \le n \le$ number of class variables   Forms all combinations of *n* class variables. You can optionally use commas between terms.   **Ranges** *n*   *n* TO *n*   *n* TO *n* BY *n*   ○ 7+

TYPES *combination* . . . ;   Specifies class combinations (in addition to any formed by the WAYS statement).   **Combinations** ()   Overall total.   *variable*variable* . . .   A specific combination of variables.   (*variable variable* . . .)* . . .   Uses each variable listed between the parentheses to form combinations.   ○ 7+

ID *variables*;   Also includes these variables in the output.

VAR *variables / option*;   Analysis variables: the proc computes statistics for these variables.   **Option** WEIGHT=*variable*   The weight variable for these analysis variables.   ○ 7+

FREQ *variable*;   The frequency variable.

WEIGHT *variable*;   The weight variable.

OUTPUT OUT=*SAS dataset   variable definitions / options*;   Creates an output SAS dataset, with one observation for each combination of CLASS variable values.

OUTPUT statement variable definitions

statistic=   Creates variables of this statistic for the VAR variables, with the same names.

statistic=*new variables*   Creates variables of this statistic for the VAR variables, with the new names indicated.

statistic(*variables*)=   Creates variables of this statistic for selected VAR variables, with the same names.

statistic(*variables*)=*new variables*   Creates variables of this statistic for selected VAR variables, with the new names indicated.

MAXID(*variable* (*ID variables*) . . .)=*new variables*   Creates variables that show the value of ID variables in the observation that has the maximum value of the indicated analysis variable.

MINID(*variable* (*ID variables*) . . .)=*new variables* Creates variables that show the value of ID variables in the observation that has the minimum value of the indicated analysis variable.

IDGROUP(*criteria options* OUT *optional n* (*variables*)=*optional new variables*) Creates output variables from the values of variables in extreme observations. **Criteria** MIN *or* MAX(*variables*) Selects observations based on the minimum or maximum value of these variables. You can specify any number of MIN and MAX criteria; a subsequent criterion is used if multiple observations meet the preceding criteria. The default or tie-breaking criterion is to select the first observation. **Options** MISSING Considers missing values. OBS Creates an output variable _OBS_ (or using _OBS_ as a prefix with a numeric suffix to form a variable name) with the observation number. LAST Selects the last observation, rather than the first, as the default or tie-breaking criterion. *n* Selects *n* extreme observations and creates *n* times as many variables (using numeric suffixes to create distinct output variable names). ○ 7+

OUTPUT statement options

INHERIT Output statistic variables take attributes from the analysis variables they are created from. ○ 7+

NOINHERIT Output statistic variables do not take attributes from the analysis variables they are created from. ○ 8+

AUTONAME Automatically generates names for output variables when names are not specified. Automatically changes output variable names to avoid creating multiple variables with the same name. ○ 7+

AUTOLABEL Combines the variable label or name and the statistic name to create the label for each output variable. ○ 8+

KEEPLEN Output statistic variables take their lengths from the analysis variables they are created from. ○ 8+

LEVELS Creates the numeric output variable _LEVEL_ that contains a generated serial number for each class combination within each value of _TYPE_. ○ 7+

WAYS Creates the numeric output variable _WAY_ that indicates how many class variables were combined. ○ 7+

Example

This step creates the SAS dataset CARTOTAL, with totals from the SAS dataset CARS:

```
PROC SUMMARY DATA=CARS NWAY;
   CLASS CAR;
   ID MAKE MODEL MODELYR;
   VAR MILEAGE DEPR;
   OUTPUT OUT=CARTOTAL SUM=;
RUN;
```

TABULATE
PROC TABULATE DATA=*SAS dataset   options*;
optional statements
TABLE *request / options*; . . .

Prints tables of descriptive statistics and frequencies of variables in a SAS dataset.

Options

MISSING CLASSDATA= EXCLUSIVE ORDER= VARDEF= EXCLNPWGT ALPHA= ○ 9+ PCTLDEF *or* QNTLDEF= QMARKERS= QMETHOD= NOTRAP THREADS ○ 9.1+ See the SUMMARY procedure for details.

TRAP Traps overflow errors. ○ 8+

FORMAT=*format* The default format for cells. **Default** 12.2

FORMCHAR(*index . . .*)='*chars*' FORMCHAR='*chars*' Overrides characters of the FORMCHAR= system option.

NOSEPS Suppresses horizontal rules between rows.

OUT=*SAS dataset* Creates an output SAS dataset. ○ 7+

STYLE=*style element or* PARENT *and/or* {*attribute=value . . .* } ODS style of the data cells. ○ 7+

CONTENTS=*name* Name of the ODS table of contents link to the first output table. ○ 8+

Statements

CLASS *variables / options*; Class variables: forms groups according to the values of these variables. **Options** MISSING GROUPINTERNAL ORDER= PRELOADFMT EXCLUSIVE MLF See the SUMMARY procedure for details. STYLE= ODS style of class variable labels. ○ 7+

CLASSLEV *variables* / STYLE=. . . ; ODS style of class values. ○ 7+

VAR *variables / options*; Analysis variables. **Options** WEIGHT=*variable* Weight variable. STYLE= ODS style of analysis variable labels. ○ 7+

FREQ *variable*; The frequency variable.

WEIGHT *variable*; The weight variable.

KEYWORD *statistics* / STYLE=. . . ; ODS style of statistic labels. ○ 7+

KEYLABEL *statistic*='*label*' . . . ; Substitutes a label for a statistic name.

TABLE *table expression / table options*; Defines the table.

Table expression

The columns, rows, and pages of a table are defined by a table expression, which consists of up to three dimension expressions that are separated by commas:

column expression
row expression, column expression
page expression, row expression, column expression

A dimension expression is made up of combinations of these elements:

ALL *class variable analysis variable statistic*
='*label*' F=*format* STYLE=. . .
(*element element . . .*) *element*element*

Joining two elements with an asterisk indicates that the elements are combined and form different levels in the table definition.

The dimension expressions are combined to form the table. The combination that forms any cell can include any number of class variables, but no more than one analysis variable and one statistic. The FORMAT_PRECEDENCE= and STYLE_PRECEDENCE= table options determine the results for cells that have multiple formats and styles.

Dimension elements

ALL   Unclassified summary.

class variable   Classes of a class variable.

analysis variable   Applies a statistic to this analysis variable.

statistic   Applies this statistic to an analysis variable.

N   A frequency count, if not combined with an analysis variable.

='*label*'   Label for a variable or statistic element.

F=*format*   Format for cell values.

STYLE(*optional part*)=*style element or* PARENT *and/or* {*attribute=value* . . . }   ODS style. (Precede with = to associate the style with a specific variable.) **Part** CLASSLEV   Class values. ⟳ 7+

(*element element* . . .)   Consecutive elements. Each element has the same level of heading.

element*element . . .   Combines elements. Later elements have lower-level headings under the headings for the earlier elements.

Statistics

The standard statistics and:

quantiles   QRANGE ⟳ 7+

PCTN<*denominator*>   A percent of a frequency.

PCTSUM<*denominator*>   A percent of a sum.

COLPCTN   ROWPCTN   PAGEPCTN   REPPCTN   A percent of a frequency. ⟳ 8+

COLPCTSUM   ROWPCTSUM   PAGEPCTSUM   REPPCTSUM   A percent of a sum. ⟳ 8+

CLM   LCLM   UCLM   Confidence limit for the mean. ⟳ 9+

Table options

CONDENSE   Combines pages, when possible.

STYLE=. . .   ODS style for the table. ⟳ 7+

CONTENTS=*name*   Name of the ODS table of contents link to the output table. ⟳ 8+

FUZZ=ε   Numbers closer to 0 than this are treated as zero values.

FORMAT_PRECEDENCE=*dimension*   STYLE_PRECEDENCE=*dimension* Uses the format and style indicated for the specified dimension in the table expression. **Dimensions** PAGE   ROW   COLUMN   COL ⟳ 9.1+

MISSTEXT='*string*'   MISSTEXT={LABEL='*string*' STYLE=. . . }   Text for cells that contain missing values.

PRINTMISS   Forms all class combinations, even empty ones.

ROW=CONSTANT *or* CONST   Row title space is divided among all row levels.   ROW=FLOAT   Row title space is divided among nonblank title elements.

RTSPACE *or* RTS=*n*   The size of the row title space.

INDENT=*n* Changes the format of nested row titles to use only one column, omit class variable labels, and indent lower-level row titles *n* characters.

BOX=*contents* BOX={LABEL=*contents* STYLE=. . . } The upper left corner box. **Contents** '*string*' The string. _PAGE_ The page dimension text. *variable* The variable's name or label.

NOCONTINUED Does not print a continuation message at the bottom of the page in a multi-page table.

Example
```
PROC TABULATE DATA=ELECTION MISSING;
  CLASS STATE CANDIDAT;
  VAR VOTES;
  TABLE STATE ALL,
    CANDIDAT*VOTES^(SUM^F=10. PCTSUM<STATE ALL>);
  LABEL CANDIDAT='CANDIDATE' VOTES='Votes';
  KEYLABEL SUM='Count' PCTSUM='Percent';
RUN;
```

TAPELABEL ♂ z
PROC TAPELABEL DDNAME=*fileref*;
Prints information from a standard tape label.

TEMPLATE
PROC TEMPLATE;
optional statements
Creates and edits ODS style and table definitions. ♂ 8+

Statements
DEFINE *type path* / *optional* STORE=*template store*; *secondary statements* END; Creates a definition. **Type** STYLE TABLE COLUMN HEADER FOOTER TAGSET ♂ 9+

EDIT *path optional* AS *path* / *optional* STORE=*template store*; *secondary statements* END; Edits a definition.

DELETE *path* / *optional* STORE=*template store*; Deletes a definition or a directory.

PATH *template store* (*optional access mode*) . . . ; Sets the search order. This statement overrides the setting of the ODS PATH statement. **Access modes** READ WRITE UPDATE

LIST *optional path* / *options*; Writes a list of definitions. **Options** STORE=*template store* SORT=*statistic optional sort order* Sorts the list. STATS=(*statistic*, . . .) *or* ALL Includes these columns in the list. **Statistics for sorting only** TYPE Type. PATH Path. **Statistics** NOTES LABEL Notes stored with the definition. SIZE Size. CREATED Creation date. LINK The definition that the definition links to. **Sort order** ASCENDING A DESCENDING D

SOURCE *path* / *options*; Decompiles the definition and writes the resulting source code to the log or to the indicated output file. **Options** NOFOLLOW Does not resolve links. STORE=*template store* FILE=*output file*

TEST DATA=*SAS dataset* / *optional* STORE=*template store*; Tests the last definition with the indicated SAS dataset.

Secondary statements

For any type: *attribute*=, NOTES

For STYLE: STYLE, REPLACE

For TABLE: COLUMN, HEADER, FOOTER, TRANSLATE, DYNAMIC, CELLSTYLE, MVAR, NMVAR, DEFINE

For COLUMN: COMPUTE AS, TRANSLATE, DYNAMIC, CELLSTYLE, MVAR, NMVAR, DEFINE

For HEADER or FOOTER: DYNAMIC, MVAR, NMVAR, TEXT, TEXT2, TEXT3

For TAGSET: DEFAULT_EVENT, DEFINE EVENT, tagset attributes (see chapter 11)

attribute=*value*; Sets an attribute.

NOTES '*notes*'; Stores notes in the definition.

STYLE *name* *optional* FROM *parent style element* *optional* '*notes*' / *attribute*=*value* . . . ; Defines a style element.

REPLACE *name* *optional* FROM *parent style element* *optional* '*notes*' / *attribute*=*value* . . . ; Defines a style element that replaces a style element of the parent style definition for the purpose of inheritance in creating the current style definition.

COLUMN *column* . . . ; Indicates the selection and arrangement of columns in the table. **Columns** *column* A column definition nested inside the table definition. *path* A separate column definition. *variable* *variable list* Variables from the SAS dataset. (*column* . . .) Arranges multiple data elements in a single column. (*column* . . .)*(*column* . . .) Places the data elements of the second list in the columns of the data elements of the first list. **Default** The default is to use all the nested column definitions as columns.

HEADER *header* . . . ; Indicates the selection and sequence (from top to bottom) of headers above the table. **Headers** "*text*" Header text, with line breaks at the split character. If the SPLIT= attribute is not in effect, and the first character of the text is not a space, letter, or digit, it is used as the split character. _LABEL_ The label of the output object. *header* A header definition nested inside the table definition. *path* A separate header definition.

FOOTER *footer* . . . ; Indicates the selection and sequence (from top to bottom) of footers below the table. **Footers** "*text*" Footer text, with line breaks at the split character. If the SPLIT= attribute is not in effect, and the first character of the text is not a space, letter, or digit, it is used as the split character. _LABEL_ The label of the output object. *footer* A footer definition nested inside the table definition. *path* A separate footer definition.

COMPUTE AS *expression*; Computes a value for the column.

CELLSTYLE *condition* AS *style element and/or* [*attribute*=*value* . . .], . . . ; Conditionally applies styles to column values. The style is applied for the first true condition in the statement. In a table definition, this statement applies only to numeric columns.

TRANSLATE *condition* INTO *character expression*, . . . ; Conditionally substitutes a character value for the value of a column. The INTO expression is applied for the first true condition in the statement. This substitution takes the place of the format that would otherwise be applied to translate the value to text. In a table definition, this statement applies only to numeric columns.

DYNAMIC *variable optional* 'notes' ... ; Makes variables available for use in expressions in the definition and in any nested definitions.

MVAR *macro variable name optional* 'notes' ... ; Makes macro variables available for use as character variables in expressions in the definition and in any nested definitions.

NMVAR *macro variable name optional* 'notes' ... ; Makes macro variables, converted to numeric values, available for use as numeric variables in expressions in the definition and in any nested definitions.

TEXT *value* ... ; The text of the header or footer. **Values** _LABEL_ The label of the output object. 'text' The constant value. *variable optional format* The value of a variable from a DYNAMIC, MVAR, or NMVAR statement.

TEXT2 *value* ... ; Alternative text for the header or footer if the text of the TEXT statement is too long.

TEXT3 *value* ... ; Alternative text for the header or footer if the text of the TEXT2 statement is too long.

DEFINE EVENT *name; secondary statements* END; Defines an event.

DEFAULT_EVENT='*event*'; This event executes when a requested event is not in the tagset.

Expressions

These rules apply to CELLSTYLE and TRANSLATE conditions and the INTO expression of a TRANSLATE statement. Use the special variable name _VAL_ to get the value of the current column. Otherwise, you cannot refer to values of table columns. You can use names declared in DYNAMIC, MVAR, and NMVAR statements. You can use WHERE operators.

The COMPUTE AS expression uses the same rules, except that you can use the names of columns as part of the expression, and you cannot use the special name _VAL_.

Secondary statements for DEFINE EVENT

STYLE=*style element*; Applies a style.

event action / optional event condition; Applies the action if the condition is true.

FILE=*page*; Directs output to a specific page. **Pages** BODY CONTENTS PAGES FRAME CODE STYLESHEET

PURE_STYLE=YES *or* NO; Whether to allow the use of any style element.

Event actions

PUT *items* Writes output.

PUTL Writes a new line to the output.

PUTLOG *items* Writes a log message.

PUTQ *items* Writes output as a quoted string.

FLUSH Writes any buffered output.

BREAK Ends execution of the event.

NDENT Adds one level of indentation.

XDENT   Subtracts one level of indentation.

SET $*event variable value*   Assigns the value to the variable.

UNSET $*event variable* or ALL   Removes the variable or all previously defined variables.

TRIGGER *event optional event part*   Executes another event.
Event parts START   FINISH

BLOCK *event*   Blocks the event. The event is inactive until a subsequent UNBLOCK action.

UNBLOCK *event*   Unblocks the event.

OPEN *stream*   Opens or creates the stream.

PUTSTREAM *stream*   Writes the stream to the output file.

CLOSE   Closes the current stream and redirects output to the output file.

DELSTREAM *stream*   Deletes the stream.

Output items

'*text*'   A character constant.

event variable   A variable.

'*text*'   *event variable*   A text/variable pair, written only if the variable has a value.

Event conditions

ANY(*variable, variable, . . .*)   Tests whether any of the variables has a value.

CMP('*string*', *variable, . . .*)   Tests whether the string matches the variable(s).

CONTAINS(*string, substring*)   Test whether the string contains the substring.

EXIST(*variable, . . .*)   Tests whether all the variables have values.
Alias EXISTS

NOT *condition*   The negative of the condition.

IF *condition*   WHEN *condition*   The same as *condition*.

TIMEPLOT

PROC TIMEPLOT DATA=*SAS dataset options*;
optional statements
PLOT *plot requests / plot options*;

Plots variables in a sequence, with one row for each observation or group of observations.

Options

MAXDEC=*n*   The maximum number of decimal positions to print.

UNIFORM   Uses the same horizontal scale for all BY groups.

SPLIT='*char*'   Uses variable labels and splits column headings wherever this character appears in the label. ⑤ 9+

Statements

CLASS *variables*;   Variables that define groups of observations. The input SAS dataset should be grouped by the class variables. Instead of printing one row for each observation, the PLOT statements print one row for each class group. If a symbol variable is not used, only the first observation in the class group is plotted.

ID *variables*; Additional variables to be printed.

PLOT *plot requests / plot options*; Defines one or more plots.

Plot requests

variable The first character of the variable name is the plotting symbol.

variable or (variables) = 'symbol' or symbol variable The first nonblank character of the symbol constant or formatted symbol variable is the plotting symbol.

Plot options

AXIS=*value, value, . . .* AXIS=*start* TO *stop* BY *interval* Defines the horizontal axis.

JOINREF Connects the leftmost plotting or reference symbol in a line to the rightmost plotting or reference symbol with hyphens, unless the line does not contain any plotting symbols. HILOC Connects the leftmost plotting symbol to the rightmost plotting symbol with hyphens.

NOSYMNAME Does not print the name of the symbol variable if there is a CLASS statement.

NPP Does not print the value of the plotted variables.

OVERLAY Puts the entire PLOT statement on one plot.

OVPCHAR='*char*' The character that is printed when plotting symbols overlap. **Default** '@'

POS=*n* The plot width.

REF=*numbers* Prints reference symbols at the points specified on each line. REF=MEAN(*variables*) Prints reference symbols on each line at the point that represents the mean of each variable.

REFCHAR='*symbol*' The reference symbol. **Default** '|'

REVERSE Arranges the axis in descending order.

TRANSPOSE

PROC TRANSPOSE DATA=*SAS dataset* OUT=*SAS dataset options*; *optional statements*

Transposes: converts observations to variables and variables to observations. If you use a BY statement, BY groups are transposed separately.

Options

PREFIX=*prefix* The prefix for output variable names if you do not use an ID statement.

LET Allows duplicate ID values.

NAME=*variable* The name for the output variable that contains the input variable names. **Default** _NAME_

LABEL=*variable* The name for the output variable that contains the input variable labels. **Default** _LABEL_

Statements

VAR *variables*; These variables are transposed. By default, numeric variables not named in other statements are transposed.

COPY *variables*;   These variables are copied without transposing.

ID *variable*;   The input variable that forms output variable names.

IDLABEL *or* IDL *variable*;   The input variable that forms output variable labels.

Examples

This step converts the variable TEMP to a separate variable for each different value of MONTH in the input SAS dataset:

```
PROC TRANSPOSE DATA=AREATEMP OUT=AREAMON;
BY TOWN;
ID MONTH;
VAR TEMP;
RUN;
```

If there is only one observation in each BY group in the SAS dataset AREAMON, the step below converts the numeric variables in that SAS dataset to the variable TEMP1. The number of output observations per BY group is determined by the number of numeric variables.

```
PROC TRANSPOSE DATA=AREAMON OUT=AREATOWN
NAME=MONTH PREFIX=TEMP;
BY TOWN;
RUN;
```

TRANTAB

PROC TRANTAB TABLE=*name option*;
optional statements
Loads a translation table for editing. (Run-group)

Option

NLS   Loads one of the SAS System internal translation tables: SASXPT, SASLCL, SASUCS, SASLCS, or SASCCL.

Statements

LOAD TABLE=*name option*;   Loads a translation table for editing.
Option NLS

LIST *area option*;   Writes the translation table in the log, using hexadecimal notation.

CLEAR *area option*;   Sets all positions in the translation table to zero.

INVERSE;   Inverts area one, the device-to-host area of the translation table, to create area two, the host-to-device area of the translation table.

SWAP;   Exchanges areas one and two of the translation table. To edit area two, use the SWAP statement, one or more REPLACE statements, and another SWAP statement.

REPLACE *position value(s)*;   Sets position(s) in the translation table, beginning at the indicated position, with the indicated value(s). The position can be a number from 0 to 255 or a character in the table. The values can be numbers from 0 to 255, characters, and/or character strings.

SAVE *area option*; SAVE TABLE=*name area option*; Stores the edited translation table.

Area options ONE Area one; the device-to-host area of the translation table. TWO Area two; the host-to-device area of the translation table. BOTH Both areas.

UNIVARIATE
PROC UNIVARIATE DATA=*SAS dataset options*;
optional statements
Computes statistics for individual variables.

Options for computation
EXCLNPWGT Disregards (excludes) observations that have nonpositive weight values. ⊙ 7+

VARDEF=N *or* DF *or* WEIGHT *or* WGT *or* WDF

ROUND=*number* . . . Variable values are rounded before processing. Use either one roundoff number or a separate one for each variable in the VAR statement. **Default** 0

PCTLDEF=1 *or* 2 *or* 3 *or* 4 *or* 5 Mathematical definition of percentiles.

Options for statistical measures and output
FREQ A frequency table.

MODES A table of modes. ⊙ 7+

NEXTROBS=*n* Number of observations in the list of extreme observations. **Default** 5 NEXTRVAL=*n* Number of distinct values in the list of extreme values. **Default** 0 ⊙ 7+

NORMAL NORMALTEST Tests for normal distribution.

ROBUSTSCALE Table of robust estimators of scale. ⊙ 7+

PLOTS PLOT Plots. PLOTSIZE=*n* Size of plots. NOBYPLOT Does not produce the side-by-side BY-group box plots. ⊙ 7+

CIBASIC Confidence interval for normal mean and standard deviation. TYPE=TWOSIDED LOWER UPPER Type of confidence limit. ALPHA=*x* $0 < x \leq .5$ Confidence level. ⊙ 7+

CIPCTLDF CIQUANTDF Nonparametric (distribution-free) confidence intervals for percentiles. TYPE=SYMMETRIC ASYMMETRIC LOWER UPPER Type of confidence limit. ALPHA=*x* $0 < x \leq .5$ Confidence level. ⊙ 7+

CIPCTLNORMAL CIQUANTNORMAL Normal confidence intervals for percentiles. TYPE=TWOSIDED LOWER UPPER Type of confidence limit. ALPHA=*x* $0 < x \leq .5$ Confidence level. ⊙ 7+

LOCCOUNT A frequency table of comparison to μ_0. ⊙ 7+

MU0=μ_0 , . . . The null-hypothesis mean or center value. Use either one value or a separate one for each variable in the VAR statement. **Default** 0 ⊙ 7+

TRIMMED=*n or x*, . . . $0 < x \leq .5$ Table of trimmed means after trimming *n* observations or the indicated fractional proportion of the observations. Indicate either one value or a separate one for each variable in the VAR statement. TYPE=TWOSIDED LOWER UPPER Location to trim. ALPHA=*x* $0 < x \leq .5$ Confidence level. ⊙ 7+

WINSOR=*n or x*, . . . 0 < *x* ≤ .5 Table of Winsorized means after replacing *n* extreme observations or the indicated fractional proportion of the observations with the value of the next less extreme observation. Indicate either one value or a separate one for each variable in the VAR statement. TYPE=TWOSIDED LOWER UPPER Location to substitute less extreme observations. ALPHA=*x* 0 < *x* ≤ .5 Confidence level. ↻ 7+

ALL The output of the options FREQ MODES NEXTRVAL=5 PLOT CIBASIC CIPCTLDF CIPCTLNORMAL. ↻ 7+

NOPRINT Suppresses all print output.

Graphics: GOUT=*catalog* ANNOTATE=*SAS dataset* ↻ 8+

Statements

VAR *variables*; Analysis variables. Statistics are computed for these variables.

ID *variables*; Additional variables that are copied to the output SAS dataset and printed in the table of extreme observations.

FREQ *variable*; The frequency variable.

WEIGHT *variable*; The weight variable.

OUTPUT OUT=*SAS dataset options*; Defines an output SAS dataset, which contains one observation per BY group (or only one observation if there is no BY statement).

OUTPUT statement options

statistic=variables Names output variables that contain the indicated statistic for the analysis variables. Provide one variable name for each analysis variable. In addition to the usual statistics, these statistics can be used: MEDIAN Q1 Q3 QRANGE P1 P5 P10 P90 P95 P99 MODE GINI MAD QN SN STD_GINI STD_MAD STD_QN STD_QRANGE STD_SN NORMAL PROBN MSIGN PROBM SIGNRANK PROBS T PROBT

PCTLPTC=*number* . . . 0 ≤ *number* ≤ 100 Creates variables that contain the indicated percentiles for the analysis variables.

PCTLPRE=*prefixes* Defines prefixes used to create variable names for percentiles. Provide one prefix for each analysis variable.

PCTLNAME=*suffixes* Defines suffixes used in place of the percentile numbers to create variable names for percentiles.

Statements for graphics output

CLASS *variable (variable options) optional variable (variable options) / option*; One or two class variable for use in comparative plots in the HISTOGRAM, PROBPLOT, or QQPLOT statements. **Option** KEYLEVEL=*value or value value* Identifying value(s) for the class group (level) that determines the axis for the comparative plot. ↻ 8+

HISTOGRAM *variables / distribution(distribution options) . . . appearance options*; Produces a histogram. **Alias** HIST ↻ 8+

PROBPLOT *variables / distribution(distribution options) . . . appearance options*; Produces a probability plot. ↻ 8+

QQPLOT *variables / distribution(distribution options) . . . appearance options*; Produces a quantile-quantile plot. ↻ 8+

INSET *inset statistic options   distribution(distribution options)
/ inset appearance options*;   Adds a statistical table inset to the
graphics output of the preceding statement. ⟳ 8+

Class variable options

MISSING   Considers missing values of the variable.

ORDER=   Values are displayed in order determined by: INTERNAL
Values. FORMATTED Formatted values. DATA Order of appearance in the input data. FREQ Descending frequency.

Distributions

BETA   Beta. **Options** ALPHA=*x* BETA=*x* SIGMA=*x* THETA=*x*

EXPONENTIAL   Exponential. **Options** SIGMA=*x* THETA=*x*

GAMMA   Gamma. **Options** ALPHA=*x* SIGMA=*x* THETA=*x*

KERNEL   Kernel. Valid for histogram. **Options** C=*x* . . .
K=NORMAL *or* QUADRATIC *or* TRIANGULAR . . . W=*width*
LOWER=*x* . . . ⟳ 9+ UPPER=*x* . . . ⟳ 9+

KERNEL   KERNEL*n* Kernel, for histogram inset. **Options**
C=*x* . . . TYPE=NORMAL *or* QUADRATIC *or* TRIANGULAR . . .
BANDWIDTH=*width* AMISE

LOGNORMAL   Lognormal. **Options** SIGMA=*x* ZETA=*x* THETA=*x*
For plot: SLOPE=*x*

NORMAL   Normal. **Options** MU=*x* SIGMA=*x*

WEIBULL   Weibull. **Options** C=*x* SIGMA=*x* THETA=*x*

WEIBULL2   Two-parameter Weibull. Valid for plot and inset.
Options C=*x* SIGMA=*x* SLOPE=*x* THETA=*x*

Options for all distributions

COLOR=*color* L=*line type* W=*width*

For histogram: FILL MIDPERCENTS NOPRINT PERCENTS=*n* . . .

For histogram inset: AD ADPVAL CVM CVMPVAL KSD KSDPVAL

Appearance options

ANNOTATE= CAXIS= CFRAME= CHREF= CTEXT= CVREF=
DESCRIPTION= FONT= HMINOR= LHREF= NAME= VMINOR=
CTEXTSIDE= CTEXTTOP= ⟳ 8.2+

Reference lines: HREF= HREFLABELS= VREF= VREFLABELS=
FRONTREF ⟳ 9+

Histogram layout: BARWIDTH= FORCEHIST GRID HOFFSET=
HREFLABPOS= LGRID= MIDPOINTS= NOBARS NOFRAME
NOHLABEL NOPLOT NOVLABEL NOVTICK RTINCLUDE
TURNVLABELS VAXIS= VAXISLABEL= VOFFSET= VREFLABPOS=
VSCALE= WAXIS= WGRID=   ENDPOINTS= ⟳ 8.2+

Histogram style: CBARLINE= CFILL= CGRID= HEIGHT=
INFONT= INHEIGHT= PFILL= WBARLINE=

Plot layout: NADJ NOFRAME PCTLMINOR RANKADJ SQUARE
CFRAMESIDE= CFRAMETOP= INTERTILE= NCOLS= NROWS=
⟳ 8.1+

Probability plot layout: GRID LGRID= PCTLORDER=

Comparative: ANNOKEY CFRAMESIDE= CFRAMETOP=
INTERTILE= NCOLS= NROWS=

Comparative histograms: CPROP= MAXNBIN= MAXSIGMAS=

Inset statistic options

descriptive statistic *quantile* GINI MAD QN SN STD_
GINI STD_MAD STD_QN STD_QRANGE STD_SN MSIGN
NORMALTEST PNORMAL PROBM PROBN PROBS SIGNRANK
statistic='*label*' *statistic*=(*format*) *statistic*='*label*' (*format*)

Inset appearance options

CFILL=*color* CFILL=BLANK CFILLH=*color* CHEADER=*color*
CSHADOW=*color* CTEXT=*color* FONT= FORMAT= HEADER=
HEIGHT= NOFRAME POSITION= DATA REFPOINT=

UPLOAD ○ SAS/CONNECT

PROC UPLOAD *options*;
optional statements

Copies a file from the local session to the remote session.

Options

DATA=*SAS dataset* OUT=*SAS dataset* Transfers the SAS dataset.
INCAT=*catalog* OUTCAT=*catalog* Transfers the catalog. IN=*libref*
OUT=*libref* Transfers the library. INDEX=YES *or* NO Whether to
copy indexes. CONSTRAINT=YES *or* NO Whether to copy integrity
constraints. DATECOPY Copies SAS dataset creation and modification dates. EXTENDSN=YES Increases the length of short numeric
variables by 1. MTYPE=(*member type*, . . .) Copies only these
member types in the library. ENTRYTYPE=*entry type* Copies only
this entry type in the catalog. GEN=NO Omits historical generations
of generation datasets from the library. V6TRANSPORT Creates a
transport file for transfer.

INFILE=*file* OUTFILE=*file* Transfers the text file. BINARY Uses a
binary transfer instead of a text transfer.

AFTER=*date* Transfers only files that have been modified since the
date given.

STATUS=YES *or* NO Whether to display the Transfer Status dialog.

Statements

SELECT *or* EXCLUDE *members or entries* / *option*; Copies only
selected members of a library or entries of a catalog. **Options**
MEMTYPE=*member type(s)* ENTRYTYPE=*entry type*

TRANTAB *translation table* *options*; Selects a translation table
for text translation. **Options** TYPE=(*entry type*, . . .) Applies the
selected translation table to these entry types. OPT= Translates
only: DISP Display text. SRC Programs. (DISP SRC) Both.

19

Products

Base SAS encompasses only a fraction of the functionality that a SAS program can address. Other SAS products provide additional language elements and, especially, procedures. This chapter lists procedures and other features of a few popular SAS products.

SAS/ACCESS

A set of products for access to DBMS data and other file formats.

ACCESS   Create logical connection to DBMS data.

DBLOAD   Add SAS data to DBMS tables.

DBF   Import and export DBF files.

DIF   Import and export DIF files.

IMPORT   EXPORT   (options)   For importing and exporting DBMS data and other external data.   ⏿ 7+

—

LIBNAME statement options: For connecting to databases and other external data.

SQL components: For retrieving data from and passing SQL statements to databases.

SAS/AF

BUILD   Create and manage AF applications.

—

BUILD command and related commands for creating AF applications.

SAS/CONNECT

Connects to SAS sessions on other computers.

ADMIN   Messaging server administration.

DOMAIN   Messaging server setup.

DOWNLOAD   Transfer file from remote to local.

UPLOAD   Transfer file from local to remote.

—

SIGNON and SIGNOFF commands and statements: For remote sessions.

RSUBMIT command, RSUBMIT and ENDRSUBMIT statements: Submit SAS statements to a remote session for execution.

KILLTASK statement: Ends a remote session or task. ⟳ 8.2+

RDISPLAY command and statement: Displays log and output windows for a remote session. ⟳ 7+

RGET command and statement: Retrieves remote log and output to display in Log and Output windows.

LIBNAME statement options: For Remote Library Services.

SQL components: For Remote SQL Pass-Through (RSPT), an SQL connection to a database on the remote system.

SAS/ETS

Statistical analysis of time series data.

ARIMA   Autoregressive moving average models.

AUTOREG   Autoregression error model.

COMPUTAB   Program-based spreadsheet reporting.

COUNTREG   Analyzes count data. ⟳ 8.2+

DATASOURCE   Imports economic data from various sources.

ENTROPY   Generalized Maximum Entropy. ⟳ 9+

EXPAND   Sample frequency conversion.

FORECAST   Univariate forecasting models.

LOAN   Loan computations.

MDC   Discrete choice modeling (multinomial). ⟳ 8.2+

MODEL   Nonlinear simultaneous equation models.

PDLREG   Multiple time series regression with delayed effects.

QLIM   Models with limited dependent variables. ⟳ 8.2+

SIMLIN   Predictions from linear structural equations.

SPECTRA   Frequency (spectral) analysis.

STATESPACE   State space model for multivariate time series.

SYSLIN   Estimation for interdependent linear equations.

TIMESERIES   Converts transactional events to a time series. ⟳ 9+

UCM   Unobserved Components Models. ⟳ 9+

TSCSREG   Time series cross section regression.

VARMAX   Vector autoregressive model for time series. ⟳ 8.1+

X11   X12   Seasonal adjustments of time series data.

—

Functions for financial computations, financial calendars, and time series tests.

SAS/FSP

Full-screen user interface style.

FSBROWSE   FSEDIT   Full-screen view of SAS datasets.

FSLETTER   Form letters.

FSVIEW   Tabular view of SAS datasets.

SAS/Genetics

Genetics.

ALLELE   HAPLOTYPE   FAMILY   CASECONTROL   PSMOOTH
INBREED   HTSNP   Genetic marker statistics and tests. ⊙ 9+

SAS/GIS

Geographical information systems and other spatial data applications.

GIS   Creates and maintains spatial databases.

SAS/GRAPH

Graphics.

GCHART   GRADAR   GAREABAR   GBARLINE   Creates charts.

GCONTOUR   GPLOT   G3D   G3GRID   Creates plots.

GMAP   GPROJECT   GREDUCE   GREMOVE   Creates maps.

GPRINT   GSLIDE   Creates graphic text.

GFONT   Creates and manages fonts.

GANNO   GREPLAY   Displays graphics.

GIMPORT   MAPIMPORT   Imports CGM files and ESRI Shapefiles.

GKEYMAP   Manages SAS/GRAPH character encoding.

GOPTIONS   Displays graphics system options.

GDEVICE   Manages graphics device drivers.

GTESTIT   Graphics device testing.

—

Data Step Graphics Interface: Functions and CALL routines for creating graphics.

Graphic options: Global settings for graphics.

GOPTIONS statement: For setting graphic options.

AXIS statement: Defines the range and appearance of an axis.

PATTERN statement: Defines the color and form of fill patterns.

SYMBOL statement: Defines the shape and color of plot symbols and connecting lines.

LEGEND statement: Creates legends for charts, plots, and maps.

Options in TITLE and FOOTNOTE statements: Apply graphic formatting to title and footnote lines.

SAS/INSIGHT

INSIGHT   Visual exploratory data analysis.

SAS/MDDB Server
MDDB   Builds multidimensional databases.

SAS/OR
Operations research and project management.

ASSIGN   Network cost models.

LP   NLP   Linear and nonlinear programming.

INTPOINT   Interior Point optimization. ○ 8.2+

NETFLOW   TRANS   Network flow models.

CPM   PM   Project management.

DTREE   Decision tree models.

GANTT   Graphical scheduling for project management.

NETDRAW   Network diagrams.

BOM   Tree processing of bill-of-material data. ○ 8.2+

AATRANS   Linear least squares for sparse data. ○ 9+

SAS/QC
Statistical quality control.

CAPABILITY   Evaluates a process result against a standard.

CUSUM   Creates cumulative sum control charts.

FACTEX   Constructs orthogonal factorial experimental designs.

ISHIKAWA   Creates and edits Ishikawa diagrams.

MACONTROL   Creates moving average control charts.

ANOM   Creates analysis of means charts. ○ 9+

OPTEX   Constructs efficient experimental designs.

PARETO   Creates Pareto (relative frequency) charts.

RELIABILITY   Analysis of reliability and failure data.

SHEWHART   Creates Shewhart control charts.

—

Functions: For computations related to quality analysis.

SAS/SHARE
Allows multiple users simultaneous access to SAS libraries.

SERVER   Starts a SAS/SHARE server.

OPERATE   Manages a SAS/SHARE server.

—

LIBNAME statement options: For shared libraries.

SAS/STAT
Statistical modeling and analysis.

ACECLUS   Estimates cluster shapes (covariances).

ANOVA   Analysis of variance for balanced data.

BOXPLOT   Creates box plots of distribution statistics.

CALIS   Estimation and hypothesis testing for structural models.

CANCORR   Canonical correlation.

CANDISC   Canonical discriminant analysis.

CATMOD   Categorical modeling of contingency table data.

CLUSTER   Hierarchical clustering.

CORRESP   Correspondence analysis.

DISCRIM   Derives a discriminant criterion for classifying observations based on quantitative measures.

DISTANCE   Measures dissimilarity between observations.   9+

FACTOR   Common factor and component analysis.

FASTCLUS   Disjoint clustering.

FREQ   Statistics and tests of frequency tables.

GAM   Generalized additive models.   8.2+

GENMOD   Estimates generalized linear models.

GLM   The method of least squares for general linear models.

GLMMOD   Design matrixes for general linear models.

GLMPOWER   Power and sample size computations.   9.1+

INBREED   Pedigree statistics.

KDE   Kernel density estimation.

KRIGE2D   Spatial prediction model.

LATTICE   Analysis of lattice experiments.

LIFEREG   Parametric estimation of failure data.

LIFETEST   Nonparametric estimation of failure data.

LOESS   Nonparametric estimation of regression surfaces.

LOGISTIC   Logistic regression analysis.

MDS   Multidimensional scaling models.

MI   Multiple imputation for estimating missing values.   9+

MIANALYZE   Statistical inferences from multiple imputation.   9+

MIXED   Mixed linear models.

MODECLUS   Clustering from nonparametric density estimates.

MULTTEST   Multiple hypothesis tests.

NESTED   Analysis of hierarchical (nested) experiments.

NLIN   Least squares estimates of nonlinear models.

NLMIXED   Nonlinear mixed models

NPAR1WAY   Nonparametric tests on a one-way classification.

ORTHOREG   Least squares estimation for general linear models.

PHREG   Proportional hazards model of failure data.

PLAN   Designs for factorial experiments.

PLS   Linear predictive methods.

POWER   Power and sample size computations.   9.1+

PRINCOMP   Principal component analysis.

PRINQUAL   Generates transformations of variables.

PROBIT   Estimation of discrete event data.

REG   Regression.

ROBUSTREG   Robust regression for data with outliers. ↻ 9+

RSREG   Quadratic response surface regression models.

SCORE   Applies coefficients to data values to generate scores.

SIM2D   Spatial simulation.

STDIZE   Standardizes numeric variables.

STEPDISC   Stepwise selection of discriminant variables.

SURVEYFREQ   Frequency tables and tests of association. ↻ 9+

SURVEYLOGISTIC   Logistic regression of survey data. ↻ 9.1+

SURVEYMEANS   Estimates population means from survey data.

SURVEYREG   Regression analysis of survey data.

SURVEYSELECT   Random sampling.

TPSPLINE   Penalized least squares method for nonparametric regression model.

TRANSREG   Transformation regression.

TREE   Tree diagram of cluster data.

TTEST   *t* tests.

VARCLUS   Clustering based on maximum variance.

VARCOMP   General linear models with random effects.

VARIOGRAM   Measures of spatial continuity.

SAS Words

Legend

**Symbol Type
(chapter)**

c command/window (13)

call CALL routine (17)

color color (3)

dev device (10)

dso dataset option (10)

eng engine (10)

et entry type (10)

f function (16)

fileref fileref (10)

fmt format (15)

infmt informat (14)

lib library (10)

mt member type (10)

mvar macro variable (8)

ods ODS driver/ destination (11)

oo object class (7)

oper operator (7)

p proc (18, 19)

s·d data step statement (5)

s·g global statement (4)

s·p proc step statement (6)

so system option (9)

stats statistic (12)

$... fmt infmt
* s·g
A c color
ABORT s·d
ABS f
ACCESS c mt
ADDRLONG f
AF c
ALLPERM call
ALTER dso
ALTLOG so
ALTPRINT so
AND oper
ANY... f
ANYDT... infmt
APPEND p
ARCOS f
ARRAY s·d
ARSIN f
ATAN f
ATAN2 f
ATTRC f
ATTRIB s·d s·p
ATTRN f
AUTOADD c
AUTOEXEC so
AUTOFLOW c
AUTOSPLIT c
AUTOWRAP c
AWS... c so
B c color
BAND f
BASE eng
BATCH so
BEST fmt infmt
BETA f
BETAINV f
BETWEEN oper
BFIND c
BINARY fmt infmt
BINDING so
BITS infmt

BLACK color
BLKSIZE so
BLSHIFT f
BLUE color
BNOT f
BOR f
BOTTOMMARGIN so
BOUNDS c
BROWN color
BRSHIFT f
BUFNO dso so
BUFSIZE dso so
BXOR f
BY s·d s·p
BYE c
BYERR so
BYLINE so
BYSORTED so
BZ infmt
C c color
CALENDAR p
CALL s·d
CANCEL c
CAPS c so
CARDIMAGE so
CARDS s·d fileref
CAT f
CATALOG c dev mt p
CATAMS et
CATCACHE so
CATNAME s·g
CATS f call
CATT f call
CATX f call
CBT et
CBUFNO so
CC so
CDF f
CEIL f
CEILZ f
CENTER so
CEXIST f

CHANGE c
CHARCODE so
CHART p
CHOOSEC f
CHOOSEN f
CIMPORT p
CINV f
CL c
CLEANUP so
CLEAR c
CLOSE f
CMDMAC so
CMPOPT so
CNONCT f
CNTLLEV dso
COALESCE f
COALESCEC f
COLLATE f so
COLOR c
COLORPRINTING so
COLS c
COMAMID so
COMB f
COMDEF so
COMMA fmt infmt
COMMAND c
COMMAX fmt infmt
COMMPORT dev
COMPARE f p
COMPBL f
COMPCOST call
COMPGED f
COMPLEV f
COMPOUND f
COMPRESS dso f so
CONFIG so
CONNECTREMOTE so
CONNECTSTATUS so
CONNECTWAIT so
CONSTANT f
CONTAINS oper
CONTENTS p
CONTINUE s·d
CONVERT p
CONVX f
CONVXP f
COPIES so
COPY c p
CORR p
COS f
COSH f
COUNT f
COUNTC f
CPARMS et
CPORT p
CPUID so

CPUCOUNT so
CSS f stats
CSV ods
CU c
CUROBS f
CV f stats
CYAN color
D c fmt
DACC... f
DAIRY f
DATA mt s·d
DATALINES s·d fileref
DATASETS p
DATASTMTCHK so
DATDIF f
DATE f fmt infmt so
DATEPART f
DATETIME f fmt
   infmt
DAY f fmt
DBCS so
DBCSLANG so
DBCSTAB p
DBCSTYPE so
DCLOSE f
DDE dev
DDMMYY fmt infmt
DECLARE s·d
DELETE c s·d
DEP... f
DEQUOTE f
DES c
DESCRIBE s·d
DESKTOP c
DETAILS so
DEVIANCE f
DEVICE so
DFLANG so
DHMS f
DICTIONARY lib
DIF f
DIM f
DINFO f
DIR c
DISK dev
DISPLAY p s·d
DKRICOND so
DKROCOND so
DLDMGACTION dso
   so
DM s·g
DMDB mt
DMR so
DMS so
DMSEXP so
DMSLOGSIZE so

DMSOUTSIZE so
DMSSYNCHK so
DNUM f
DO s·d
DOCUMENT ods p
DOLLAR fmt infmt
DOLLARX fmt infmt
DOPEN f
DOPTNAME f
DOPTNUM f
DOWNAME fmt
DREAD f
DRIVEMAP dev
DROP dso s·d
DROPNOTE f
DSNAME f
DSNFERR so
DTDATE fmt
DTMONYY fmt
DTRESET so
DTWKDATX fmt
DTYEAR fmt
DTYYQC fmt
DUMMY dev
DUPLEX so
DUR f
DURP f
E fmt infmt
ECHO so
ECHOAUTO so
EDPARMS et
ELSE s·d
EMAIL dev
EMAIL... so
ENCODING dso
ENCRYPT dso
END c s·d
ENDRSUBMIT s·g
ENDSAS c s·g
ENGINE so
EQ oper
ERF f
ERFC f
ERROR s·d
ERRORABEND so
ERRORBYABEND so
ERRORCHECK so
ERRORS so
EURO infmt fmt
EUROCURR f
EUROFR... fmt
EUROTO... fmt
EUROX infmt fmt
EXECUTE call s·d
EXIST f
EXP f

EXPLODE c p
EXPLORER c so
EXPORT p
FACT f
FAPPEND f
FCLOSE f
FCOL f
FDELETE f
FETCH f
FETCHOBS f
FEXIST f
FGET f
FILE c s·d
FILECC so
FILECLOSE dso
FILEEXIST f
FILENAME c f e·g
FILEREF f
FILL c
FIND c f
FINDC f
FINFO f
FINV f
FIP... f
FIRSTOBS dso so
FLOAT fmt infmt
FLOOR f
FLOORZ f
FMTERR so
FMTSEARCH so
FNONCT f
FNOTE f
FOLDER et
FONT et
FONT... so
FONTREG p
FOOTNOTE s·g
FOOTNOTES c
FOPEN f
FOPTNAME f
FOPTNUM f
FORMAT et p s·d s·p
FORMATC et
FORMCHAR so
FORMDLIM so
FORMS p so
FORMULA et
FPOINT f
FPOS f
FPUT f
FRACT fmt
FRAME et
FREAD f
FREQ p
FREWIND f
FRLEN f

FSDEVICE so
FSEP f
FSLIST c p
FTP dev
FULLSTATS so
FULLSTIMER so
FUZZ f
FWRITE f
G color
GAMINV f
GAMMA f
GE oper
GENMAX dso
GENNUM dso
GEOMEAN f
GEOMEANZ f
GETOPTION f
GETVARC f
GETVARN f
GLOBAL et
GOPTIONS et p s
GOTO s·d
GRAY color
GREEN color
GREY color
GRSEG et
GSUBMIT c
GT oper
GWINDOW so
HARMEAN f
HARMEANZ f
HASH oo
HBOUND f
HELP c et
HEX c fmt infmt
HFS dev
HHMM fmt
HITER oo
HMS f
HOME c
HOUR f fmt
HSCROLL c
HTML ods
HTMLDECODE f
HTMLENCODE f
I c
IB fmt infmt
IBR fmt infmt
IBUFSIZE so
ICON c so
IDXNAME dso
IDXWHERE dso
IEEE fmt infmt
IF s·d
IFC f
IFN f

IMAGE et
IMPLMAC so
IMPORT p
IN dso oper
INCLUDE c
INDEX dso f mt
INDEXC f
INDEXW f
INFILE s·d
INFMT et
INFMTC et
INFORMAT s·d s·p
INITCMD so
INITSTMT so
INPUT f s·d
INPUTC f
INPUTN f
INT f
INTCK f
INTNX f
INTRR f
INTZ f
INVALIDDATA so
IORCMSG f
IQR f
IRR f
IS MISSING oper
IS NULL oper
ITEMSTOR mt
JC c
JL c
JR c
K color
K... f
KEEP dso s·d
KEYS c et
KURTOSIS f stats
LABEL call dso s·d
  s·p so
LAG f
LARGEST f
LBOUND f
LE oper
LEAVE s·d
LEFT f
LEFTMARGIN so
LENGTH f s·d
LENGTHC f
LENGTHM f
LENGTHN f
LETTER et
LGAMMA f
LIBNAME c f s·g
LIBRARY lib
LIBREF f
LIKE oper

LINESIZE c so
LINK s·d
LIST et s·d
LISTING c ods
LISTTASK s·g
LOCK c s·g
LOG c et f so fileref
LOG2 f
LOG10 f
LOGBETA f
LOGCDF f
LOGISTIC call
LOGPARM so
LOGPDF f
LOGSDF f
LOSTCARD s·d
LOWCASE f
LT oper
M c color
MACRO et so
MAD f
MAGENTA color
MANAGER c
MAPS so
MARKUP ods
MASK c
MAUTOSOURCE so
MAX f oper stats
MCL c
MCU c
MDDB mt
MDY f
MEAN f stats
MEANS p
MEDIAN f stats
MEMLIST c
MEMRPT so
MEMSIZE so
MENU et
MERGE s·d
MERGENOBY so
MERROR so
META... so
MFILE so
MIN f oper stats
MINGUO fmt infmt
MINUTE f
MISSING call f s·g so
MLOGIC so
MMDDYY fmt infmt
MMSS fmt
MMYY fmt
MOD f
MODE stats
MODIFY s·d
MODZ f

MONNAME fmt
MONTH f fmt
MONYY fmt infmt
MOPEN f
MORT f
MPRINT so
MRECALL so
MSG so
MSGCASE so
MSGLEVEL so
MSTORED so
MSYMTAB et
MSYMTABMAX so
MULTENVAPPL so
MVARSIZE so
MVS dev
MZOOM c
N color f stats
NAMEPIPE dev
NEGPAREN fmt
NENGO fmt infmt
NETENCRYPT... so
NETMAC so
NETPV f
NEWS so
NLITERAL f
NMISS f stats
NORMAL f
NOT oper
NOT... f
NOTE f
NOTEPAD c
NOTES so
NOTIN oper
NPV f
NTITLE c
NULLS c
NUMBER so
NUMBERS c
NUMKEYS so
NUMMOUSEKEYS so
NVALID f
O c color
OBJECTSERVER so
OBS dso so
OBSBUF dso
OCTAL fmt infmt
ODS s·g
OPEN f
OPLIST so
OPTIONS c p s·g
OPTLOAD p
OPTSAVE p
OR oper
ORANGE color
ORDINAL f

ORIENTATION so
OTHERWISE s·d
OUTPUT c et ods s·d
OUTREP dso
OVP so
P color
PAGE s·g
PAGEBREAKINITIAL
   so
PAGENO so
PAGESIZE c so
PAPER... so
PARM so
PARMCARDS s·p so
   fileref
PARMS et
PASTE c
PATHNAME f
PCL ods
PCLEAR c
PCTL f
PD fmt infmt
PDF f ods
PEEKCLONG f
PEEKLONG f
PERCENT fmt
PERM f
PIB fmt infmt
PIBR fmt infmt
PINK color
PIPE dev
PK fmt infmt
PLOTTER dev
PMENU c et p
POINT f
POINTOBS dso
POISSON f
POKELONG call f
PRINT c p so fileref
PRINTCMD so
PRINTER dev ods
PRINTERPATH so
PRINTINIT so
PRINTMSGLIST so
PRINTTO p
PROB... f
PROC s·p so
PROCLEAVE so
PROFILE et
PROGRAM c et mt
PROPCASE f
PRT stats
PRTDEF p
PRTEXP p
PRX... call f
PS ods

PTRLONGADD f
PUT f s·d
PUTC f
PUTLOG s·d
PUTN f
PVP f
PW dso
PWENCODE p
PWREQ dso
QRYPROF et
QTR f fmt
QTRR fmt
QUANTILE f
QUERY c et
QUIT s·p
QUOTE f
QUOTELENMAX so
R c color
RAN... call f
RANGE f stats
RANK f p
RB fmt infmt
RCHANGE c
READ dso
RECALL c
RED color
REDIRECT s·d
REGISTRY p
REMOTE so eng
REMOVE s·d
RENAME dso s·d
REPEAT f
REPEMPTY dso
REPLACE dso s·d so
REPORT et p
REPT et
REP_MGRLOC so
RESET c
RESOLVE f
RETAIN s·d
RETURN s·d
REUSE dso so
REVERSE f
REWIND f
RFIND c
RIGHT f
RIGHTMARGIN so
RMS f
ROLE dso
ROMAN fmt
ROUND f
ROUNDZ f
RSASUSER so
RSUBMIT c s·g
RTF ods
RTRACE so

RTRACELOC so
RUN s·d s·p
RX... call f
S so
S2 so
S370F... fmt infmt
SASAUTOS so
SASCMD so
SASCOLOR c
SASCONTROL so
SASFILE s·g
SASFRSCR so
SASHELP lib so
SASINITIALFOLDER
  so
SASMSG so
SASMSTORE so
SASSCRIPT so
SASUSER lib so
SAVE c
SAVING f
SCAN call f
SCANQ call f
SCL et
SCREEN et
SDF f
SECOND f
SELECT s·d
SEQ so
SEQENGINE so
SERROR so
SET call s·d so
SETINIT c so
SGIO so
SIGN f
SIGNOFF c s·g
SIGNON c s·g
SIN f
SINH f
SKEWNESS f stats
SKIP s·g so
SLEEP call f
SLIST et
SMALLEST f
SOFTMAX call
SOCKET dev
SORT p
SORT... so
SORTEDBY dso
SORTSEQ dso
SOUND call
SOUNDEX f
SOURCE et so
SOURCE2 so
SPEDIS f
SPILL dso

SPLASH so
SPLASHLOC so
SPOOL so
SQL p
SQL... mvar
SQRT f
SSN fmt
STANDARD p
STARTLIB so
STARTSAS s·g
STATS so
STAX so
STD f stats
STDERR f stats
STDIZE call
STFIPS f
STIMEFMT so
STIMER infmt so
STNAME f
STNAMEL f
STOP s·d
STREAMINIT call
STRIP f
SUBMIT c
SUBPAD f
SUBSTR f
SUBSTRN f
SUBTOP c
SUM f stats
SUMMARY p
SUMSIZE so
SUMWGT stats
SYMBOLGEN so
SYMDEL call
SUMEXIST f
SYMGLOBL f
SYMLOCAL f
SYMGET f
SYMPUT call
SYMPUTX call
SYNCHIO so
SYNCOLOR c
SYNCONFIG c
SYNTAXCHECK so
SYS... mvar
SYSGET f
SYSIN so
SYSLEAVE so
SYSMSG f
SYSPARM f so
SYSPRINT so
SYSPRINTFONT so
SYSPROCESSID f
  mvar
SYSPROCESSNAME f
  mvar

SYSPROD f
SYSRC f
SYSTASK s·g
SYSTEM call f
T stats
TABS c
TABULATE p
TAN f
TANH f
TAPE dev eng
TAPECLOSE so
TAPELABEL p
TBUFSIZE so
TC c
TCP... so
TEMP dev
TEMPLATE p
TERMINAL dev so
TERMSTMT so
TF c
THREADS so
TIME f fmt infmt
TIMEPART f
TIMEPLOT p
TINV f
TITLE et s·g
TITLES c
TNONCT f
TOBSNO dso
TOD fmt
TODAY f
TOPMARGIN so
TRANSLATE f
TRANSPOSE p
TRANTAB dso et p so
TRANWRD f
TRIM f
TRIMN f
TRUNC f
TS c
TYPE dso
UNBUFLOG so
UNIFORM f

UNIVARIATE p
UPCASE f
UPDATE s·d
URL dev
URLDECODE f
URLENCODE f
USER lib so
USS f stats
UTILLOC so
UUID... f so
V*n*... eng
V6CREATEUPDATE so
VALIDFMTNAME so
VALIDVARNAME so
VAR c f s·p stats
VARFMT f
VARINFMT f
VARLABEL f
VARLEN f
VARNAME f
VARNUM f
VARRAY f
VARTYPE f
VECTOR so
VERBOSE so
VERIFY f
VFORMAT f
VIEW mt
VIEWTABLE c
VINARRAY f
VINFORMAT f
VLABEL f
VLENGTH f
VNAME call f
VNEXT call
VNFERR so
VTYPE f
VVALUE f
W color
WAITFOR s·g
WAITSAS s·g
WAKEUP f
WEDIT c

WEEKDATE fmt
WEEKDATX fmt
WEEKDAY f fmt
WHEN s·d
WHERE dso s·d s·p
WHEREUP dso
WHITE color
WINDOW s·d
WORDDATE fmt
WORDDATX fmt
WORK lib so
WORKINIT so
WORKTERM so
WPOPUP c
WRITE dso
WSAVE c et
X c s·g
XCMD so
XML eng ods
XSYNC so
XWAIT so
Y color
YEAR f fmt
YEARCUTOFF so
YELLOW color
YEN fmt infmt
YIELDP f
YRDIF f
YYMM fmt
YYMMN fmt infmt
YYMMDD fmt infmt
YYMON fmt
YYQ f fmt infmt
YYQR fmt
Z fmt
ZD fmt infmt
ZDB infmt
ZDV infmt
ZIP... f
ZOOM c
LAST so
NEW s·d

Index

The Author

When the first edition of *Professional SAS Programmers Pocket Reference* was published a decade ago, Rick Aster was already known around the world as one of the most recognized experts in SAS programming. His prodigious SAS consulting career began with projects for the U.S. Department of Energy, followed by work in insurance, banking, and marketing. He cowrote the landmark book *Professional SAS Programming Secrets*, released in 1991, and has since authored a dozen books and audio titles on SAS. He has participated in projects that won regulatory approval for new drugs, delivered a data warehouse for one of the world's largest banks, and forecast sales for Fortune 500 companies. His most enduring accomplishment lies in teaching hundreds of students to unleash the power of SAS.